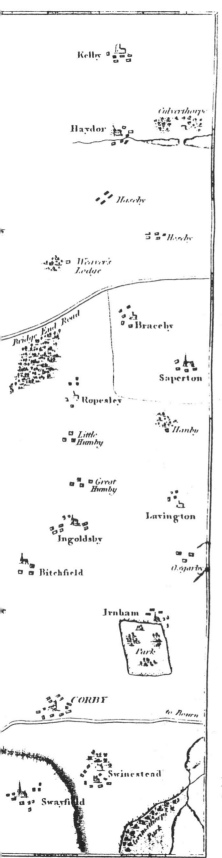

Part of Lincolnshire comprehending the Soke of Grantham from E. Turnor, *Collections for the history of the town and soke of Grantham*, London, 1806

THE

PUBLICATIONS

OF THE

𝕷incoln 𝕽ecord 𝕾ociety

FOUNDED IN THE YEAR

1910

VOLUME 83

ISSN 0267—2634

GRANTHAM DURING THE INTERREGNUM

THE HALL BOOK OF GRANTHAM

1641—1649

TRANSCRIBED BY

BILL COUTH

The Lincoln Record Society

The Boydell Press

First published 1995

A Lincoln Record Society Publication
Published by The Boydell Press
an imprint of Boydell & Brewer Ltd
PO Box 9, Woodbridge, Suffolk IP12 3DF, UK
and of Boydell & Brewer Inc.
PO Box 41026, Rochester, NY 14604-4126, USA

ISBN 0 901503 56 8

British Library Cataloguing-in-Publication Data
Grantham During the Interregnum: Hall Book of
Grantham, 1641–49. – (Publications of the Lincoln
Record Society, ISSN 0267–2634; Vol. 83)
 I. Couth, Bill II. Series
 942.538062
 ISBN 0-901503-56-8

The paper used in this publication meets the minimum requirements
of American National Standard for Information Sciences –
Permanence of Paper for Printed Library Materials, ANSI Z39.48–1984

Printed in Great Britain by
St Edmundsbury Press Ltd, Bury St Edmunds, Suffolk

CONTENTS

CONTENTS

GENERAL EDITOR'S NOTE

Mr Couth made a complete transcript of the text of the Hall Book which contains 201 folios and covers the years 1633 to 1649. For this edition it has been necessary to begin at folio 97v and to cover only the years 1641 to 1649. We are thus able to present a picture of the town and its government during the two civil wars and in the early period of the Commonwealth. For the sake of conciseness and in the interests of layout, it has been decided to omit the marginal headings which added nothing to the text and took up a great deal of space. Biographical notes are added to the index of persons.

ACKNOWLEDGEMENTS

I would like to thank a number of people and institutions.

Mr Cann, chief executive of South West Kesteven District Council, which holds the Hall Book at the Grantham Civic Centre, gave permission for it to be read and copied. The staff at the Grantham Library and Museum provided facilities for its study both in the original and on microfilm. The manuscript department of the Nottingham University Library produced from Professor Alan Rogers' microfilm some excellent copies of its pages which eased the burden of transcription. Dr Richard Mobbs of the Computer Centre of the University of Leicester was generous with his time and expertise and so speeded transcription, as did advice about computers from Laura and Andrew Kirton. Dr Dorothy Owen's knowledge, encouragement and kindness improved the clarity and conciseness of the transcript. Lastly there are others who in a formal and informal manner contributed unknowingly to the finished work.

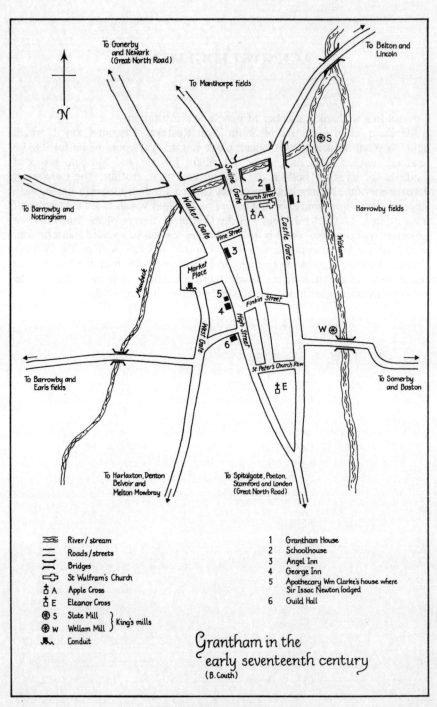

To Gonerby
and Newark
(Great North Road)

To Belton and
Lincoln

To Manthorpe fields

N

Swine Gate

Walker Gate

Church Street

2

1

To Barrowby and
Nottingham

Harrowby fields

A

Vine Street

Castle Gate

3

Maudcock

Witham

Market
Place

5

Finkin Street

4

S

High Street

6

West Gate

W

St. Peter's Church Row

To Barrowby and
Earls fields

E

To Somerby
and Boston

To Harlaxton, Denton
Belvoir and
Melton Mowbray

To Spitalgate, Ponton,
Stamford and London
(Great North Road)

≈	River / stream	
≡	Roads / streets	
⟨	Bridges	
⌂	St Wulfram's Church	
♁ A	Apple Cross	
♁ E	Eleanor Cross	
⊛ S	Slate Mill	} King's mills
⊛ W	Wellam Mill	
⨇	Conduit	

1	Grantham House
2	Schoolhouse
3	Angel Inn
4	George Inn
5	Apothecary Wm Clarke's house where Sir Issac Newton lodged
6	Guild Hall

Grantham in the
early seventeenth century
(B. Couth)

Sketch plan of the centre of Grantham c.1640

THE HALL BOOK OF GRANTHAM

1641–1649

f. 97 An assemblie by Thomas Mattkine gen Alderman of the Borough of Grantham aforesaid the comburgesses & burgesses of the same in Corpus Christi Queare within the Prebendarie Church of Grantham aforesaid the Frydaye after St Lukes daye being the xxii daye of October Anno Domini 1641
First the said Mr Mattkine did sitt downe in Corpus Christi Queare within the Prebendarie Church aforesaid
Then nexte unto did sitte Mr Arthure Rhoades
Then were there three comburgesses sente downe into the bodie of the Church Mr George Lloyde Mr Robert Colcrofte & Mr Edward Christian
Out of which three one of them was chossen to sitte uppon the cushione or place of electione Mr George Lloyde.
Then were there three (sic) comburgesses sett uppon the cushione or place of electione viz Mr Mattkine, Mr Rhoades, Mr George Lloyde & Mr Colcrofte
Oute of which three one was to bee chossen Alderman of the Towne & Borough of Grantham for this yeare nexte ensewing
And by the generall assente of this assemblie Mr George Lloyde was chossen Alderman of this Towne & Borough for this yeare now nexte to come
Whereuppon the said Mr Thomas Mattkine discharged himself from the place & office of the Alderman according to auntiente custome, and the said Mr George Lloyde being elected Alderman as aforesaid for the yeare to come did att this assemblie take his oathe according to the auntiente & laudable custome of this Borough.

f. 98 First Court of George Lloyd 29 October 1641

Mr George Loyde Alderman

First Twelve Comburgesses		*Second Twelve*	
Mr Alexander More	jur	George Briggs	jur
Mr Lewes Somersall	jur	Thomas Fishare	jur
Mr Arthure Rhoades	jur	Edward Rawlinson	jur
Mr Richard Conye	jur	Edward Towne	jur
Mr Henrie Cole	jur	Gilbert Chauntler	
Mr John Mills	jur	Brian Newball	
Mr Richard Pearson	jur	Thomas Shorte	
Mr Robert Colcrofte	jur	John Bracewell	jur
Mr Edward Christian	jur	William Hodgkinson	jur
Mr Thomas Mills	jur	John Rawlinson	jur
Mr Christopher Hanson	jur	John Fearon	jur
John Bee	jur		

Nomina Officiariorum ibidem

Coroner	Thomas Mattkine	gen	Markett	Brian Godley	jur
Escheator	Edwarde Christian	gen	Sears	John Kirke	jur
Church	John Rawlinsone	jur	Prisors	John Simpsone	jur
Masters	John Fuller	jur	of Corne	William Bristowe	jur
Chamber-	Edwarde Towne	jur	Leather	Richard Kellam	jur
lins	James Gibsone	jur	Sealers	Raphe Goddwine	jur
High	George Briggs	jur		Anthonie Wallitt	jur
Constables	Thomas Fysher	jur	Parishe Clarke	Thomas Somersall	jur

Underconstables

Markett	Robert Trevillian	jur	Sexton	Alexander Bothomley jur	
Place	Richard Archer	jur	Scavengers	John Trigge	
High	Thomas Wallette	jur		Richard Poole	
Streete	John Watsone	jur	*Nomina Comunum huius cur*		
West	William Parker	jur	Markett	Robert Trevillian	
Gate	Thomas Graunte	jur	Place	Richard Hartlington	
Walker-	Augustine Winter	jur		James Gibsone	
Gate	Francis Bacon	jur		Thomas Doughtie	
Swine-	Henrie Ferman	jur		James Walker	
Gate	Thomas Mussone	jur		Edward Bristowe	
Castle	Thomas Hanson	jur			
Gate	William Grococke	jur			
Key Keepers	Mr Alderman	jur			
for the	Edward Towne	jur			
Comon	John Rawlinson	jur			
Hutch					
Collectors for the Schoole house rents	Richard Pearsone	gen			
Sergeants at Mace	Matthew Whiting	jur			
	Richard Poole	jur			
Gaoler & Bayliffe	_____				

Adhuc nomina comunium huius curie

Westgate	John Kirke	High Street	Thomas Lane	
	Edward Still		Thomas Wallett	
	Christopher Fisher		John Fuller	
	John Wythey	Walkergate	Robert Tompson	
	John Hutchine		Augustine Winter	
	Thomas Marshall		George Hardackers	
Swinegate	William Parker		Francis Bristowe	
	Henrie Ferman	Castlegate	John Scotte	
	John Phiper			

Mille Masters now chossen

for Well Lane Mills	John Fearone	For the Slate Mills	John Bracewell	
	William Clarke		Francis Bristowe	

Att this courte Thomas Mattkine gen Alderman delivered uppe in open courte by the Inventorie thereof all the townes plate unto the said Mr Lloyde gen now Alderman (viz) twoe silver cannes, twoe beare bolls, one wine bolle, one guilte cuppe, twoe silver tunes, one beker, a silver salte & cover, the horse race cuppe & casse and thirteen silver spoones.

Att this courte William Graye being a stranger borne came into this courte and brought in tenn poundes which hee tendred for his freedome according to order

& auntiente custome of this Borough,and in regard hee formerlie maried a free mans daughter of this Borough haveing lived heare manie yeares,and being well accepted of and made free of the companie of shoomakers which trade he useth & professeth.

This courte was willing & did agree that hee sholde paye butt three poundes vis viiid and the reste to be given him backe againe of his said tenn pounds which was then paied to the chamberlins and thereuppon hee being desirous to be incorporated & made free, this courte did assente, whereuppon hee tooke his oath of allegiance, and was sworne free burgesse, and paid his due fees to the Clarke & Sergeants.

Att this courte uppon a petitione exhibited by one William Kellam a poore man borne within this Borough being by reasone of sicknes growen into extreame povertie ytt was granted unto him that twoe men shold gather the releiffe of all well disposed people within this Borough towards the supplie of his presente wants.

f. 99 Second Court of George Lloyd 5 November 1641

The accounte of George Briggs & William Clarke chamberlins for this Borough of Grantham for Thomas Mattkines yeare late Alderman of the said Borough.

	£	s	d
The totall some of the receipts of George Briggs chamberline is	143	12	8
The totall some of his payements as by his booke appeareth is	143	17	7
Soe then remained due to him which was paid unto him by William Clarke in open courte	0	5	6
The totall some of William Clarke the other chamberline as by his booke appeareth for his receipts	276	x	1
The totall some of his payments as by his said booke appeareth is	258	15	5
Receaved more of George Hardacker for the tolle of the Slate Mills	3	16	11
Soe then there is in the accountants handes	21	2	3

which was paid by the said chamberlines in open courte the laste courte daye.

Ytt is fullie concluded & agreed uppon by this courte that this Borough shall forthwith purchase & buye of one Edward Walker of Canosbie [Rauceby?] in the countie of Lincolne shoemaker whoe affirmeth himself to be nexte heire to Nicholas Walker late Rector of Colsterworth in the said countie Docter of Divinitie deceased a litle closse in Houghton neare Grantham & certaine feilds in truste for the borough of Grantham to such uses as the said Docter Walker in his leif tyme by his letter did declare himself hee wolde give the same to this corporacone and to give the said Edward Walker for performance & sale thereof sixteen poundes xiiis iiiid for the said closse.

Third Court of George Lloyd 18 November 1641

Att this courte ytt ordered everie inhabitante within this Borough within the High Street, Walkergate & the waye leading from the Markett Place to the Church shall clens the manure & rubbish before theire dores in the streets before tomorow at eight being Satterdaye in paine of everie one that shall neglecte the same to forfeit xiid to this corporacon to be presented by constables of everie warde & leavies to the releif of this Borough according to auntiente custome.

Att this courte Thomas Baylie & William Broughton being both free borne did desire to be incorporated & admitted free men of this Corporacon & Borough whereunto this Borough did freelie assente and soe the said parties did paye to the chamberlins iis vid a peece & xviiid to the Clerke & Sergeants tooke theire severall oathes & soe were admitted free men of this Borough.

Agreed this courte to goe to the vestrie to take oute certaine writings for the setting out the house & groundes adioyning uppon Loves house & groundes in Westgate.

Uppon mocon made by Mr Alexander More for new securitie to be given to Mr Hall for £100 poundes borowed by this corporacon ytt was now agreed that new securitie shold be given for the true payemente thereof.

The musicons formerlie hired refussing to receave the liveries as the chamberlines doe affirme was this courte againe dismised and to have theire ii quarters wages for this winter half yeare.

The letting of the closse in the tenure of Widdowe Bristowe late Docter Walkers in Houghton feilde respitted till the next courte

William Grococke alsoe had daye given him till next courte to give answere what hee will doe about the lease of his house.

Att this courte Mr Arthure Rhoades, Mr Edward Christian, Edward Towne, Thomas Fisher, John Phiper & John Scotte are nominated & appointed to veiwe & see the woode & trees growing & being in a litle closse in Houghton late Nicholas Walker Docter of Divinitie & purchassed by this corporacon and to make sale thereof as speedelie as they can for the use & benefitt of this borough and thereof to yeld an instant accounte.

Whereas att the seconde courte of Thomas Wickcliffe gen Alderman held the third daye of November 1626 ytt was then agreed uppon that non of the presente or succeeding chamberlins nor anie other person or persons whatsoever clayming or pretending to have anie authoritie to erecte lette or appointe anie stalls or standings uppon the markett or faire dayes within this Borough shall att anie tyme hereafter lette for the hire or otherwise bargaine for, dispose of or appointe to anie inhabitante of this towne or anie forriner whatsoever anie more stalls or standings than one a peece: that is to say to everie such severall inhabitante or foriner as aforesaid but onlie one stall or standing & noe more uppon paine of everie chamberlin and other user soe offending contrarie to this order to forfeit vs a peece to the comon boxe and ytt was then alsoe further agreed that everie inhabitante of this Borough or foriner which att anie tyme or tymes thereafter shall use or have anie more stalls or standings then one uppon anie markett or faire dayes within this towne shall likewise forfeit vs shillings a peece to the comon boxe for everie such defalt which saide order is this courte confirmed and agreed uppon still to continue & stand in force.

Fourth Court of George Lloyd 4 December 1641

Whereas there is a £100 owing to Mr Hall ytt is this courte agreed that yf the said Mr Hall will call in his said money ytt shalbe paid unto him by a £100 which Mrs Walton of this towne promisseth to lende to this corporacon.

Att this courte ytt is fully concluded & agreed uppon that William Grococke whoe maried Widdowe Duckers daughter shall have a lease sealed unto him of a messuage or tenementc in the High Street in Grantham wherein hee the said William Grococke & the said Widdowe Ducker now dwell for the tenure of one & twentie yeares to begin & comence after the ende of Humfire Duckers old lease uppon the payemente of £xxv of lawfull English money uppon the feast daye of the Annuncyacon of the Blessed Virgine Marie nexte ensewing for a fine to the use of this Borough and entring into such covenants as other the townes tenants doe and payeing yearlie the auntiente rente of xxiis viiid during the said terme and one couple of well fed capons or iis vid in money in lue thereof putting in further sufficiente securitie to the towne for performance of the covenants conteined in the said lease. In earnest of which said bargaine the the said William Grococke & Widdowe Ducker paid & delivered into Mr Aldermans hands the some of vs.

The stalls letting respited till Mr Aldermans next courte.

Att this courte uppon some speciall causes ytt was agreed that Francis Bristow shold gather & take the toles at faires & marketts which Robert Wright the elder hath heretofore usuallie used to take & gather to the end the said Francis Bristowe shold trulie inform this Borough of the true valeur thereof.

100 Att this courte Anne Bristowe of Spitlegate widdowe came & desired to be admitted tenante to a litle closse in Houghton feilde late Docter Walkers and now belonging to this Borrough and this courte did then lett unto her the said closse for the terme of xxitie yeares to comence att the feast of the Annuncyacon of the Blessed Virgine Marie nexte ensewing in consideracon of the somme of tenn poundes of lawfull money of Englande to be paid for a fine to the use of this Borough att the feast of the Annuncyacon of the Blessed Virgine Marie before specified and entring into such covenants for maintenance & repaire of the fences & other things as other tenants usuallie doe and payeing the yearlie rente of xxxs p ann to this Borough during the said terme and one couple of good fatte capons or iis vid in money in lue thereof. In earnest of which said bargaine and agreemente the said Widdowe Bristowe paide into Mr Aldermans hands xiid.

Att this courte came the Reverente learned divine Docter Saundersone of Boothebie Panell and gave this courte to understande that Mr Beniamine Nelsone whoe hath lattelie taken to farme parte of the schoolehouse lands, was departed this leif, and soe desired this courte that they wold be pleased to graunte him leave to assigne the same over to certaine other tenantes viz to William Threaves, Robert Kellam & Robert Wilcocke of Gonnerbie, John Patchett of Belton & John Miller of Litle Gonnerbie. Which this courte taking into consideracon desired the said Dr Saunderson that administracon might be taken after the death of the said Mr Nelsone and then they wold shew him all lawfull respects nott preiudicing this corporacon.

Fifth Court of George Lloyd 21 January 1641

Articles of Agreemente att this courte concluded & agreed uppon between the Alderman & Burgesses of the Borough of Grantham in the countie of Lincoln of the one parte and Richard Attkinsone of Grantham aforesaid carpenter of the other as followeth: Imprimis the said Alderman & Burgesses for divers good causes & consideracons hereunto especiallie moveing, have given & graunted power & authoritie unto the said Richard Attkinson to place, sett & lett all the stalls & standings in the faires & marketts belonging to this Borough in the markett place there for foriners onelie and to take the profitts & benefitte thereof in as large & ample manner as one Richard Tomlinson by virtue of a demise thereof made unto him from the Alderman & Burgesses of Grantham hath & of righte ought to have & use the same to holde the said power & authoritie and the profitt & benefitt of placing,setting & letting all the said stalls & other the premisses before mentioned to be demised to him the said Richard Attkinson his executors & assignes from the feast of St Michaell the Archangell which shalbe in the yeare of our Lord 164– for & during the full end & terme of xxitie yeares from thence next & immediatellie following fullie to be complette & ended: yelding & payeing therefore yearelie & everie yeare during this demise to the Alderman & Burgesses of Grantham aforesaid & theire successors the instant & intire somme of £xx of lawfull English money att foure severall dayes & termes in everie yeare viz in & uppon _____ daye of _____ and in & uppon the _____ and in & uppon _____ and in & uppon _____ by even & equall portions

And ytt is further concluded & agreed uppon between the said parties that the Alderman & Burgesses aforesaid shall within or aboute foure monnethes before the expiracon of the demise made as aforesaid to the said Richard Tomlinson buy all the stall geares that shall belonge to the said Richard Tomlinson as used in the markett to & for the use & benefitt of him the said Richard Attkinson during the aforesaid terme of xxi yeares to him letten or else shall within three monnethes before the expiracon of the said demise made to the said Richard Tomlinsone paye unto the said Richard Attkinsone £xxv of lawfull English money and in consideracon thereof hee the said Richard Attkinsone att his owne propper costs & charge is to finde & provide sufficiente stall geares & all bordes & implements thereto belonging as by the iudgemente of foure sufficiente men shalbe thought fitting & expediente for the performance of that service and the well furnishing of the markett.

Provided alwayes & ytt is further concluded & agreed uppon between the said parties to those presents that hee the said Richard Attkinsone att the insealing & deliverance of his lease of the premisses above specified shall enter into one obligacon of the somme of £100 with twoe sufficyente sueriets to the Alderman & Burgesses of this Borough & theire successors as well for the true payemente of the said rente as alsoe for the maintenance of leaving & yelding uppe of the said stall geares and all things thereunto belonging either by the Alderman & Burgesses bought aforesaid of the said Richard Tomlinsone or by him to be provided aforesaid att the ende & expiracon of the said demised terme into the handes possessione of the Alderman & Burgesses & theire successors for the tyme being in as good order & plight as they were unto him delivered or were by him provided as aforesaid att the tyme of his entrance uppon the said demise & for the true performance of all other covenants graunted in the said demise. And yf anie controversie or difference shall happen or arise by reason of the placing or displacing of anie manner of persone or persons in setting of the said stalls that then & soe ofte as anie such thing shall fall or happen the same to be decided determined & ended by the Alderman for the tyme being & twoe of his bretheren or by such persons whome the Alderman & his bretheren shall appoint.

Sixth Court of George Lloyd 28 January 1641

Att this courte uppon the humble request of Robert Wrighte the elder a poore inhabitante within this Borough haveing receaved great losse by a packe of wares latelie stolne from him being the greatest parte of his substance whereby hee did maintaine himself his weif and famelie libertie is given by Mr Alderman & his bretheren that twoe of the inhabitants of this Borough shall in his behalf gather the charitable benevolence of the inhabitants of the said Borough for & towards the releiffe & maintenance of him the said Robert Wright.

Uppon a certifficate brought to Mr Alderman, and read in open courte toutching the losse & hurte which one Thomas Pickard a dyer had & receaved aboute twoe yeare sithence by reasone of a soden floode & deluge of water which then happened and caried away the greatest parte of his wares & substance whose losse being by the said certifficate under the hands of Master Alderman of Stamforde and divers gentlemen & other credible persons more fullie declared craveing on his behalf the charitie of well disposed people. Ytt is this courte by Mr Alderman & his bretheren nominated & appointed that the churchwardens of this borough shall gather the charitable benevolence of all well disposed people within this Borough for & towards the succor & releife of him Docter Pickard in these his wants.

Seventh Court of George Lloyd 25 February 1641

Att this courte came in Mr Hugh Wilkinson schoolemaster of the free schoole within the Borough & towne of Grantham,and there did declare himself that by reason he was growen onto in yeares hee founde himself nott so fitte & able to take paines in teaching schollars as heretofore hee had done,and likewise that hee did nott give that contentmente to the towne in that funcone which hee & they desired and taking into consideracon that the towne did conceave that great hurte & detrimente mighte growe unto the same thereby hee in his love & good respecte which hee did beare thereunto acquainted Mr Alderman & his bretheren & the residue of the said courte that to give them contentment hee wold be willing to surrender uppe his place of schoolemaster att the feast of the Annuncyacon of the Blessed Virgine Marie nexte comeing uppon such propositions & condicons as hee then propounded which his loveing offer the said courte tooke in good parte

And in the said courte likewise came in one Mr Charles Hoole & made sute unto the said courte for the said place and did bring with him letters of comendacon from divers neighbouring knights docters of divinitie & gentlemen in his behalfe which were read in the courte that hee might succeed the said Mr Wilkinsone in that place & functione. Butt some of the said courte did move that there mighte bee further respitte & tyme of consideracon had before anie direct answere should bee given to the said sute to the ende there mighte be some further inquirie after some other persons, whoe perhapps mighte become suters for the place, the courts desire being to have the place furnished with the fittest & ablest man that might be gotten. The courte well approving this mocone respitte was taken & graunted for a fortnighte when ytt was agreed the Alderman should keepe annother courte and att that courte Mr Charles Hoole should have further answere.

The churchwardens accounte now published butt noe certentie made of ytt.

Symon Frith to paye xs to the churchwardens which was owing by his father.

f. 101 **Eighth Court of George Lloyd 11 March 1641**

Att this courte the aforenamed Mr Charles Hoole came with the certifficat aforesaid expecting then an answere from the courte to his said sute and att the same courte on Mr Cockes a stranger appeared & was likewise a suter unto the said courte for the said place butt broughte noe certifficate or letters of comendacons in his behalf,whereuppon the Alderman propounded the consider-acon of this buisnes to the courte whether of these twoe suters were fittest to be elected, and there being then presente in courte the Alderman & eleavon of his bretheren & of the seconde xii nine whereof the Alderman & tenn of his bretheren & five of the seconde twelve did declare themselves for Mr Charles Hoole by reasone of the certifficate & comendacons the receaved from the said gentlemen & other neighbours. Whereuppon ytt was then putte to the comoners whoe being the maior parte gave theire voyces for Mr Cockes.

Anthonie Thwaites att this courte being a stranger borne came into the courte & broughte in £x which hee tendred for his freedome according to order & auntiente custome of this Borough and in regarde hee maried a weif haveing manie children being a widdowe whose former husbande was likewise free of this borough haveing lived heare manie yeares & brought uppe his charge which were like to be chargeable to this Borough. This courte was willing & did agree he sholde paye butt twentie shillings and the reste to be given him backe againe of his said tenn poundes, which was then paid to the chamberlines,and thereuppon hee being desirous to be incorporated & made free this courte did assente whereuppon hee tooke his oathe of alegiance, was sworne free Burgesse and payd the due fees to the Clerke & Sergeants.

Ninth Court of George Lloyd 22 March 1641

Att this courte ytt was fullie concluded & agreed uppon that Mr Alderman & some of his bretheren with the keybearers & others sholde this daye goe to the vestrie to open the comon hutch to take oute the charter of Kinge Edward the sixte to shew & peruse aboute the electione of an new schoolemaster which was done accordinglie,and the said charter lefte in the handes & custodie of Mr Alderman.

Tenth Court of George Lloyd 25 March 1642

Att this courte ytt was likewise agreed to goe to the vestrie to open the comon hutch to use the comon seale for the sealing two indentures of demise made from the Alderman & Burgesses of this Borough the one to Anne Bristowe widdowe the other to one William Grococke which was done accordinglie in regarde whereof & uppon other occassions this courte was then dismissed.

Eleventh Court of George Lloyd 15 April 1642

Att this court uppon motions made concerning a peece of grounde called the More lyeing neare Grantham in Manthorpe feilde and being then by divers affirmed that the towne of Grantham in tymes paste usuallie kepte theire swine there and being now abridged thereof; ytt was agreed that a bill of complainte should be drawen & preferred to the Steward of the Courte Leete holden for the manor of Grantham that redresse mayo bo had therein & the Borough of Grantham inioye theire auntiente rightes & custome of keeping theire swine there as formerlie they have done.

Ytt was likewise agreed that one Boarene carpenter or milne righte should be talked withall to the ende that hee maye give direccons what tymber woode should be bought & provided for the amending of the mille called the Slate Mill belonging to the towne & Borough of Grantham and then a course should forthwith be taken for the buyeing & ecareing of the said wood & tymber.

Att this courte overseers for comon works belonging to this Borough being formerlie appoynted by Mr Alderman were now againe published viz Mr Edward Christian, Edwarde Rawlinson, John Scotte and Francis Bristowe And alsoe agreed that the lane adioyning Grantham called Barowbie lane should now by the said overseers be amended.

Att this courte questions being made whether the election of Mr Cockes to be schoolemaster of the free schoole belonging to this Borough was thoughte to be legall or nott by reasone that the schoole was nott then voyd after longe debate the same being putt to voyces the maior parte of the said courte voted that ytt was noe legall electione and desired that there mighte be somme speedie course taken to finde out some eminante man to supplie & settle in that place.

Twelvth Court of George Lloyd 20 April 1642

Ytt was this courte ordered that the interest money due to Mr William Welbie uppon Mr Hicksons bonde shold forthwith paied ine and hee to have new bondes given him for £200 with the interest att a certaine daye yett to come by Mr Robert Colcrofte Edward Rawlinson Mr William Clarke and Robert Trevillian

Att this courte ytt was ordered that Mr Hugh Wilkinson nowe shoolemaster of the free schoole belonging to this borough of Grantham att such tyme as he shall resigne & surrender uppe his righte & interest of & in the said schoole with the approbacon & good likeing of Mr Alderman & his bretheren for the tyme being shall after his said surrender have & be allowed by the towne & Borough of Grantham the somme of £xx a yeare during his natural leif & noe longer. And to have ytt confirmed under the comon seale of the borough for securitie of the said somme in that behalf. And in the meane tyme hee to keep his interest & righte in the said schoole till such tyme as the parte of this courte shall be agreed whoe shalbe the newe schoolemaster.

Mr Edward Christian & Thomas Fysher appoynted to buye & provide wood & tymber for to amend the Slatte Mille.

A motione made this courte to send twoe to inquire out an new schoolemaster butt nott agreed whoe those twoe shalbe that sholde be sente.

Att this courte Henrie Cole sonne of Henrie Cole one of the comburgesses a free
man borne desired to be incorporated & admitted a free man of this corporacon
whereunto this courte did freelie assente soe hee paid the chamberlins iis vid, vid
a peece to the Clarke & Sergeants,tooke his oathes & was admitted free.

A distresse graunted to Robert Trevillian against Christopher Browne for
departing the court without license unexecuted or brought in.

f. 102 **Thirteenth Court of George Lloyd 13 June 1642**

Att this courte by a generall consente and agreemente of the same Mr Robert
Colcrofte one of the comburgesses of this Borough was nominated and
appoynted to be elected Alderman of this Borough att the daye of electione for
one wholle yeare from thence next ensueing.

Att this courte John Rawlinson & Francis Bristowe are nominated and appoynted
to be coalebuyers for this presente yeare.

Att this courte cam Richard Archer one of the pettie constables of this Borough
and for some reasons to him the said Richard Archer best knowen haveing as ytt
seemeth betake himself to some other course of living hath now craved the good
will of Mr Alderman the rest of the comburgesses his bretheren and the wholle
courte, to resigne his said office, & to be freed from his attendance att this
courte, unto which request of his for the good will which they beare unto him the
wholle courte did freelie condiscend,whereuppon hee was by Mr Alderman
knocked of from his said office, and likewise released & freed from his service
& attendance on this or the like courtes,and William Cole was sworne constable
in his steade.

Att this courte ytt was likewise agreed that the comen armes belonging to this
towne & Borough of Grantham sholde be made fitt & shewed before the
gentlemen whoe were appoynted for taking the nexte veiwe of armes att
Grantham.

Villa sive Burgus in Grantham in Com Lincoln

Mr More	Mr Colcrofte
Mr Cole	Mr Christian
Mr John Mills	Mr Hansone
Mr Pearsone	

The said Mr Alderman did acquainte the gen comburgesses above named with
his extraordinarie occassions to travell the nexte daye into Yorkshire aboute
some specyall affaires, and made his request unto them for the same whereunto
they did generallie condiscende whereuppon the said Mr George Lloyd
Alderman did att the same tym appoint Mr John Mills above named to bee his
Deputie Alderman during his said necessarie occassione of absence and the said
Mr Mills did then by the appoyntmente aforesaid take the oathe of Deputie
Alderman in the presence of all his said bretheren the comburgesses.

Fourteenth Court of George Lloyd 18 July 1642

A letter sente from Edwarde Skipwith Esq to Mr Alderman & his bretheren
whereby hee doth declare himself to give to the poore of this Borough forever

(five poundes) to be disposed of by Mr Alderman & his bretheren for the tyme being in manner following (viz) that they shall putt the same forth uppon interest according to the statute in that case provided and sixe shillings of the interest money to be bestowed yearelie uppon Whitson week on twoe doozen of three pennie householde breade and then given unto foure & twentie of the poorest and most needfull people (widdowes being first respected) inhabiting in the High Streete & Castlegate, or uppon St Peeters Church Rowe, att the discretion of the churchwardens & overseers for the poore that yeare and that the other twoe shillings parte of the said interest, shalbe yearelie towards the maintenance of the roape & buckett belonging to the well one Peeter Hill, soe as sixe of the poorest & meanest householders which shalbe charged to the same, att anie tyme maye be thereby freed from payeing anie taxe or assessmente towards the providing of the roape or buckette of theire said assessmente nott rendering foure pence per house which gratuitie was by the wholle court thankefullie receaved.

Att this courte ytt was agreed & Edward Towne did then condiscende & promise to become bounde with Mr Colcrofte & others in the roometh of William Clarke to Mr William Wellbie of Denton for the payemente of moneys as this Borough of Grantham shall owe & are indebted unto him.

Robert Wood att this courte being a stranger borne came into this courte & brought in £x which hee tendred for his freedome according to order & auntiente custome of this Borough being now a freeholder within this Borough & likelie to prove a good townsman,this courte was willing and did agree that hee shoulde paye butt twentie nobles and the rest to be given him backe againe of the said £x which was then paid to the chamberlines and thereuppon hee beinge desirous to be incorporated and mad free this courte did assente whereuppon hee tooke his oath of alegiance was sworne free burgesse,and payd the due fees to the Clerke & Sergeants.

Fifteenth Court of George Lloyd 22 July 1642

Att this courte Edward Skipwith of this Borough esquire for the good will hee beareth to this corporacon and to supplie the same with some moneys for the presente wante hee perceaveth the Borough standeth in need of, hath freelie & of his owne accorde proffered & doth now lende unto this Borough £xx of lawfull English money gratice till the feast of St Micaell the Archangell next ensueing, which is kindelie receaved and this courte doe promise att the said feast of St Michaell to repaye the same againe.

Att this courte came William Knowstubbs a mussicione & George Reade a couper both being strangers & brought in ten poundes a peece which they tendred for theire freedomes according to order & auntiente custome of this Borough and in regard they were poore men & like to prove good townes men,nor like to hurte anie freeman being of theire trades within this borough this courte was willing & did agree that they should paye butt five poundes a peece and the rest to be given them back againe of theire tenn poundes a peece which was then paid to the chamberlines and thereuppon they being desirous to be incorporated & made free, this courte assente whereuppon they tooke theire severall oathes of allegiance, were sworne free burgesses and paid theire due fees to the Clerke & Sergeants.

Att this courte William Mattkine sonne of Thomas Mattkine one of the comburgesses of this Borough being a free man borne desired to be incorporated & admitted a free man of this corporacon whereunto this courte did freelie assente whereuppon hee tooke his oath of allegiance & was sworne free paid to the chamberlines iis vid & vid a peece to the Clerke & Sergeants.

Att this courte likewise Robert Smith & John Harison being strangers borne formerlie apprentices within this Borough did now each of them desire to be admitted free men of this borough which was freelie agreed unto by this courte and the said severall parties did paye to the comon boxe vs a peec and xviiid a peece to the Clerke & Sergeants tooke theire oathes of allegiance & soe were sworne free men of this Borough.

Att this courte ytt is alsoe ordered & agreed that an assessmente of £20 shall from ten dayes after this courte be made by Mr John Mills, Mr Pearson Thomas Fysher & Thomas Shorte assessors by this courte nominated & appointed for making the said assessmente to & for the paving the High Streete & other places wanting of this Borough in which assessmente making the said assessors are to charge & assesse at such & greater rates & taxacons in the assessmente all such persons as are most hurtefull & offensive in the streets with caridges or theire dores most broken and in need of repaire then such ordinarie people as are nothing neare soe hurtefull, the said assessmente to be allowed by sixe other justices & then to be brought to Mr Alderman.

f. 103 Whereas likewise att this courte Mr Robert Colcrofte William Hodgkinson Robert Trevillian and Francis Bristowe stand ioyntelie & severallie bounden for the debt of this Borough unto William Welbie gen in the somme of sixe hundred poundes for the paymente of three hundred poundes in or uppon the daye of which shalbe in the yeare of Our Lord 1643 being att the request of this courte. Itt is therefore by the generall consente of this courte agreed uppon & ytt is the firme promise of the same that the said Mr Colcrofte William Hodgkinson Robert Trevillian & Francis Bristowe & everie of them theire & everie of theire heires, executors & administraters & everie of them shall by this Borough from tyme to tyme & att all tymes hereafter be secured saved kept harmeles & indempmnefied of & from the said bonde & the conditon thereunder written and of & from all & everie forfeiture penaltie & paymente,and of all & everie somme & somes of money in theire conteined & mentioned.

Ytt is this courte further ordered that the order made in Mr Alexander Mores tyme A D 1630 that everie constable of this towne respectivelie within theire severall wardes shall weekelie everie Frydaye night forever hereafter repaire to the houses of everie housholder within this towne & shall there take notice in writing of them or of some in theire famelies (yf they will give them notice) what quantitie of corne or mault everie such housholder hath in the wholle weeke ymmediatelie grounde before att one of the Kings mills belonging to this towne,and att which of the said mills theire said corne or mault was grounde. And to deliver the same next morning to Mr Alderman, shall continue still in force,and anie constable neglecting or denieing to doe the same shall forfeit for everie offence to be payed to Borough twelve pence to be leavied.

Sixteenth Court of George Lloyd 16 September 1642

Att this courte John Castle miller of the Slate milne uppon his submissione & faithfull promise made that hee wold make the said Slate milne serve the towne well & sufficyentlie to grinde all such mault corne or graine as shalbe brought unto him. This courte was contente againe to continue him miller of the said milne uppon condicon that hee behave himself trustlie & honestlie to this borough in his said place

Att this courte ytt was alsoe ordered & agreed that the towne clerke shall search & peruse over the orders formerlie made for the providing of bucketts and att the nexte courte to certefie what bucketts are wanting by the first & seconde twelve & the comoners that what are wanting maye forthwith be provided according to the former orders.

Whereas there is a peece of grounde lyeing in Manthorpe feild neare Grantham Slate millne called the myers uppon which peece of grounde the inhabitants of the Borough of Grantham have formerlie & tyme oute of minde used to hearde & keepe theire swine there. Ytt is this courte concluded & agreed uppon that yf the inhabitants of this Borough or anie of them shall soe be disposed, they maye hereafter heard & keepe theire swine uppon the said peece of grounde in as free manner as formerlie they have done.

Att this courte Edward Rawlinsone of this Borough executor of the laste will & testamente of Thomas Pickering of the said Borough deceased brought in fortie shillings in open courte to the chamberlins which the said Thomas Pickering gave to Thomas Oldfeilde the younger his foure children now living (viz) tenn shillings a peece and to be putte into the towne of Granthams hands to interest to increase to theire severall uses & to be payed then severallie, when they shall accomplish theire severall ages of xxitie yeares, yf anie of them shall dye before they accomplish theire said ages of xxitie yeares then the survivor or survivors of them to have the said legacies with the interest thereof equallie to be divided amongst them.

Whereas there is an order that noe swine shalbe suffered to goe abroad in the towne streets uppon penaltie of forfeiting a 1d for everie swine soe offendinge, and John Trigge being the Beadle giving informacon that Edward Hawden Baker had certaine swine goeing openlie in the markett place to the annoyance of the inhabitants of the towne and in contempt of the said order; Thomas Graunt & William Parker constables for the markett place warde was by this courte commanded to distreane the said Edwarde Hawden by his goodes & cattells for the forfeiture for suffering his said swine soe to goe abroad contrarie to the said order,and the said constables in obedience to this courte did distreane the said Edwarde Hawden by a bible butt the said Edwarde Hawden did in further contempte sweare by god they shoulde take noe distresse there & shutt the dores & kept them in thausting them about the house untill by force they gate oute giving them ill language by calling them Jackes, they said constables making affidavitte whereuppon this court thought fitte to graunte the good behavior againste him the said Edwarde Hawden.

(Seventeenth Court of George Lloyd 7 October 1642)

Whereas the house & groundes adioyning to the house & groundes called Loves in Castlegate are much abused & made comon & used & inioycd by those that have noe righte thereunto to the greate damage & hurte of this corporacion Ytt is therefore this courte ordered that the chamberline shall forthwith cause the gates & dores towarde the streete to be well & surficyentlie nayled & barred uppe & alsoe cheined that non maye have anie more regall or passage there till further order & direction comannded by Mr Alderman & his bretheren.

Att this courte John Fearon & Edwarde Bristowe are chosen & appointed to be overseers of the markett place well, for the yeare following and to see ytt kepte in order as ytt ought to bee. James Gibsone likewise the chamberline is appointed forthwith to sende to London for a cocke to be sett uppon the conduitte pipe in the markett place.

Att this courte it was ordered that everie inhabitante within this Borough haveing anie houses or groundes adioyning uppon the River called mowbecke shall uppon wednesdaye nexte being the xvii daye of this instante October well & sufficyentelie scoure & clenge soe much of the River mawbecke as theire said houses & groundes shall ioyne thereunto,and manthorpe to doe the like uppon notice thereof given by Henrie Ferman Thomas Mussone ii of the pettie constables of this Borough and the towne of Grantham to doe the like at Walkergate Brigge.

Att this court William Kirke sonne of John Kirke being a free man borne desired to be incorporated & admitted a freeman of this corporacon whereuppon this courte did freelie consente soe hee payed the chamberline iis vid the Clarke & Sergeants vid a peece tooke his oathe of alegiance and freedome & was admitted a freeman of this borough.

f. 104   Eighteenth Court of George Lloyd 18 October 1642.

The Accounte of Richarde Pearsone gen comburgesse of the towne of Grantham & Thomas Doughtie collectors for the schoolehouse rentes

Imprimis they charge them selves with one wholle yeares rentes of the landes due the laste Michaellmas 1642 amounting to the somme of	£46	5s	0d
Deductions for moneys uncollected of the said rents			
Imprimis behinde for one wholle yeares rente of Richard Buttlers house in the markett place ending att Michaellmas laste	£1	0s	0d
Behinde of Charles Granby for his house in parte of his rente due as before	£0	5s	4d
Of Mr Hackeley for landes late in the tenure of Widdowe Clifton deceased	£0	12s	6d
The new house this yeare unletten	£1	6s	8d
The house & grounde late in thc tenure of Thomas Loaves this yeare unletten	£0	13s	4d

Mr Goodyeare for the oute rente of twoe shoppes in the markett place	£0	1s	0d
Summa	£3	18s	10d

Paide to Mr Wilkinsone schoolemaster & the usher for twoe quarters	£15	0s	0d
To him for midsomer & michaellmas quarters laste	£10	0s	0d
Paid to the Bayliffe for an oute rente due to the Kings Majestie 16s 8d & for acquittance 4d	£0	17s	0d
Now layed oute for a balke for the new house & to William Skevington & his man for ii dayes worke	£0	11s	0d
To Richard Nixe & Atkinson for 3 dayes worke & a halfe att the new house with beare bestoweds uppon them		3s	9d
To William Hornewood for work there & for nayles	0	0s	8d
for slates & for lyme	£0	7s	4d
To Edwarde Marshall & three others working there	0	3s	10d
Payed a laborer one daye to serve the slaters & drinke for them	£0	1s	0d
For ii rigge tyles & clenging the rubbish in the house	£0	1s	4d
Paid for nayles,alsoe poles,a piece of wood a pecke of lyme,a locke for the outer dore & for beare	£0	4s	7d
Payd Robert Trevillian for furdeale bordes & a locke iron bandes & other thinges	£0	9s	10d
Allowance for gathering uppe the rents	£0	5s	0d
Paid in money to the ohamberline uppon this accounte in open courte which was in the collectors handes £14		1s	0d
whereuppon they have discharged theire accounte	£28	5s	2d

Tho accounte of Thomas Mattkine gen comburgesse Coroner of the towne & soake of Grantham

There was a carte wheele presented by the Jurie to be the death of one Cooke which was by the same slaine in Barkeston feild which wheele being Sir Edward Husseys was valued to be worth	£0	10s	0d

And comaunde given to Richard Poole the Sergeante to call for the same.

The accounte of Edwarde Christian comburgesse & Escheator of the towne & soake of Grantham

Receaved by him for the finding one inquisicone after the death of William Crale	£0	15s	0d
Whereof discharged by him in fees & other dues	£0	18s	8d
Soe remaineth due to him which was paid him.by the chamberline	£0	3s	8d

The Accounte of the Mille masters of the profitte and charges of the mills from the xxxth daye of October 1641 untill the   daye of   1642

The receipts of John Bracewell & George Hardackers for the slate milles as by theire booke appeareth till the daye of 1642	£64	16s	9d

Tho receipts of John Fearon & William Clarke for for the
Well lane milles for ii monieths ending xvii daye of
November 1641 £18 00s 0d
Receaved of John Fearone for the residue of the profitte
of the Well lane mills till the daye   of   1642

Mr Aldermans Accounte

Receaved of Mr Skipwith which hee lente the towne
gratis £20 00s 0d
Receaved more of him which hee gave for ever to the
towne payeing 8s per ann as is cxpressed in the courte
booke the some of £05 00s 0d
Receaved more of Mr Welbie to make uppe the some the
towne oweth him £300 the some £02 06s 8d
Delivered a bill in courte of his layeings oute this yeare
which was then allowed him £29 17s 8d
Christopher Hanson since for his house & himself about
the towne buisnes £00 03s 6d
Soe then the some totall £30 01s 2d
Soe hee hath laid out more than hee hath receaved £2 14s 6d

f. 106 An assemblie holden by George Lloyde gen Alderman of the Borough of
Grantham aforesaid the comburgesses & burgesses of the same in Corpus
Christi Queare within the Prebendarie Church of Grantham aforesaid the
frydaye after St Lukes daye being the xxith daye of October 1642

first the said Mr Lloyde did sitte downe in Corpus Christi
Queare within the Prebendarie Church aforesaid.

Then next unto did sitte Mr Arthure Rhoades & Mr Colcroft

Then were there three comburgesses sente downe into the bodie of the Church
(viz) Mr Edward Christian Mr Thomas Mills & Mr Christopher Hansone.

Oute of which three one of them was ohossen to sitte uppon the cushione or
place of electione (viz) Edward Christian

Then were there three comburgesses sett uppon the cushion or place of
electione (viz) Mr Arthure Rhoades Mr Robert Colcrofte Mr Edward
Christian

Out of which three one was to be chossen Alderman of the towne Borough of
Grantham for this yeare next ensewing.

And by the generall assente of this assemblie Mr Robert Colcrofte was
chossen Alderman of this towne & borough for this yeare next to come.

And the said Mr Robert Colcrofte being elected Alderman as aforesaid for the
yeare to come did att this assemblie take his oathe according to the auntiente
& laudable custome of this Borough.

107 First Court of Robert Colcroft 28 October 1642

Mr Robert Colcrofte Alderman

First Twelve			*Second Twelve*	
Mr Alexander More	jur		Thomas Shorte	jur
Mr Lewes Somersall	jur		William Hodgkinson	jur
Mr Arthure Rhoades	jur		Edward Rawlinson	jur
Mr Richard Conye	jur		George Briggs	jur
Mr Henrie Cole	jur		Edward Towne	jur
Mr John Mills	jur		Gilbert Chauntler	jur
Mr Richard Pearson	jur		Thomas Fysher	jur
Mr Thomas Mattkine	jur		Brian Newball	jur
Mr George Lloyde	jur		John Bracewell	jur
Mr Edward Christian	jur		John Rawlinson	jur
Mr Thomas Mills	jur		John Fearone	jur
Mr Christopher Hanson	jur		John Bee	jur

Nominated Officials

Coroner	George Lloyde	gen jur	Parish	Thomas Somersall	jur
Escheator	Thomas Mills	gen jur	Clarke		
Church	John Rawlinson	jur	Sexton	Alexander	
masters	John Scotte	jur		Bothomeley	jur
Chamberlins	Thomas Fysher	jur	Scavengers		
	John Phiper	jur		John Trigge	
High	William Hodgkinson	jur		Richard Poole	
Constables	Thomas Shorte	jur	Millemasters for the Towne		
Under Constables			Mille	Brian Newball	jur
Markett	Thomas Secker	jur		Christopher Fysher	jur
Place	Thomas Hansone	jur	For the Slate Mille		
High	Thomas Wallett	jur		John Fearone	jur
Street	Robert Woode	jur		William Cole	jur
West	William Parker	jur	*Nominated Commoners*		
gate	Thomas Graunte	jur	Markett Place		
Walker	Francis Bacon	jur		Robert Trevillian	
gate	Edward Watsone	jur		James Gibsone	
Swine	Henrie Ferman	jur		William Cole	
gate	William Darnill	jur		William Clarke	
Castle	William Grococke	jur		Thomas Doughtie	
gate	William Graye	jur		James Walker	
Key keepers	Mr Alderman	jur		Edward Bristowe	
for the	Thomas Fysher	jur		Edward Still	
Common Hutch	John Rawlinson	jur		John Lenton	
Collectors	William Cole	jur		Henrie Browne	
for the Schoole-	Christopher Hanson	jur	High Streete		
house rents	Robert Clarke	jur		John Watsone	
Sergeants	Mathewe Whiting	jur		Thomas Wallett	
att Mace	Richard Poole	jur		Thomas Lane	
Gaoler & Baylif	Richard Poole	jur			

Markett	William Cole	jur	Westgate	
Seers	William Broughton	jur		William Parker
	William Kirke	jur		Thomas Graunte
Prisors	Edward Bristowe	jur		Christopher Fysher
of Corne	Augustine Winter	jur		John Wythey
Leather	Richard Baylie	jur		John Hutchine
Sealers	Henrie Wright	jur		Thomas Marshall
	Anthonie Wallett	jur		
	Thomas Lane.			

Nominated Commoners

Walker	Augustine Winter	Castle	Thomas Hanson
gate	Francis Bacon	gate	William Grococke
	Robert Tompson		John Scotte
	George Hardakers		Thomas Sparowe
Swine	John Phiper		
gate	Henrie Ferman		
	Thomas Mussone		

Att this courte came in Richard Sentance & William Knowstubbs with twoe of the servants of the said Knowstubbs musicians & desired to be the townes waites for this yeare to come whereunto Mr Alderman & this courte doth assente and Mr Alderman by the chamberlins did give unto them xiid a peece and soe the said Sentance & Knowstubbs have severallie bounde themselves to serve the towne as theire waytes for this yeare to come.

The churchmasters to paye Russell & Nixe xs for certain dayes workes they loste aboute veiwing the steeple (viz) to Russell viis to Nixe iiis.

Second Court of Robert Colcroft 18 November 1642.

Att this courte Mr George Lloyd late Alderman delivered uppe in open courte by the inventorie thereof the townes plate unto the said Robert Colcrofte gen now Alderman (viz) twoe silver canes, twoe beare boles, one wine bolle, one guilte cuppe, twoe silver tunnes, one beaker, a silver salte & cover, the horse race cuppe & casse & thirteen silver spones.

Three charter boxes delivered then alsoe in by the said Mr Lloyde viz the great charter box & twoe other charter boxes with the severall charters & other the writings in them conteined delivered then alsoe in open courte one green deske with divers evidences & writings therein conteined as by a note of particulars under the hand of Mr Alexander More Esq one of the comburgesses of this borough & therein locked doth apeare.

Uppon a letter this courte sente to Mr Alderman from Mr Doctor Saunderson Doctor of Divintie and this daye openlie read in courte in the behalf of Mrs Wilcocks his wives sister whoe inioyeth the benefitt of a lease of the schoolehouse lands granted to the said Docter Saunderson & Mr Brian Nelson her brother, he did by the said letter desire Mr Alderman & the rest of the courte that they wold be pleased to make uppe the xix yeares yett remaineing & unexpired in the lease to bee made uppe to xxi yeares which request Mr Alderman & the courte was willing & did graunte uppon such termes as was formerlie graunted for performance of such covennants as are comprised within a longer lease and soe that ytt was nott further preiudiciall to them.

Third Court of Robert Colcroft 16 December 1642

The accompts of James Gibson one of the chamberlins of the borough of Grantham for Mr George Lloyd his yeare late Alderman of the said borough.

The totall somme of the receipts of said James Gibson as by his booke of receipts appeareth is	£549	2s	0d
The totall somme of his payments as by his chamberlins booke appeareth is	£545	3s	8d
Soe remaineth due to him	£000	1s	7d

Att this courte Joane Hutchine widdowe late weif of Hutchine of Grantham yeoman deceased hath lente unto this corporacon the somme of fiftie poundes of lawfull English money for six monneths which the corporacon doth promise shalbe againe repaid unto her with the use & interest due for the same att the end & expiracon thereof.

Att this courte Edward Skipwith of Grantham Esq out of his love and well wishing to learning, and the better to make & incourage the viccars of Grantham (in the winter & colde tyme of the yeare to follow theire studdies) by an note under his hand did declare himself in manner following viz I give unto the towne of Grantham fiftie shillings the yearlie interest whereof being foure shillings I will that ytt be bestowed in some fitte & conveniente firewood by the discretion of the churchwardens for the tyme being to be allowed yearlie for the maintaineing of a fire within the librarie att such tyme as the viccars of the said towne or either of them shall have need or require during the tyme of theire studdie within the said librarie which fiftie shillings hee did deliver to the towne.

Att an assembly holden by Robert Colcrofte gen Alderman of the said borough and the comburgesses of the same hereafter named the firste daye of Febuarie A.D 1642.

The names of the comburgesses

Alexander More comb	Richard Pearson comb
Arthure Rhoades comb	Thomas Mattkine comb
Richard Cony comb	Edward Christian comb
Henrie Cole comb	Christopher Hanson comb

Att this assemblie the Alderman aforesaid being taken prisoner by the Captain authorised thereunto by a Committee of Parliamente now att Lincolne and being by them sent to Lincolne to appeare before the said committee the said Alderman ymmediatelie before hee was sente to Lincolne did nominate & appoynte Mr Alexander More one of the aforenamed comburgesses to be his deputie, and in his absence to supplie his place & office of Alderman, and the said Mr More did thereunto consente, and did take his oath, and was sworne deputie according to the tenor of a charter in this casse graunted to the Alderman and burgesses of Grantham aforesaid by His Soveringe Lorde the kings Majestie that now is.

f. 109   First Court of Alexander More Deputy Alderman 3 February 1642

Att this courte Arthure Rhoades gen one of the comburgesses of this borough by a generall consente thereof is chossen coroner for the borough of Grantham and the soke & liberties thereof in the roometh of Mr Lloyde one other of the comburgesses being coroner before butt now being absente & residing out of the liberties could nott execute & perform his said office,whereuppon the said Mr Rhoades in open courte took his oath & was sworne coroner.

Att this courte ytt was likewise fullie agreed that whereas the townes plate being in the custodie & keeping of Mr John Mills one of the comburgesses of this borough and being taken away by the Captaines now in Grantham authorised by a Committee of Parliamente now att Lincolne that hee the said Mr John Milles shall in noe account hereafter be made chargeable or lyable to make good the same, butt shall hereby clearlie forever be freed & discharged thereof.

Att this courte Gilbert Chauntler is elected & chossen one of the millmasters of the slate mille in the absence of John Fearon whoe was millmaster formerlie.

An assemblie helde the xixth daye of Februarie A D 1642 att the Guilde Hall in Grantham in the counsayle chamber ther by the persons hereafter named,

Alexander More deputie Alderman	Seconde Twelve	Commoners
Lewis Somersall comburg	Thomas Shorte	High Con- James Gibson
	William Hodgkinson	stables William Clarke
Arthure Rhoades comb	George Briggs	Robert Trevillian
Richard Conye comb	Edwarde Towne	William Cole
John Mills comb	Brian Newball	Henrie Ferman
Richard Pearson comb	Thomas Fysher	Francis Bristowe
Thomas Mattkine comb	John Fearone	John Phiper
Edward Christian comb	John Rawlinson	Edward Bristowe
Thomas Mills comb	John Bee	Thomas Doughtie
Christopher Hanson comb		John Scotte
		Thomas Lane
		Thomas Sparowe
		Thomas Wallett

Att this assemblie ytt was generallie & fullie agreed that the now Deputie Alderman Mr Alexander More Esq shold receave & take into his possession by the deliverie of Captaine Ascough of all the townes plate by his appoyntemente & comande, formerlie taken from & oute of the possession of John Mills one of the comburgesses of Grantham aforesaid, and uppon the receipt thereof shold give unto the said Captain Ascough an acquittance for the same and ytt was further by the said assemblie fullie agreed that yf ytt shold fall out that the said plate or anie parte thereof shold be taken out of the possession of the said Alexander More against his will or consente by anie person or persons whatsoever haveing or pretending to have anie lawfull power or authoritie stated doe or by anie other forme or violence,that then the towne of Grantham is to beare & sustaine the losse & damage thereof & the said Alexander More to stande & remaine free from all trouble & detremante thereof.

Att an assemblie holden by Robert Colcrofte gen Alderman of the said borough and the comburgesses hereafter named the fifte day of May A D 1643 Anno Regni R Caroli decimo nono.

the names of the comburgesses Arthure Rhoades comb Henrie Cole comb Thomas Mattkine comb. John Mills comb Thomas Mills comb Richard Pearson comb.

Att this assemblie the said Mr Alderman acquainted the gentlemen above named with his necessarie absence and the causes whereof hee could nott continue att home whereunto they all assented and Mr Alderman did appoynte & nominate the said Mr Arthure Rhoades to be Deputie Alderman during his said absence, and thereuppon the said Mr Rhoades tooke his oath of Deputie Alderman.

Att an assemblie holden by Arthure Rhoades comburgess Deputie Alderman and the comburgesses & burgesses hereafter named the xiith daye of June Anno Regni R Caroli decimo nono Anno Dm 1643.

Arthure Rhoades *comburgesse*	*Second xii*
John Mills comb	Thomas Shorte
Richard Pearson comb	George Briggs
Thomas Mattkine comb	Thomas Fysher
Edward Christian comb	John Bee
Christopher Hanson comb	

Comoners

William Cole	Thomas Graunte
Francis Bristowe	Edward Marshall
Edward Bristowe	William Grococke

Ytt is agreed att this assemblie that an assessemente hereafter shalbe mad for the maintenance & defrayeing such charges as the souldiers now lodging in Mr Caves house being aboute sixtie or more souldiers shall accounte unto the cheiffe constables of this borough bringing in how long they shall there remaine & the charge thereof.

An assemblie held the twentith daye of June A D 1643 at the Guild Hall in Grantham in the counsaile chamber there by the persons hereunder named.

	Second xii	
Arthure Rhoades comburgesse	Thomas Shorte	
deputie Alderman	William Hodgkinson	
Henrie Cole comb	Edward Rawlinson	
John Mills comb	George Briggs	Thomas Fysher
Richard Pearson comb	Brian Newball	John Rawlinson
Thomas Mattkine comb	Gilbert Chauntler	John Bee
Edward Christian	John Bracewell	
Thomas Mills comb		
Christopher Hanson comb		

Commoners

Thomas Hanson	Edward Still	John Lenton
Henrie Ferman	John Hutchine	Thomas Mussone
Thomas Graunte	Robert Woode	William Graye
William Parker	Francis Bristowe	William Grococke

Att this assemblie ytt was appointed & agreed that John Hutchine & William Darnill both of this borough shall forthwith gett all the towne bucketts to be sett in sufficyente repaire & amended and the same being soe performed then to goe aboute to gett the gratuities & benevolence of well disposed people within this towne towards the charges of soe needfull & necessarie a worke & to yeld an instant account of this theire doeings. Ytt was now likewise agreed that fortie shillings being now assessed uppon John Phiper by commissioners att Newarke towards the payment of one hundred & fiftie pounds imposed uppon this borough shold in his behalfe & att his wives request be layed downe & paid by the chamberline in parte of the money owing him by the towne of Grantham.

f. 110 Fourth Court of Robert Colcroft 31 July 1643

Att this courte by a generall consente and agreemente of the same Mr Edward Christian one of the comburgesses of this Borough was nominated & appointed to be elected Alderman att the daye of electione for one wholle yeare from thence nexte ensewing.

Att this courte John Rawlinson & Francis Bristowe colebuyers chossen and appointed in Mr Lloyds tyme of being Alderman made their accounte of £31 14s 2d being the stocke of buyeing coales for the poore within the Borough of Grantham (viz) delivered them by the former yeares colebuyers £17 18s 2d given by the Ladie Pakenham £x by Thomas Hussey £v by Mistress Hussey £iii 16s being parte of £v shee gave the towne of which stocke there is lefte 30s besides the coales delivered to the souldiers when they laye in the towne & other expenses then layed out amounted to £13 10s 9d or more soe there is remaineing now in theire hands besides the losses £16 13s 5d which is this courte ordered forthwith to be payde to John Bee & William Darnill whoe are now chossen colebuyers for this nexte yeare following and are to paye or otherwise satisfy for such coales as were the laste yeare borowed to & for the use of this corporacon.

Att an assemblie holden by Robert Colcrofte gen Alderman of the said borough and the comburgesses & burgesses hereafter named the twentieth daye of August Anno Regni R Caroli decimo nono Anno Dni 1643.

Robert Colcroft gen Alderman	Second xii
Alexander More as comburgesse	Thomas Short*
Lewis Sommersall comb	William Hodgkinson*
Arthur Rhoades comb	Edward Towne
Henrie Cole comb	Brian Newball
John Mills comb	Thomas Ffysher
Richard Pearson comb	John Bracewell
Thomas Mattkine comb	John Rawlinson
Edward Christian	John Bee
Thomas Mills comb	* cheiffe constables

Att this assemblie Mr Alexander More above named delivered uppe to Mr Alderman with the approbacon & good likeing of this assemblie all the townes plate which hee had receaved from the hands of Captaine Ascough aboute Februarie laste whoe had taken the said plate formerlie from this borough togeather with three charter boxes with severall charters in them and a greene deske with divers writings therein locked: all of which were in the keeping &

custodie of Mr More & by him were delivered as aforesaid and hee thereof discharged.

First Court of Arthur Rhodes Deputy to Robert Colcroft.

Att this courte Mr Edward Rawlinson by a generall consente of the said court is chossen one of the comburgesses in the roometh of Lewis Somersall gen deceased the said Mr Rawlinson paid to the clarke and sergeants xviiid for theire due fees and soe did take the severall oathes incydente & propper to a comburgess of this Borough.

Att this courte likewise John Scotte is elected & chossen one of the second twelve in the roometh of the said Mr Edward Rawlinson and hath alsoe in open courte taken his corporall oathe incydente & propper to the said place and degree & paid the clarke and sergeants theire due fees.

And ytt was alsoe agreed that the persons hereafter named	James Gibson
shall & doe remain in the callendar or bill for the second	John Phiper
twelve.	Henrie Ferman

The accompte of Thomas Mills Escheator for the towne & soake of Grantham

| Receaved by himself which he had for insufficyente yards wands & measures & being unsealed | £0 | 11s | 0d |

Which hee paid to Thomas Fysher chamberline in open courte Item he seized a half stone weight insuffycente & giving them naught which hee tooke from Samuel Coddington which hee brought into this court & left in the custodie of the towne clarke to be disposed of as this court shall hereafter consider of.

The Mille Masters accompte of Well Lane Mille and first the receipts of Brian Newball

The receipts of Brian Newball one of the said mille masters as by his booke appeareth	£89	6s	1d
His disbursements to the miller & loadsman & other charges	£22	1s	8d
More paid to the chamberline	£63	1s	7d
Soe paid & disbursed in all	£85	3s	3d
Soe paid & disbursed in all	£04	5s	9d

The receipts and payments of Christopher Fysher the other mille master of the said mille.

His receipts as by his booke appeareth is	£70	7s	0d
His disbursements to the miller & loadsman & other charges	£15	8s	4d
More paid to the chamberline	£33	0s	0d
Soe paid & disbursed in all	£48	8s	4d
Resteth in his hands due to the towne	£21	18s	8d

There was paid this courte by Anthonye Twaits to Brian Newball rent for a closse belonging to the mill £3 butt regard of some losses the said Twait sustained in the spring this courte was content to give him five shillings again the remainder being 55s the said Brian Newball paid presentlie in open courte to the chamberline.

There was this courte paid by Thomas Fysher the chamberline to one William White a poore man of this Borough by this courte appoyntemente in parte of money due unto him from this town the somme of tenn shillings.

William Coale his receipts of the mills

Imprimis for _____ weekes	£37	0s	0d
The weeklie charges	£28	10s	1d
Paid more into the chamberlins hands	£05	0s	0d
Soe then remained in his hands	£03	9s	11d
Paid after for rente unto the mille	£00	17s	0d
For his wages	£00	5s	0d
Soe there remains in his hands	£02	7s	10d

Which hee hath paid into the chamberline

f. 111 More disbursements & payments of William Coles oute of the schoolehouse rents

Paid & lente more oute of this (viz) to John Scotte & Francis Bristowe which they laide out about the pumpe 50s & moneys owing to Mrs Colcrofte malte £1 7s 6d

in all	£3	17s	6d
Paid hereof to the chamberline	£5	6s	5d

Soe there remaineing in the hands of the schoolehouse rents

besides what hee uncollected	£0	17s	0d

Att an assemblie holden by Arthure Rhoades comburgesse deputie Alderman of this Borough of Grantham aforesaid the comburgesses and burgesses of the same in Corpus Christi Quoare in the Prebendarie Church of Grantham aforesaid the fridaye after St Lukes day being the xix daye of October 1643.
First the said Mr Rhoades as deputie Alderman did sit down in Corpus Christi Quoare in the roometh of Mr Alderman & himselfe.
Then next unto him did sitt down uppon the cushion or place of electione Mr Edwarde Christian.
Then were there three comburgesses sent down into the bodie of the church (viz) Mr Thomas Mills Mr Christopher Hansone Mr John Mills.
Oute of which one was chossen to sitte uppon the cushion or place of electione Mr Thomas Mills.
Then were there three comburgesses sat uppon the cushion or place of election (viz) Mr Arthure Rhoades Mr Edward Christian & Mr John Mills.
Oute of which there was one to be chossen Alderman of the town or borough of Grantham for this yeare now nexte ensewing.
Whereuppon the said Mr Rhoades as deputie Alderman discharged himself from the place of deputie Alderman according to antiente custome and the said Mr Christian being elected Alderman as aforesaid for the yeare to come did att this assemblie take his oath according to antiente & laudable custome of this Borough.

112 First court of Edward Christian 27 October 1643

Mr Edward Christian Alderman

First 12 comburgesses	*The Second 12*	
Mr Alexander More	Gilbert Chauntler	jur
Mr Arthure Rhoades	John Rawlinson	jur
Mr Richard Conye	George Briggs	jur
Mr Henrie Cole	Edward Towne	jur
Mr John Mills	Brian Newball	jur
Mr Richard Pearsone	Thomas Shorte	jur
Mr Thomas Mattkins	John Bracewell	jur
Mr George Lloyde	Thomas Fysher	jur
Mr Robert Colcrofte	William Hodgkinson	jur
Mr Thomas Mills	John Fearon	jur
Mr Christopher Hansone	John Bee	jur
Mr Edward Rawlinsone	John Scott	jur

Nomina Officiariorum

Coroner	Robert Colcrofte	gen jur
Church	John Scotte	jur
wardens	John Hutchine	jur
Escheator	John Mills	gen jur
Chamber-	William Hodgkinson	jur
lins	Thomas Secker	jur
High	Gilbert Chauntler	jur
Constable	John Rawlinson	jur
Under	Markett Place	
Constable	Edward Watson	jur
High Street		
	Thomas Wallett	jur
	Thomas Lane	jur
Westgate		
	Robert Wood	jur
	Edward Hardon	jur
Walkergate		
	John Byshoppe	jur
	William Bristowe	jur
Swinegate		
	William Graye	jur
	Thomas Mussone	jur
Castlegate		
	William Growcocke	jur
Keepers of the Common Hutche		
	Mr Alderman	jur
	William Hodgkinson	jur
	John Scotte	jur
Sergeants att Mace		
	Mathew Whiting	jur
	Richard Poole	jur.

Market Place

	John Poole	jur
	John Pecke	jur
	Edward Still butcher	jur
Prisors of Corne		
	George Hardakers	jur
	Richard Kellam	jur
Leather Sealers		
	John Primett	jur
	Thomas Newball	jur
	Raphe Goodwine	jur
	William Haskerd	jur
Millemasters Wellane Mille		
	George Briggs	jur
	Edward Bristowe	jur
For the Slate Mille		
	Edward Towne	jur
	Francis Bristowe	jur
Parish Clarke		
	Thomas Somersall	jur
Sexton		
	Alexander Bothemeley	jur
Scavengers		
	John Trigge	
	Widow Poole	
Collectors of the Schoolehouse Rents		
	Thomas Mattkine	jur
	Augustine Winter	jur
Aldermans Clerk		
	Robert Clerk	gen jur

Nomina Communum Curie Infra Script

Markett Place	High Street
William Cole	Thomas Wallett
John Bischoppe	Robert Woode
Edward Bristowe	Thomas Lane
James Walker	Walkergate
John Lenton	Augustine Winter
Edward Still	George Hardakers
Westgate	Francis Bristowe
William Parker	Swinegate
Christopher Fysher	William Darnill
John Hutchine	Castlegate
John Newball	Anthonie Wallett

Att this court came in William Knowstubbs & Richard Sentance & desired to be continued the town waits for this yeare to come whereunto the courte assented and they are retained and hired now in open courte by xiid a peece paid & delivered unto them by the chamberline.

Agreed att this courte that Thomas Oldfeild the elder of this Borough should hire a litle parcell which hee tooke from a hang house hee formerlie sett uppe uppon a parcell of grounde belonging to the house in Walkergate where hee now dwelleth, and thereuppon hee promised forthwith to departe & leave his said house to this Borough to be disposed of as the towne shall thinke fitte.

Att this courte a letter was sente from John Phipher toutching some moneys which he therein did expresse to be owing unto him by the Borough and therein desired therein hee might have the same which letter was then openlie red in courte which being then considered of by reason of his wives then presente necessitie ytt was then concluded & agreed that the churchwardens for her presente releif shold paye unto her £iii in parte of the said debt and the remainder of his debt that cold appeare to be iustlie due his reckoning & accounte mad perfecte shold be paid after a now assessment made & agreed uppon for the church.

Ytt was then ordered & agreed that all accountants belonging to this borough whoe have nott now perfected theire said accounts shold perfecte theire accounts & bring in such money as shall by them be due to this borough before nine of the clocke the next courte be lyable to anie former order toutching accountants.

f. 113 An assemblie holden by Edward Christian gen Alderman of the Borough of Grantham and the comburgesses burgesses comoners & freemen hereafter named at the Guilde Hall the last day of October in the nineteenth yeare of Kinge Charles Anno Dm 1643 as followeth (viz)

Mr Alderman	*Second Twelve*
Arthure Rhoades *comburgesse*	Gilbert Chauntler
John Mills comb	John Rawlinson
Richard Pearson comb	George Briggs
Thomas Mattkin comb	Edward Towne
Thomas Mills comb	William Hodgkinson
Christopher Hanson comb	Thomas Fysher
Edward Rawlinson comb	John Scotte

Comoners	Freemen	
William Cole	Mr Skipwith	Richard Kellam
Henrie Ferman	Edward Hawden	Bryan Godley
Thomas Graunte	Edward Lenton	John Worth
Francis Bristowe	Edward Marshall	George Reevline
George Hardaker		Robert Nidde
William Darnill	Edward Charles	John Massone
Thomas Mussone	Robert Smith	
William Graye	Thomas Kidde	
Robert Wood	Nicholas Becke	
Edward Watson	Anthonie Robinson	
John Hutchin	William Blacke	
Thomas Hanson	John Osborne	
William Grococke	William Beecrofte	
Anthonie Wallett	John Pecke	
John Byshoppe	Henrie Speedie	
Edward Bristowe	Anthonie Twaite	
James Walker	William Bristow	
T Marshall		
Thomas Lane		

Att this assemblie ytt was fullie concluded & agreed uppon by all the parties above named that an assessemente of £300 shall forthwith be made & leavied by the inhabitants of the borough of Grantham to raise the said somme of £300 for freeing the said Borough of the imposssition & taxe which Sir Thomas Fairefax one of the Parliamente generalls imposed & laid uppon this Borough as alsoe the redeeming Mr Alderman the comburgesses & others which hee then tooke prisoners to Nottingham till the said some shalbe paid & performed.

Assessors att the said courte by the same nominated & appointed to make the said assessmente.

Mr Richard Pearson	Comoners
Mr Edward Rawlinson	William Cole
George Briggs	John Hutchine
William Hodgkinson	Thomas Wallett
George Hardakers	
William Darnill	
William Grococke	

Att an assemblie holden by Edward Christian gen Alderman of the Borough of Grantham the comburgesses burgesses & comoners hereafter named at the Guilde Hall the sixt daye of November in the nineteenth yeare of the reigne of our soveraigne Lord Kinge Charles Anno Dmi 1643 as followeth

Mr Alderman	Second xii
Arthure Rhoades comburgesse	Gilbert Chauntler cheiff
John Mills comb	John Rawlinson constables
Richard Pearson comb	George Briggs
Christopher Hanson comb	Edward Towne
Edward Rawlinson comb	Thomas Shorte
	John Bracewell

Thomas Fysher
William Hodgkinson
John Scotte

Comoners

Thomas Graunte	John Hutchin
Edward Watson	Thomas Marshall
William Cole	John Byshoppe
Edward Bristowe	Augustine Winter
James Parker	George Hardakers
John Lenton	Thomas Musson
Thomas Lane	William Graye
Thomas Wallett	William Darnill
Robert Wood	William Grococke
William Parker	Anthonie Wallett
John Wythey	Thomas Sparowe

Att this assemblie Mr Alderman againe moveing that the assessemente of £300 imposed by Sir Thomas Fairefaxe (one of the Parliamentary generalls) uppon this Borough might be leavied & gathered for the releasing himself & other gentlemen then imprisoned att Nottingham for the same ytt was nott then agreed nor condiscended unto. Whereuppon Mr Alderman then moved the towne wold be pleased to allow him & the rest of them then imprisoned such reasonable charges as they shold be att during theire tyme of imprisonment & inlargemente to which ytt was fullie concluded & answered that Mr Alderman should onelie be alowed six pounds towards his charges & would graunte noe more

f. 114 An assemblie holden by Arthure Rhoades comburgess & the comburgesses and burgesses of Grantham aforesaid in the Guilde Hall of Grantham upon the feast daye of the purifficacon of the Blessed Virgine Marie comonlie called Candlemas Daye being the seconde daye of Februarie in the xixth yeare of King Charles 1643 by those whose names are underwritten.

Athure Rhoades Deputie Alderman	John Rawlinson cheiff
Richard Pearson *comburgess*	constable
Robert Colcrofte comb	Thomas Shorte
Thomas Mills comb	John Scotte
Edward Rawlinson comb	

Comoners

Edward Watson	John Byshoppe
Robert Woode	William Bristowe
Edward Bristowe	George Chambers
John Lenton	Francis Bristowe
Thomas Lane	William Darnill
Anthonie Wallett	William Graye
Christopher Fysher	Henrie Ferman
Anthonie Wallett	

Att this assemblie uppon a warrante sente to this Borough from Sir Peregrine Bertie knight high sheriffe of the countie of Lincolne Sir William Thorolde knight Sir Charles Hussey knighte Sir Jervice Nevill knighte Sir Robert Tredway knight & Thomas Harrington esq dated the 24th of Januarii 1643 commissioners for our Soveraigne the Kings Majestie for the assessing & leaveing the somme of £125 with comannde for the paymente of the remainder of such other moneys as now formerlie due uppon anie other assessmentes from the towne & parish of Grantham the same to be paid into Sir Robert Thorold knighte His Majesties treasurer for Lincolnshire uppon the sixt day of this instante monneth of Februarie for the maintenance of His Majesties forces within the countie of Lincolne. Ytt was now fully concluded & desired that Mr Colcroft & Mr Thomas Mills twoe of the comburgesses of this Borough togeather with John Rawlinson cheiffe constable of the same wold take the time to goe to Belvoyre to mediate with the said Sir Robert Thorold touching the said warrante to ease the said Borough to which they were willing did condiscend & went accordinglie.

Att this assemblie three constables were anew chossen & sworne for the remainder of the yeare yett to come (viz) Robert Wood formerlie constable for Westgate butt now sworne constable for the Markett Place Christopher Fysher in his roome sworne constable for Westgate,and William Darnill in Thomas Mussons rome deceased sworne a constable for Swinegate.

Thomas Graunt chossen colebuyer in William Darnills place for the residue of the yeare to come.

First Court of Arthur Rhodes Deputy Alderman 17 February 1643

Att this courte the letting of olde Thomas Oldefeilds house in Walkergate was by the said Deputie Alderman propounded to be lett for xxi yeares and thereuppon hee demanded £30 for a fine & the olde rente whereuppon Mr Raphe Nidde & Mr Robert Clerke towne clerke being both desirous to take the same were then asked what they woulde doe in the buisnes,and first ytt was demanded of Mr Clerke what hee wold give for a fine & paye the olde rente, to which hee gave presente answere that hee wold give tenn pounds for a fine & paye the olde rent upon condicon onelie that the house & kitchine with a litle stable, & the fences might be sett in repaire & made sufficyent & tenantable :and then Mr Nidde was demanded what hee would give butt hee answered hee would nott medle therewith whereuppon this courte thought good that Mr Mattkine & Mr Edward Rawlinson, Thomas Shorte, John Scotte, William Darnill, Henrie Ferman, Francis Bristowe & Thomas Wallett should veiwe the defects of that house the house where Stente dwelleth which Thomas Doughtie holdeth & Thomas Hopps house & certifie to the next courte theire oppinions & thereuppon the same should be lett.

Second Court of Edward Christian 19 March 1643

Att this courte Mr Alderman caused a letter sente from the Governor of Belvoyre toutching the assessemente of £125 to be openlie read, and thereuppon wish the constables to use theire best furtherance & indeavors to gett what moneys they could gett in uppon the said assessmente.

Att this courte John Scotte & William Parker were nominated & appoynted to lett the standing under the covering of the pumpe in the Markett Place with as much speed as possible they can; and att as higher rate as they can raise ytt unto and att the nexte courte to certifie their doeings therein.

Five pounds given to this borough by one Mr Smith and three pounds taken & receaved for a cow supposed to be in Mr George Lloydes hands to be inquired what is become thereof. Attkinsons testimonie concerning wood brought to Gilbert Chauntlers from old Thomas Oldfeilds house saith that that parte which was cloven which hee says was worth 8s:and that which he sett which was there uncloven was worth vis viiid more.

f. 115 Third Court of Edward Christian 5 April 1644

Ytt is att this courte ordered & agreed that the Pettye Constables of everic warde within this borough shall at next courte here to be holden for Mr Alderman & bring in the names of all such strangers innemates & others as of late have come to inhabite & dwell within this borough according to an order thereof heretofore formerlie made in the seconde yeare of Thomas Wikliff gen late Alderman of this borough or else forfeit vs a yere and in the meane tyme to give warning to the said strangers & inmates that they themselves doe likewise personallie appeare att the said next court of Mr Alderman here to be holden. And further that the said Pettye Constables in theire severall wards within this borough doe alsoe search & see what ladders hookes & draggs belonging to this borough are wanting in anie of theire wardes and to testifie the same that they maye be againe made uppe & brought & layde in the Guilde Hall.

Att this courte Henrie Ferman by a generall consente of the same is elected & chossen one of the chamberlins of this borough in the roometh of Thomas Secker who was formerlie chosen one of the chamberlins for this borough butt in regard of his continuall absence from home alledging that hee durst nott continue & abide att home hee was now dismissed the said place & office and the said Henrie Ferman chosen to serve in his place & roome the remainder of the yeare now to come,and there uppon the said Henrie Ferman in open courte tooke his oath & was sworne chamberline for the remainder of this yeare now to come.

Fourth Court of Edward Christian 14 June 1644

Att this courte by a generall consente and agreemente of the same Mr Thomas Mills one of the comburgesses of this borough, was nominated & appoynted to be elected Alderman att the daye of election for one wholle yeare from thence next ensewing.

This courte being now informed that divers leases belonging to this borough (viz) the lease of the tolles of stall setting eg Mr Aldermans house called the Red Lyone, the house where olde Thomas Oldfeilde latelie dwelte, the house where Stente dwelleth, Widow Inghams house Henrie Hewitts house & Wrights house in Manthorp, the house & grounds ioyneing Loves in Grantham, a lathe in Well Lane which Skevington useth & Hopps house, were some of them ended & the rest neare expired ytt is this courte with the mutual consente thereof ordered & agreed that Mr John Mills. George Briggs, Henrie Ferman, and William Cole shall take presente veiwe of the said houses, stall setting & premisses and to certifie under theire handes what they or the maior parte of them doe esteeme the same to be severallie worth and what they may by anie wayes or meanes to lette unto for the best benefitt & advantag of this borough soe that the courte maye dispose thereof accordinglie.

At this courte Leonard Camocke of this borough chapman was called in question for scandalous & uncivill speeches uttered by him against some of the comburgesses & constables of this borough contrarie to an order thereof formerlie made for which in open courte he was fined iiis iiiid which said somme of money being tendred downe by the said Leonard Camocke & submitted to the courte the said Leonard Camocke did openlie confesse that hee uttered the said words out of his passione & infirmitie & acknowledged himself sorrye for his said offence which this courte taking into consideracon are contented & ytt is the generall agreemente of the same to restoe xxd of the said iiis iiiid to the said Leonarde & soe xxd thereof is putt into the comon boxe.

Att this courte Henrie Wright of Westgate currier was brought in & informed againste for harboring & takeing in one Thomas Gill a stranger to inhabitte & dwell as innemate within him contrarie to the order thereof made & confermed by the iudges, whereuppon a distresse was sente for to the said Wrighte & another to the said Gylls for theire said offence and warning then given to both of them forthwith to reforme & amend the same or else to suffer the penaltie of the foresaid order.

Att this courte alsoe one East a stranger being of late come to inhabitte within this borough contrarie to an order of strangers & inhabitantes before mentioned to bee confirmed by the iudges was by the constables of the High Street with a distresse of his then taken brought into the courte, and there he was warned forthwith to departe the towne with his weif & children or else to abide the penalties of the said order.

Uppon a motion this courte made by Mr Dicks one of the viccars of this borough to Mr Alderman, his bretheren & the reste of the courte there assembled toutching sanctuarie hee supposed to receave by an assessmente latelie made in this borough as hee did then alledg to which motion this courte gave good respecte, & told him they were verie loath hee should by them be anie wayes opprest and wished him propounde which wayes they might give him sattisfaction therein whereuppon hee desired that whereas hee dwelt in a house belonging to this borough called Byensdale, that they would be pleased to allow him the half yeares rente alreadie due to this borough and the half yeares rente to come due for the same for this next half yeare now comeing, hee payeing & discharging all such out rents as is issueing & payable out of the said messuage for the said terme by this borough to which his said motion this court did loveinglie & freelie condiscend & agree unto.

Fifth Court of Edward Christian 7 July 1644.

Att this courte ytt is covenanted, concluded, graunted & agreed uppon to & with Richard Tomlinson of this towne shoemaker & Richard Johnson of the same town laborer by the generall consente & agreemente of the wholle courte here assembled this presente daye that in consideracon of the fine of five poundes of lawfull English money now att this courte paid as alsoe in consideracon of five poundes more of like lawfull money of Englande to be paid to the Alderman & burgesses of this towne or borough of Grantham by them the said Richard Tomlinson & Richard Johnson theire executors administrators or assignes shall & may have receave & take to theire sole & proper uses & behoofs all & singular the benefitt & profitt of and concerning all & all manner of stalls & the setting & the placing of the same in the Markett Place of this towne for forriners onelie both att all the faires & on the markett dayes (the placing or displacing of anie person or persons that att anie tyme or tymes during presente graunte shall take or hire anie of the stalls aforesaid of the said Richard Tomlinson & Richard Johnson theire executors administrators or assignes and the altering or putting into the said stalls or standings anie other person or persons att the libertie & discretion of the said Alderman or two or three of the comburgesses of this borough for the tyme being or to such other officer or officers as they shall thereunto nominate & appointe alwayes reserved & accepted to have & to holde the said profitt or benefitt of the stalls aforesaid (except before excepted) to them the said Richard Tomlinson & Richard Johnson theire executors administrators or assignes from the teneth daye of November next ensewing the date of this presente courte for during & untill the full end & terme of thirteen yeares from thence next ensewing & then fullie to be complett & ended; yelding & payeing therefore yearlie & everie yeare during the said terme unto the chamberlins of this borough for the tyme being or to theire successors to the use of the Alderman & burgesses the rente or somme of five poundes of lawfull money of Englande att twoe dayes of payemente or feasts in the yeare that is to say the feast daye of Phillippe & Jacobe comonlie called Maye daye & the feast daye of Martine the Byshoppe comonlie called Martinmas by even & equall proportions provided they paye one of the said half yeares rentes alwayes aforehand yearlie during the said terme, and the other half yeares rente to be paid att the other of the said feasts or dayes of payemente or within tenn dayes next after the said feast (being lawfullie demanded) or else this presente graunte to be utterlie voyd & of noe effect, and yelding & payeing during the terme aforesaid unto the Alderman of Grantham aforesaid one couple of goode fatte capons att the feast of the Nativitie of the Lord God. And ytt is further concluded & agreed and the said Mr Alderman comburgessess & burgesses doe for them & theire successors promise & agree to & with the said Richard Tomlinson & Richard Johnson theire executors administrators & assignes that yff att anie tyme during this graunte ytt shall please God to vissitt this towne with the plague or lay anie other affliction uppon ytt, (which God in mercie keep from us) whereby marketts & faires cannot be in such usuall manner & order as now they are that the said Richard Tomlinson & Richard Johnson theire executors administrators or assignes shall have all of the £v rente soe longe as marketts & faires shall nott be had & kept in Grantham as were formerlie as Mr Alderman & comburgesses of this borough the maior parte of them for the tyme being shall thinke reasonable & conveniable to alow.

f. 116   Att this courte likewise John Bee & Thomas Graunt are nominated & appoynted to be colebuyers for this presente yeare and Thomas Fysher one of the laste yeares colebuyers did paye unto John Bee one of the now colebuyers £ii xviiis ivd being parte of the stocke of the coale money & all that was in the hands of the same.

Att this courte John Wythey gave this courte to understand that there was £x xiiis due for use money for his wieves childrens portions is in the townes hands & desired he might have the xiiis paid unto him & yf the towne pleased he wolde lett the £x remaine still in theire hands yf they thought fitt alowing him use for soe longe as he helde the same whereuppon the xiiis was graunted unto him and the courte wolde something consider of holding the said £x uppon use.

Mrs Anne Walton likewise demanded the use money due unto her for such money as is alsoe of hers in the townes handes & ytt was agreed yf possible shee should have parte thereof payed to her the next weeke ensueing.

Uppon bills of expenses & layeings oute by the constables of this borough toutching soldiers & comaunds and warrants from commanders as they abeade & passed nott farre of & aboute this towne & now delivered in by John Rawlinson one of the cheiffe constables amounting to the somme of £26 1s 9d ytt is this courte concluded ordered & agreed that all the money due uppon the said severall bills (except on pound five shillings which Thomas Lane has sett downe for his imprisonemente att Lincolne) shalbe forthwith paid & discharged.

Ytt was this courte ordered that Thomas Nixe the dyer should be discharged for hanging his cloath & setting his stall att the Markett Place pumpe on the markett & fayre dayes (except hee will contente to give as valuable a consideracon as anie other will give for the same.)

Sixth Court of Edward Christian 9 July 1644

Ytt was this courte ordered that all those officers which were officers & accountants during the tyme Mr Colcrofte being Alderman shall att the next courte to be holden for Mr Alderman that now is make theire personall appearance and there perfect & finish all such accounts & reckonings as during the said Mr Colcrofts yeare they were chargeable withall concerning the borough of Grantham or else everie one of them that shall herein make defalte & nott then appeare shall forfeit to the use of this borough tenn shillings to be leavied by distresse according to the anntiente custome of the said borough.

And whereas ytt was this courte founde out & made knowen that manie & great arerages due to be payed by divers persons of this corporacon uppon the assessemente to be made for the payemente of the somme of £125 taxe by his Majesty's Commissioners to & for his Majesty's service towards which divers have payed theire partes uppon the said assessemente,and manie others have either neglected or denyed to paye the same which being a thing uniuste that some should paye & othere shifte out & never paye uppon which occassion ytt hath againe pleased His Majesty's Commissioners to send out a new warrante to Mr Alderman & the High Constables of this borough thereby charging them for the leavyeing & collecting the said arerages due uppon the said assessmente whereuppon ytt is this courte ordered & agreed that the now constables of everie warde within this borough shall forthwith collect & gather all the saide arears that are behinde & unpaied, due uppon the said assessmente as shall appeare to be due by the last yeares constables bills and thereof yeld a instant & true accounte to Mr Alderman & the rest of his bretheren.

Att this courte came Richard Tomlinson & payed £v which was the remainder of the £x fine which hee was to paye for the graunte of the profitt of the stalls setting in Grantham att faires & marketts and paid the same in open courte to the chamberline & desired the courte would be pleased to graunt unto him that

Richard Johnsons name of Grantham likewise might be inserted & tyed with him in the graunte formerlie made unto him of the profitt of the stall setting before mentioned to which this requeste this courte did agree and thereuppon Richard Johnsons name was inserted & putt into the before recyed graunte to be ioyned towarde thereof togeather with him the said Richard Tomlinson as by the same graunte now fullie appeareth.

Att this courte ytt is fullie concluded & agreed uppon that Robert Tompson of this borough fellmonger shall have a lease sealed unto him of a messuage & tenemente in Grantham in a strcct callcd Walkergate wherein William Stoute now dwelleth for the terme of xxi yeares to begine & comence att the feast of St Michaell the Archanngell next ensewing uppon the payemente of £ix vis viiid of lawfull English money att Mr Aldermans next courte to be holden for the borough of Grantham for a fine to the use of this borough and entering into such covenants as other tenants doe uppon condicon alsoe that he the said Robert Tompson shall att his own propper costs & charges sett in good & sufficyente repaires the houses & fences in and aboute the premises as formerlie they have bine & soe continue them. And alsoe paye yearlie the auntiente rente of xxs,and one couple of good fatte hennes putting further sufficyent securitie to the towne for performance of the covenants conteined in this said lease in earnest of which said bargaine he payed Mr Alderman iis vid.

Att this courte Thomas Nixe of this borough dyer hath taken the standing for hanging & layeing forth his cloathe & other his dyed stuffes & comedities dyded in & aboute the covering of the pumpe in the Markett Place of this borough, for one wholle yeare, from this daye nexte ensewing for iid a weeklie rente to be paied quarterlie to the chamberlins of this borough uppon demande

Charles Penny & William Stout both of this borough have here in open courte promised to come in to Mr Aldermans next courte & then to desire to have theire freedoms.

Seventh Court of Edward Christian 7 September 1644

Att this courte Mr Robert Clerk Towne Clarke payed in open courte to Henrie Ferman chamberline of this borough five poundes in lue of a fine for the house backeside & premises where olde Thomas Oldefeilde latelie dwelt in Walkergate in Grantham aforesaid, and att his owne costs & charges is to repaire amend & build the said dwelling house walls & fences in & uppon the premises. And thereuppon this courte doth demise & lette unto the said Mr Clerke the said houses & premises for xxi yeares to comence att the feast of St Michaell the Archaungell now next ensueing & payeing yearlie the rente of twentie five shillings & one couple of good fatte henns or capons & under such covenants & agreements as other the towne tenants enter into.

Att this courte cam Mr Docter Saunderson of Boothbie & in the behalf of Mrs Wilcocke his wieves sister (to whose use a former lease was graunted of the schoolehouse houses & landes) and in regard of the uncertaintie & daunger of the tyme, alledging some hardnesse to be in letting the former lease, desired the courte wold be pleased to graunte that foure yeares more be added to the former lease & that the old lease might be delivered in made voyde and a new lease be graunted of the same which request this courte taking into consideracon, did condiscend & agree that three yeares shold be added to the former lease & an new lease thereof to be made to comence of St Michaell the Archanngell laste paste A D 1643 to hold for xxi yeares.

Att this court came Robert Tompson & payed to the chamberlins in open courte nine pounds vis viiid which was for the fine hee was to paye for a lease of houses & backeside wherein William Stout now dwelleth in Walkergate in Grantham whereuppon ytt was agreed hee should have a lease sealed accodinglie

117 Ytt is alsoe now concluded & agreed uppon by the wholle courte that a distresse should be graunted against Charles Pennye for using trading within this borough by the space of twoe monneths laste paste nott being made a freeman of this borough contrarie to an anniente order of the said borough, uppon which order ytt was agreed that anie that shold use anie trade within the same, nott being formerlie made free of this borough shold forfeitt for everie weeke soe offending tenn shillings to the use of this borough whereuppon a distresse was graunted out accordinglie of which the constables are to make theire retornes.

Att this court ytt was moved by Mr Alderman what sattisfacation & allowance should be made for the charges & expenses Mr Alderman, Mr John Mills, Mr Mattkine, Mr Colcrofte, Mr Thomas Mills, Gilbert Chauntler, Henrie Ferman & Francis Bristowe comburgesses & burgesses of this borough whoe were taken awaye by Sir Thomas Fairefax, caried to Nottingham & there imprisoned, for the payemente of £300 uppon an assessemente imposed uppon this borough by the said Sir Thomas Fairefaxe uppon which motion ytt was thought by the wholle courte verie iust & equall that in regard ytt was for the townes occassions & nott theire owne they should be allowed & payed all such reasonable charges & expenses which they or anie of them were anie wayes putt unto concerning that buisnes, and thereuppon ytt was freelie & fullie by the wholle courte concluded & agreed uppon that an assessemente shalbe made within this borough for the raising of moneys for the payemente of them theire foresaid charges & expenses.

Anthonie Thwaite & John Fysher are alsoe by this court nominated & appointed overseers for Swinegate well.

Att this courte came poore Widowe Daniell & made her povertie knowen to Mr Alderman & the rest of his bretheren & desired shee might have some succor & releiffe & ytt was then thought fitte shee should be provided for of a house for her harbour & to have further weeklie collection.

Eighth Court of Edward Christian 4 October 1644.

Whereas att the xiith courte of Docter Wilson gen late Alderman of this borough ytt was ordered that everie constable that now is or shalbe in his or theire wardes, shall within one monneth next after warning or comannde given them for the tyme being or the cheiffe constables of this borough, collect & gather all such assessments & taxacons made there for the good of the borough or else take or bring in distresses to the Hall for the same uppon paine of xxs of everie constable that shalbe founde defective therein which orders being this courte taken into consideracon and finding the constables att this presente were negligent & remiss in executing theire offices for collecting & gathering assessments made within this borough for the good of the same ytt is therefore now againe thought fitt & agreed uppon that the said former orders shall still continue remaine & be in full force as formerlie and anie constable that shalbe faltie in the execucon of his office according to that & this order shall forfeit xxs to be leavied according to the anntiente custome of this borough.

Att this courte Mr George Briggs one of the mille masters of this borough & of the towne mille gave this courte to understand that one Toppins his weif daughter to Widow Welborne deceased being indebted for malte they receaved & had from the said mille, & now haveing noe money to make presente paye were contente in parte of theire said debte to assigne over a bondc uppon which John Gregorie of this borough is within a shorte tyme to paye them £x which this courte did accept of & ordered that the mill masters of the same mill should see the sam performed accordinglie.

Att this courte Mr Alderman caused a letter to be openlie reade which was sent unto him from Mr Rowland Greenwood for money due unto him from this borough, for twoe yeares ending in June laste paste whereuppon ytt is this courte desired Mr Alderman would be pleased to answere the said letter to intreat Mr Greenwood to forbeare till after the courte daye & then what money could be raised, hee should then have what they could then procure.

Att this courte John Hickson late apprentice to William Hodgkinson deceased cordwainer being free borne desired to be made free & incorporated into this borough whereunto this court did freelie assente soe hee paid the chamberline iis vid the clarke & sergeants vid a peece tooke his oath of alegiance & freedome & was admitted a freeman of this borough.

f. 118   Ninth Court of Edward Christian 11 october 1644

Att this courte came Jonathan Parnam & paied to the chamberline in open courte £iii which was for a fine hee was to paye for the lease of a barne or lathe in the Well Lane late in the tenure or occupacon of Symon Frith of which £iii the courte considering the lathe to be in some decaye & that hee was to be att the charges for repaires thereof did agree & were contented that the chamberline shold give him xs backe againe of the said £iii which was done accordinglie.

A lease of the tole of oate meale taking within this borough was this courte lett to Joseph Drake to holde from the date thereof untill the feast of St Michaell the Archanngell next ensewing the date hereof yelding & payeing thereof during the said terme to the Alderman & Burgesses of this borough for the tyme being the somme or rente of xvis of lawfull English money the same to be payed quarterly to the chamberlins of this borough by eaven & equall portions to be devided the same to be lawfullie demanded.

Palmers boye being fatherlesse & motherlesse is by the consente of this courte putt out apprentice to Edwarde Pateman of this borough cordwainer & with him for the presente to dwell during the space of 8 yeares.

Henrie Wright a distresse a paring kniffe, cobiron for continueing a tennante being a stranger contrarie to order.
Thomas Bill a bible & a litle panne for the like delivered.

Twelth & Ultimate Court of Edward Christian 24 October 1644.

Att this courte Mr George Briggs by a generall consente of the courte is chossen one of the comburgesses of this borough in the roometh of Mr Henrie Cole deceased. And the said Mr Briggs paid to the Clark & Sergeants vid a peece for theire severall fees and soe did take his oathes incydente & propper to the comburgesses of this borough.

Att this courte likewise Henrie Ferman is elected & chossen one of the second twelve burgesses in the roometh of John Feron one of seconde twelve burgesses latelie deceased and hath in open courte taken his corporall oathe incydente & propper to the said place & degree, and payed the Clarke & Sergeants theire due fees.

Thomas Secker & William Cole are likewise this court chossen of the seconde xii burgesses (viz) Thomas Secker in the roometh of William Hodgkinson one of the seconde xii burgesses deceased, and William Cole in the roometh of John Scotte one other of the seconde xii burgesses likewise deceased butt have nott as yett taken theire oathes.
And ytt was then alsoe agreed that the persons hereafter named shall & doe remaine in the callender or bill for the seconde xii   John Hutchin
                                                    Augustine Winter
                                                    Francis Bristowe

Att this courte Thomas Graunt layed downe xxs according to an auntiente order of this borough for refusing to be constable thereunto nominated & elected by Mr Alderman & his bretheren which being putt to the courte what the courte would give him againe which being taken into consideracon in regard hee taken uppon him & executed another office within this borough was sorrie for his offence & promised hereafter to shew no such evil example ytt was all given him backe againe.

Ytt was this courte likewise thought fitt & agreed uppon that James Gibson & John Phiper being formerlie left in the callender for the second xii in regarde they laye for the space of twoe yeares or thereabouts & inhabited out of this borough & have nott paied & proffered the severall duties therein by them due & belonging to bee done & that they sholde now be cleane putt out of the said callender.

Ytt is this courte further ordered & agreed that whereas the churchwardens have formerlie ordered to make theire accounte for this borough as uppon this courte daye as regard they are usuallie chossen into theire said office aboute Christmas, they are from henceforth to make uppe theire said accounts for the said borough yearlie att Christmas before such tyme as they shall goe out of theire said office.

Att this courte Anthonie Twaits paid into the chamberline for rente of a closse belonging to this borough and desired the courte wold be pleased to consider of him & restore him some parte thereof backe in regard of the great losse hee had sustained by reason of the souldiers quartering in this borough and thereupon this courte did give him backe oute of his said rente tenn shillings.

John Castle of Paunton came into this courte & promised to paye to this borough for the tolles due uppon that road vs att the feast of St for tolls in that Martine the Byshoppe next ensewing.

Mr John Mills being escheator of this borough for the laste yeare now ended did declare unto this courte that nothing escheated or fell within his said yeare & therefore hath noe accounte to make.

Mr Colcrofte likewise coroner for this borough for the laste yeare now alsoe ended did the like & saith nothing fell within his office & soe hath noe accounte to make.

Mr Alderman his accounte & first his receipts

Imprimis receaved of Edward Towne mille master of the Slate mill att severall tymes by reason William Hodgkinson was then dead	£19	0s	0d
Receaved more of Edward Bristow mille master of the Well lane mille att severall tymes as appeareth by his booke	£22	7s	0d
	£41	7s	0d

His payements for wante of the chamberline as abovesaid

Imprimis to Mrs Porter for the laste Ladies Daye quarteridge ending the 25th daye of March 1644	£10	0s	0d
To Widow Walton in parte of use money due unto her	02	0s	0d
To William Wood on a letter of request for a losse he had by fire	0	5s	0d
Payed to Mr Clerke for his half yeares wages due att the feast of the Annuncyacon of the Blessed Virgine Marie laste paste	03	0s	0d
Payed to himself for the £20 hee is to be allowed from the towne	20	0s	0d
Payed to him more for his charges & expenses when hee was caried to Nottingham & Belvoy by reason of Sir Thomas Fairfax his comittment for the £300 assessmente being from home xxtie weekes	£07	0s	0d
In all	£43	0s	0d
Soe there remained due to him	£01	18s	0d

In all which by the consente of the courte was by the chamberline paied unto him.

The Mille Masters accounte of the Well Lane mille (viz) George Briggs & Edward Bristow from the 28th of October 1643 untill the i8th of October 1644.

Theire receipts as by theire booke appeareth be	£120	12s	2d
Theire disbursementes as by theire booke appeareth bee	£033	6s	3d
Soe the cleare profitte of the mill besides charges & disbursements which with £x 19s by a bonde made over by the expense of the towne for malte owing by him & his wief to the said mille masters they receaved from the said mill & 40s allowed to the said George Briggs upon his accounte the remainder they paied to the chamberline	£084	8s	4d

More receaved of Anthonie Twaits for rente hee paid for
the mille closse and now paid to the chamberline   £002   0s   0d

119 Edward Towne millmaster of the Slate mill his accounte from the 27th of
October 1643 untill the 29th of March 1644

Imprimis his receipts   £45   15s   1d
His disbursements & charges   £14   05s   11
Soe then due to the towne which hee paied to Mr Alderman
& the chamberline by Mr Aldermans appoymente   £31   09s   02

The accounte of Francis Bristowe the other mille master of the Slatte mille
fron the fifte of Aprill 1644 until the 18th of October 1644.   £   s   d
Imprimis the profitts & receipts of the said mille   48   04   06
His charges & disbursements as by his accounte & booke
appeareth   19   15   11
Soe clered & due to the towne for this   28   08   07

The receipts & disbursements of William Hodgkinson one of the chamberlins
of this borough deceased from October 29th 1643 till Aprill the 11th 1644 as
followeth

Imprimis his receipts as by his booke appeareth   25   03   04
His payements which hee paied & disbursed out of this   25   08   00
Soe there remained due to him out of this   00   04   08
More hee receaved Februarie the 5th 1643 for halfe a
yeares rente ending att Michaelmas before as by his booke
appeareth butt unsett downe whose or for what rente nor
how payed or disbursed   02   10   00

The accounte of Henrie Ferman the other chamberline belonging to the
borough from Aprill the 19th 1644 untill the 24th of October 1644 as
followeth
Imprimis all his receipts as by his booke in particulars
appeareth is   152   16   11
his payements as by the same booke appeareth   152   15   05
Soe then resteth due to him from the towne   000   01   06

The accounte of Thomas Mattkine gen comburgesse & Augustine Winter
collectors for the schoolehouse rentes.

Imprimis they charge themselves with the whole yeares
rents due for the said landes the laste yeare amounting to
the somme of   45   12   04
Whereof paid to Mr Wilkinsone schoolemaster   20   00   00
Paid to the chamberline   15   16   01
Payed the collectors theire allowance   00   05   00
Soe then the somme of the payments is   36   01   01
Rents uncollected & due of the said schoole house rents as
by theire booke appeareth for this yeare is besides the
house & land adioyning to Loaves   08   02   06
Areares receaved by the said collectors
Imprimis of John Skevington   00   06   08

Of Thomas Hoppe	00	01	00
Of Widowe Exon	00	00	10
Of Henrie Johnson of Manthorp	00	06	03
Of Roberts Howett	00	02	06
of Mr Hackeley for Cliftons landes	00	05	00
Soe theire wholle receipts	38	12	07
Whereof paid as above	36	01	01
Soe resteth due to the towne	02	11	06

f. 120 Att an assemblie holden by Edward Christian gen Alderman of the borough of Grantham aforesaid the comburgesses & burgesses of the same in Corpus Christi Quoare in the Prebendarie Church of Grantham aforesaid the Friday after St Lukes daye being the 25th daye of October 1644.

First the said Mr Alderman did sitt downe in Corpus Christi Quoare within the Prebendarie Church aforesaid.
Then next unto him did sitt uppon the cushione or place of electione Mr Arthure Rhoades Mr Thomas Mills.
Then were there three comburgesses sente downe into the bodye of the church (viz) Mr Hanson, Mr John Mills & Mr Edward Rawlinson.
Out of which one was chosen to sit uppon the cushione or place of electione (viz) Mr John Mills.
Then there were three comburgesses sitt uppon the cushione or place of election (viz) Mr Rhoades, Mr Thomas Mills & Mr John Mills.
Oute of which there was one to be chossen Alderman of the town or borough of Grantham for this yeare now nexte ensueing.
And by the generall assente of this assemblie Mr Thomas Mills was chosen Alderman for this borough for this yeare now nexte to come.
Whereuppon the said Mr Edward Christian did discharge himself from the place & office of Alderman according to the auntiente custome: and the said Mr Thomas Mills being elected Alderman as aforesaid for the yeare to come did att this assemblie take his oath according to the auntiente & laudable custome of this borough.

f. 121 First Court of Thomas Mills 24 October 1644

Mr Thomas Mills Alderman

The first twelve comburgesses	*The Second xii burgesses*	
Alexander More Esq comburgesse	John Bee	jur
Arthure Rhoades comburgesse	Henrie Ferman	jur
Richard Coney comburgesse	Edwarde Towne	jur
John Mills comb	Gilbert Chauntler	
Richard Pearson comb	Brian Newball	jur
Mr Thomas Mattkin comb	Thomas Shorte	jur
George Lloyde comb	John Bracewell	jur
Robert Colcrofte comb	Thomas Fysher	jur
Edward Christian comb	John Rawlinson	jur
Christopher Hanson comb	William Cole	
Edward Rawlinson comb		
George Briggs comb		

Nominated Officers

Coroner	Mr Edward Christian		Key keepers	Mr Alderman	
Escheator	Mr Hanson	jur	for the	John Rawlinson	
Church	Brian Newball	jur	Comon		
			Hutch	Brian Newball	
wardens	John Hutchine	jur		John Hutchine	
Chamb-	John Rawlinson	jur	Collectors of		
erlins	Thomas Graunte	jur	the Schoole-	Mr John Mills	
High Con-	John Bee	jur	house rents	Christopher Hanson	
stables	Henrie Ferman	jur		Mr Robert Clerke	
				Mr Aldermans Clerk	

Under Constables

			Sergeants	Mathew Whiteing	
Markett	Edward Watson	jur	att Mace	Richard Poole	
Place	John Bishoppe	jur	Gaoler & Bayliffe		
	Edward Still	jur	Prisors of	John Wythey	
High	Thomas Wallett	jur	Corne	John Peeke	
Street	Thomas Kidde	jur	Markett	Henrie Cole	
	Richard Baylie	jur	Sayers	William Kirke	
Weste	Edward Hawden	jur		William Broughton	
gate	Henrie Speedie	jur	Leather	John Primett	
	Thomas Baylie	jur	Sealers	Thomas Marshall	
Walker	William Bristowe	jur		William Haskerd	
gate	George Wraye	jur		Henrie Right	
Swine	William Darnill	jur	Mille masters	Thomas Fysher	
gate	William Graye	jur	for the Well	Augustine Winter	
	John Fysher		Lane Mille		
Castle	Daniell Coddington	jur	For the Slatte	William Cole	
gate	Robert Smith	jur	Mille	George Hardackers	
	Thomas Sparowe	jur	Parish clarke	Thomas Somersall	
			Sexton	Alexander Bothomley	
			Bedles and	John Peake	
			Scavengers	Widow Poole.	

Nominated Commoners

Markett Place			Westgate		
Edward Watson	jur		Edward Hawden	jur	
John Byshoppe	jur		Christopher Fysher	jur	
Edward Still	jur		Henrie Speedie	jur	
Robert Wood	jur		William Parker		
Thomas Secker			John Wythey	jur	
Robert Trevillian	jur		John Hutchine	jur	
Thomas Graunte	jur		Thomas Marshall	jur	
Thomas Hanson	jur		Thomas Baylie	jur	
Christopher Browne			Walkergate		
James Gibson			William Bristowe	jur	
Thomas Doughtie			George Wraye		
James Walker	jur		Augustine Winter	jur	
John Kirke	jur		Robert Tompson		
Edward Bristowe			George Hardakers	jur	

Edward Still	jur	Francis Bristowe	
John Lenton	jur	Swinegate	
High Street		William Darnill	jur
Thomas Lane	jur	William Graye	jur
Thomas Wallett	jur	John Fysher	jur
Thomas Kidde	jur	Castlegate	
Richard Baylie	jur	William Grococke	
		Thomas Sparowe	
		Robert Smith jur	

Att this courte Mr Alderman according to auntiente order & custome of this borough did nominate & appoynte twelve pettie constables for this borough for the yeare following, for everie ward twoe constables (viz) for the Markett Place Edward Watson, John Byshoppe, for the High Street Thomas Wallett, Thomas Kydde, for Westgate Henrie Hawden, Henrie Speedye, for Walkergate William Bristowe, George Wraye for Swinegate, William Darnill, William Graye, for Castlegate Daniell Coddington, Robert Smith, after which nominacon & appoyntment some of the said constables (in regard the troublesommes of the tymes) desired Mr Alderman to nominate & appoynte some more constables in some of theire said wardes to be helpfull & assistante unto them Whereuppon Mr Alderman did nominate & appoynte five more constables (viz) for the Markett Place Edward Still butcher, for the High Street Richard Baylie, for Westgate Thomas Baylie, for the High Street Richard Baylie, for Swinegate John Fysher, and for Castlegate Thomas Sparowe.

f. 122 Second Court of Thomas Mills 10 January 1644

The courte being moved by Mr Richard Conye comburgesse toutching money due by this borough to Joseph Clerke sonne of Raphe Clerke late of this borough comburgesse deceased ytt was this courte ordered that the somme of nine pounds fifteen shillings should att or aboute this daye fortnight to be paid to the said Mr Conye to & for the use of the said Joseph for which said somme of nine poundes xvs the said Mr Conye on the receipt thereof is to give a lawfull & sufficyente discharge.

This courte being further moved concerning the payemente of certaine use money likewise now due to Anne Walton widow ytt was this courte likewise concluded & agreed uppon that with what conveniente speed can be shee shold have & be paied the same, shee alsoe payeing & allowing for moneys as are by her behinde in areare & unpayed uppon anie former assessmente or towne duties belonging to this borough.

Third Court of Thomas Mills 1 February 1644

Ytt is this courte ordered that the now churchmasters shall first make demand of all the areares due & unpaid uppon anie assessemente made for quarterings belonging to the church of Grantham anie tyme for three yeares laste paste before Mr Alderman that now is entred to bee Alderman of this borough and to certifie to Mr Alderman & his bretheren the names of those that shall refuse to paye the same that such further order may thereuppon be taken for the getting in thereof as to Mr Alderman & his bretheren shalbe thought fitt & conveniente.

Att this courte likewise Thomas Wayte & Richard Braunston being strangers borne butt formerlie apprentices within this borough did now each of them desire to be admitted & made free men of this borough which by this courte was fully agreed unto and the said severall parties did paye to the common boxe vs a peece & xviiid to the Clerk & Sergeants tooke theire oathes & soe were made freemen of this borough.

Fourth Court of Thomas Mills 11 April 1645

Whereas William Darnill late of the borough of Grantham victuler deceased att his death desired the towne of Grantham would be pleased to accept & take into theire handes fiftie poundes of money of which hee intended should be in parte of portions for his children, the town allowing use for the same; which this courte taking into consideracon, and haveing care for the good of the children as for sattisfactione of the request of the said Darnill: ytt was this courte ordered & agreed that the said fiftie pounds shalbe had & receaved by the chamberlins of this borough and that the executors or such others whoe ar intrusted to deale for the said children shall have securitie for the repayemente of the said fiftie pounds togeather with the use thereof to & for the use & benefitte of the said children under the comon seale belonging to this borough according & in such manner & forme as others uppon the like occassions have formerlie had the same.

Ytt was therefore this courte further ordered & agreed uppon that the said fiftie pounds being soe receaved as above said shalbe payed by the chamberlins (in casse Mr Skipwith wilbe contented & pleased to forbeare this borough for fiftie pounds which is owing unto him by this borough) to James Ferman in parte of the money due by bonde to Sushanna Ferman his late mother deceased which he challengeth to be due unto him by waye as executor to his said mother deceased.

Ytt is likewise this courte concluded & agreed that parte of the moneys alreadie due to William Clarke of this towne from this borough shall by the chamberlins of this borough be payed unto him out of such moneys as they shall next receave from the mille masters belonging to this borough.

123 Fifth Court of Thomas Mills 9 May 1645

Att this courte by a generall consente & full agreement of the same Mr John Mills one of the comburgesses of this borough was nominated & appoynted to be elected Alderman att the nexte daye of election for one wholle yeare then nexte ensueing which office this courte hopeth hee will accept of accordinglie.

Att this courte Gilbert Chauntler & James Walker are nominated & appoynted colebuyers for this yeare nexte ensueing.

Att this courte the chamberlins receaved fiftie pounds to pay moneys belonging to William Darnills children which was by them payed & disposed of, as the court did then order & agree, and ytt was thereuppon further ordered that the executors of the said William Darnill or such others as are instructed aboute the said childrens money shall have such securitie for the same from the Alderman & Burgesses & theire successors by waye of covenante under the comon seale of this borough as shalbe reasonablie devised advised or required; the same to be done & performed with what conveniente speed may be and in the meane tyme this courte doth further promise from tyme to tyme to paye the yearlie interest after the rate of of eighte poundes per cent for the said fiftie pounds from the tyme of the receipts thereof to the executors or those that are interested for the saide children for & towards theire educacon & bringing uppe.

Ytt was this courte likewise ordered & agreed that the use money of the fortie poundes of Marie Searsons children of Lincoln spinster (viz) Margarett Searson, Marie Searson & Christopher Searson which was formerlie putt into the townes handes by William Clarke her brother to raise portions for the said children shall forthwith be cast uppe and then the totall somme of both principall & interest being allowed & agreed uppon securitie & assurance for the same to be alsoe concluded given under the comon seale of this borough by Mr Alderman & the Burgesses of this borough & theire successors for the tyme being for the payemente of such sommes of money as according to the casting uppe & agreemente, shall thereuppon grow due to the said children as they shall accomplish theire severall ages on & by the said agreement agreed uppon & expressed.

Ytt was further agreed uppon that the constables belonging to everie warde within this borough shall before Satterdaye nexte comeing provide & furnish theire said severall wardes with twoe ladders for everie warde for the use of this borough and yf the constables of anie warde shalbe fayling herewith the same to forfeite to the use of this borough xxs to be leavied for what other forfeite was according to the custome of this borough.

Fifth Court of Thomas Mills 5 September 1645

This courte being now informed that a quarters stipend which was due to Mr Wilkinson late schoolemaster of this borough before the death of the said Mr Wilkinson was unpaied ytt was now ordered & agreed that the said quarters stipende being five poundes should by the collectors of the schoolehouse rents of this borough be paied to the said Mr Wilkinsons daughter to whome the same is now due.

Ytt was this courte alsoe ordered that notice should the next Sabeth daye be openlie declared in the church that there should bee a meeting in the church uppon Wednesdaye nexte by Mr Alderman & his bretheren aboute one of the clocke in the afternoone to agree uppon an assessemente to be made for repaire of the glass windowes & other needfull things aboute the church to the end that all parishioners belonging to the same whome ytt shall concern might then be likewise there.

Seventh Court of Thomas Mills 9 September 1645

Ytt was this courte ordered that the High constables of this borough shall give warning to the pettie constables of the same that the nexte court holden by Mr Alderman they bring in notes what inmates or other newcome inhabitants are latelie come & inhabite & dwell within anie of theire severall wardes.

Att this courte ytt is by a generall consente ordered & agreed that everie inhabitant within this borough of Grantham shall before the tenth daye of October next att theire owne costs & charges sufficyentlie pave & amend the streets wherein they dwell which heretofore have bine paved as far as theire buildings & walls adioyning to theire said streets foure yardes from the said buildings & walls in paine of everyone that shall faile in the performance thereof to forfeite to this borough for everie yard soe unpaved & nott amended as aforesaid six pence: and shall alsoe from tyme to tyme att theire owne propper costs & charges maintaine the same and yf anie defecte shalbe in anie of theire said pavements, notice thereof being given to the parties soe neglecting or offending by anie of the constables of the said warde or other officers thereunto appoynted yf the same shall nott then forthwith be amended the parties soe neglecting & offending to forfeite to this borough for everie such defalte five shillings both which penalties & forfeitures are to be leavied by distresse & sale of the offenders goodes according to the anntiente custome of this borough, and to be ymployed to the amende of the said pavements.

Att this courte alsoe John Wythey is chossen & appoynted one of the overseers of the weste well.

124 Eighth Court of Thomas Mills 30 September 1645

Att this courte ytt was fullie ordered & agreed that the usher now to be chossen for the free schoole of Grantham shall have for his yearlie stipende and allowance the somme of sixteen poundes per annum over & besides all such gratuities & benevolence as hee shall receave from the parenths & frendes of such children as shall by them be putt unto him to be educated & instructed.

Att this courte uppon some occassions moved ytt was ordered & agreed that the chamberline of this borough shall for this presente provide & bespeake the dinner att Mr Aldermans election which shalbe nexte chossen att some inne or other conveniente place as to them shalbe thought fitte for that purpose.

This courte being moved & intreated by Mr Edward Christian one of the comburgesses of this borough that they wold be pleased to graunt unto him a lease of the house or inne where he dwelleth in Walkergate called the Red Lyone whereuppon ytt was this courte freelie concluded & agreed uppon in regard the said Mr Christian hath by cassualtie of fire & other crosses & losses latelie befallen him, receaved greate damage & losse shall have a lease thereof graunted him att Michaellmas laste paste for one & twentie yeares hee payeing yearlie the anntiente rente due for the same & under such covenants & agreements as other the townes tennants usuallie doe covenante & agree unto.

Ninth Court of Thomas Mills 6 October 1645.

This courte being somewhat urged by Mr Rowland Greenwood for the payeinge unto him eight & thirtie poundes of lawfull English money alreadie due unto him for the use of certaine moneys due unto him by this corporacon to the children of James Chambers deceased ytt was this courte agreed that the chamberlins of this borough should presentlie paye unto him the said Mr Greenwood the somme of twentie poundes, and the remainder which was eighteen pounds being taken into further consideration, nott knowing well for the presente how to paye the same, ytt were by those whose names are underwritten & hereafter mentioned, wishing the welfare of this corporacon propounded that yf this borough wold be soe pleased & that they mighte have theire moneys payed unto them againe by this corporacon att or before the nativitie of our Lord God nexte comeing, they for presente woulde laye downe the same in manner following Mr George Briggs xls, Henrie Ferman xls, John Rawlinson xls, Robert Trevillian xls William Clarke xls, Thomas Doughtie xls, Edward Bristowe xxxs, William Parke xxxs, Thomas Graunt xxs, William Grococke xxs & Thomas Baylie xxs uppon which theire free offer & payemente this courte doth order the said parties shall have theire severall moneys soe by them lente repayed unto them againe att or before the nativitie of our Lord God above said according to theire desires, whereuppon they paid to the chamberlins theire said moneys to sattisffie the said Mr Greenwood.

f. 125 Tenth and Ultimate Court of Thomas Mills 24 October 1645

Mr Alderman his accounte & first his receipts

Imprimis receaved of Thomas Graunte chamberline	23	00	00
Of Alexander Bothomeley for tole	00	05	07
Of Mr John Bee of cole money	03	00	07
The somme of his receipts	26	06	02
His payements & disbursements			
Imprimis paied to Mr Greenwood	08	00	00
To Peake	00	01	00
To Alexander Bothomeley	00	01	00
To Thomas Myles	00	03	11
Paied Mr Holland	05	00	00
To Captaine Bee	01	10	00
Paid Mr Chauntler for cole money	03	00	07
Layed out & given to poore people passengers & strangers for this yeare	00	18	06
Paied to worke folks & givene them to drink	00	07	09
Spente uppon necessarie occassions	00	09	02
Layed oute Mr Newtons money more	00	03	04
His disbursements	19	15	03

Soe remaining in his hands £6 10s 11d which this courte was contente & did freely agree to alow Mr Alderman towards his charges & expenses uppon his imprisonement att Nottingham for the assessemente then demanded uppon this borough by Sir Thomas Fayrefaxe.

The accounte of John Mills gen comburgesse one of the collectors of the schoolehouse rents his partner being dead

Imprimis the wholle rente of the schoolehouse lands wherewith hee is charged	46	05	08
Receaved thereof by his booke of receipts appeareth	27	05	01
Payed by the said collector as followeth			
To Mr Wilkinson & his daughter for three quarters stipende	15	00	00
To Slaters for slate, lyme & workmanshippe aboute mending the schoolehouse as by a note appeares	02	08	08
The allowance for collecting	00	05	00
Soe the somme of the disbursements & payements	17	13	08

Rents uncollected as followeth

Imprimis Richard Elston for his rente	03	00	00
Butlers house	01	00	00
Thomas Shorte jun	00	10	00
Charles Grandby	00	05	04
Mr Wilkinson his executors	00	08	06
Mr Mattkine for Newhouse closse	01	04	00
Widow Griffine	00	13	04
Mr Archer	00	08	08
Loves his house	00	13	04
Mr Harley	01	04	00
Jonathan Parnam	01	00	00
William Taylor	00	03	00
Widow Winter	01	00	00
Widow Walgrave for three quarters	00	15	00
Mr Rowland Greenwood	00	08	00
Henrie Johnson quarters	00	18	09
William Clarke	00	06	00
The chamberlins	00	06	08
The somme uncollected	19	00	07
Soe then remaineth in the collectors hand due of the schoolehouse rents which hee hath now paied into the chamberlins	9	12	5

The accounte of Brian Newball churchwarden & first his receipts as followeth from the 28th of December 1644

Receaved of John Hutchine for areares due to the church	6	14	5
For the great bell ringing	3	17	4
Receaved of the assessmente	2	15	0
Receaved more for rents	1	13	8
Soe the totall of his receipts	15	00	5
His payements from December 28 1644 till Julie 21 1645 as by his booke of particulars appeareth is	5	19	2
Soe then due to the church from him which is paied to the ensueing churchwarden	9	00	5

The Mille Masters accounte
And first the accounte of Thomas Fisher one of the mille masters of the Well Lane Mills from the first of November 1644 till the 11th of April 1645.

Imprimis the proffitts by him receaved as by his booke appeareth is	127	13	10
His charges & disbursements as by his booke alsoe appeares	21	10	11
Soe then cleared & due by him to the towne which hee hath payed into the chamberlins	106	02	11

The accounte of Edward Bristowe another of the mille masters of the Well Lane Mills from the 18th of Aprill till the 16th of Maye 1645.

The proffitts by him receaved	29	11	10

His charges & disbursements	4	11	9
Soe cleared by the towne which hee hath payed in butt onlie £1 2s 6d	25	00	1

The accounte of Thomas Hanson another of the mille masters of the Well Lane Mills from the 23th of Maye till the 23th of October 1645

Imprimis the proffitts by him receaved as by his booke of particulars appeareth is	112	11	10
His charge & disbursements	30	18	8
Soe cleared during his tyme which hee hath paied into the chamberlins	71	02	2
Cleared more for annother moneth of that mille	10	13	6
Soe cleared in alle for his tyme with this moneth	81	15	8
Then cleared in all by that mill	222	18	10

The accounte of William Cole one of the mille masters of the Slate Mill from the six of November till April 11th 1645

The proffitts by him receaved as by his booke appeareth is	66	19	11
his charge & disbursements	20	13	5
Soe cleared & due to the town which hee hath payed to the chamberlins	46	06	6

The accounte of George Hardakers annother mille master of the said mill from the 18th of Aprill till October 1645

Proffitts by him receaved as by his booke appeareth is	75	15	0
His charge & layeings oute	22	03	9
Cleared by him	53	14	6
Soe cleared in all by the Slate Mill	99	15	0

The accounte of John Rawlinson & Thomas Graunte chamberlins for the borough of Grantham for Mr Thomas Mills his yeare Alderman of this borough.

The totall somme of the receipts of John Rawlinson chamberline from November 10th 1644 till Maye the 10th 1645	184	16	8
More moneys after by him receaved as by his particulars	77	08	10
Ytt doth appeare with tenn pounds Widow Lane weif of Thomas Lane deceased putt into the townes hands for raising settlements for her children			
The somme of his receipts in all	262	05	6
The totall somme of his payements as by his bookes & notes appeares is	261	15	6
Soe then remaines due to the towne by him	000	10	0
Which tenn shillings he hath payed into the next chamberline			

The totall somme of the receipts of Thomas Graunte chamberline as by his notes appeareth is	167	08	11
His payements & disbursements	154	12	11
Soe remaines due in his hands to the towne which hee hath payed to the next chamberline	12	16	00

The accounte of Thomas Graunte colebuyer chossen in the roometh of
William Darnill for of the yeare Mr Christian being Alderman

Moneys by him receaved Julie the 12th 1644			
Receaved the saule daye in courte	3	17	4
Of the collectors	0	11	2
Of the chamberline	4	12	10
More of him	3	00	0
Laide downe in moneys	5	16	1
	17	17	5

Which thus layed oute & bestowed			
Layed out for coales	16	15	3
Paied Robert Thompson for house rente	00	15	4
To Robert Ulliott	00	05	0
Spente uppon neighbours that brought coales att 12d a hundred	00	01	2
	17	17	5

Which coales were after sold out to the poore as followeth			
Imprimis 228 hundred waite some att 14d the hundred some att 16d	13	07	1
More sold 50 hundred waite	03	00	7
More for 4 strike of small coales	00	03	0
Payed Goodweif Gibson which was borowed of her before 6 hundred	00	07	0
Delivered to the Almshou ii hundred	00	12	10
Oweing by Goodweif Darnill for ii hundred	00	02	4
	17	12	10

Whereof there was due to himself which hee had laide out of his owne moneys	05	16	1
More hee paied to Mr Chauntler now coalemaster for the yeare following	10	15	9
Soe then discharged by him as appeareth	16	11	10

Att an assemblie held by Thomas Mills gen Alderman of the borough of
Grantham the comburgesses & burgesses of the same in Corpus Christi Quoire
within the Prebendarie Church of Grantham aforesaid the Fridaye nexte after St
Lukes daye being the foure & twentieth daye of October Anno Regni R Caroli 21
Anno Dm 1645.
First the said Mr Thomas Mills Alderman did sitt downe in Corpus Christi
Quoare in the Prebendarie Church aforesaid.
Then next to him being sick was to sitt uppon the cushion Mr Arthure Rhoades
next to him did sitt Mr John Mills.
Then were there three comburgesses sente downe into the bodye of the church
Mr Hansone, Mr Edward Rawlinson & Mr Richard Conye.
Out of which one was chossen to sitt uppon the cushione of place of electione
(viz) Mr Christopher Hanson.
Then were there three comburgesses sett uppon the cushione or place of
electione (viz) Mr Arthure Rhoades,Mr John Mills & Mr Christopher
Hanson.

Out of which there was one to be chossen Alderman of the towne or borough of Grantham for the yeare to come.

And by a generall assente of this assemblye Mr John Mills was chossen Alderman of this borough for this yeare now nexte ensueing.

Whereuppon the said Mr Thomas Mills did discharge himself from the place & office of the Alderman according to the anntient custome.

And the said Mr John Mills being elected Alderman as aforesaid for the yeare next to come did att this assemblie take his oathe, according to the anntient & laudable custome of this borough.

f. 127 First Court of John Mills 1 November 1645.

Mr John Mills Alderman.

The first xii comburgesses			*Second xii*	
Alexander More Esq comburgesse			John Bracewell	jur cheiffe
Arthure Rhoades comburgesse			William Cole	jur constables
Richard Conie comb		jur	Gilbert Chauntler	jur
Richard Pearson comb		jur	Thomas Shorte	jur
Thomas Mattkine comb		jur	John Bee	jur
Robert Colcrofte comb		jur	Henrie Ferman	jur
Edward Christian comb		jur	John Rawlinson	jur
Thomas Mills comb		jur		
Christopher Hanson comb		jur		
Edward Rawlinson comb		jur		
George Briggs comb		jur		

Coroner	Thomas Mills	jur	Gaoler	Richard Poole	jur
Escheator	George Briggs	jur	Bayliffe	Richard Poole	jur
Church	John Bee	jur	Prisors	George Hardakers	jur
wardens	Robert Trevillian	jur	of Corne	Daniell Coddington	jur
Chamb-	Henrie Ferman	jur	Markett	John Clarke	jur
lins	Thomas Doughtie	jur	Sayers	John Poole	jur
High Con-	John Bracewell	jur	Mill	James Gibson	jur
stables	Willam Cole	jur	Masters for	Thomas Graunte	jur
Pettie Constables			the Well	John Wythey	jur
Markett Place	Thomas Hanson	jur	Lane Mills	William Parker	jur
High	John Fysher	jur	Millmasters	John Rawlinson	jur
Street	Henrie Cole	jur	the Slate Mills	William Graye	jur
West	Henrie Speedie	jur	Leather	Augustine Minocke	jur
gate	Thomas Baylie	jur	Searchers	Raphe Goodwine	jur
Walker	George Wraye	jur		William Grococke	jur
gate	William Poole	jur		William Jordane	jur
Swine	Nicholas Beck	jur	Thomas Somersall Church Clarke		
gate	Robert Smith	jur	Alexander Bothomeley Sexton		jur
Castle	Edward Hawden	jur	John Pecke Bedle.		
gate	Thomas Knotte	jur	Key	Mr Alderman	jur
Collectors of	Mr Richard Pearson	jur	Keepers	Henrie Ferman	jur
the Schoole-			Sergeants	Mathew Whiting	jur
house Rents	Mr Robert Clerk		att Mace	Richard Poole	jur
	Town Clarke.				

Nominated Commoners

Edward Still	jur	Thomas Wallett	jur	George Hardakers	jur
Robert Ropp	jur	Richard Baylie	jur	William Graye	jur
Robert Trevillian	jur	William Grocock	jur		
William Clarke	jur	Edward Bristow	jur	Daniell Coddington	jur
Thomas Graunte	jur	William Parker	jur		
James Gibson	jur	John Wythey	jur		
Thomas Doughtie	jur	John Hutchine	jur		
Thomas Hanson	jur	Thomas Marshall	jur		
James Walker	jur	William Bristow	jur		
John Kirke	jur	Robert Tompson	jur		

Richard Shepperson att this courte being a stranger borne yett haveing served Richard Conye one of the comburgesses of this borough as journeman for manie years desired to be incorporated & made a freeman of this borough and according to order & the auntiente custome of this borough brought into this courte tenn poundes which hee tendred for his freedome, which this courte considering of & in hope hee wold make a good member hereafter in this corporacon was willing & did agree hee shold paye onelie £iii vis viiid and the rest to bee given him backe againe of the said £x which £iii vis viiid was then payed to the chamberlins and the said Richard Shepperdson tooke his oathe of allegiance & freedome paid vs to the chamberlins & xviiid to the Clarke & Sergeants & soe was admitted a freeman into this corporacon.

128 Second Court of John Mills 7 November 1645.

Writings & charters delivered uppe to the now Alderman in open court. In the Great Charter Box.

Kinge James his charter
Kinge Charles his charter
The Charter of Executor
In annother charter boxe
Queen Elizabeths charter
For the escheator
The Schoolehouse charter
Writings concerning the librarie
Orders for the schoolehouse
A writing from the Alderman of Stamforde.
In annother charter boxe

The Green Deske with divers writings therein of which there was noe inventorie taken And some new acquittances now delivered to Mr Alderman by the laste yeares chamberlins which was now likewise putt into the green deske.
There was alsoe now delivered to Mr Alderman the greater parte of the Statute seale.

A coppie of Edward 4th charter
Kinge Henrie the 8th his charter
Queen Elizabeth her charter
Judge Dyers award
The Comoners booke
A writing with manie seals
Twoe scrutchins of the townes.

Att this courte Richard Pearson sonne of Richard Pearson one of the comburgesses of this borough, Andrew Poole sonne of Richard Poole late of this borough deceased, Richard Blacke sonne of Richard Blacke of this borough deceased and Thomas Fearone sonne of William Fearone of this borough shoemaker being all of them free borne,did everie of them desire to be incorporated & admitted free men of this corporacon whereunto this courte did freelie ascente and the said parties did paye to the chamberlins theire due fees being iis vid a peece & xviiid a peece to the Clarke & Sergeants tooke theire severall oathes & soe were admitted free men of this borough.

Att this courte likewise Thomas Barker a stranger borne haveing served his apprentishipp with Mr Richard Conye one of the comburgesses of this borough desired now to be incorporated & made a freeman of this borough which was freelie agreed unto by this courte,and the said Thomas Barker did paye to the comon boxe vs & xviiid to the Clarke & Sergeants tooke his severall oathes of allegiance & freedome & soe was admitted a freeman of this borough.

Third Court of John Mills 14 November 1645

Att this courte a letter sente from Mr William Burye as concerning the payement of £76 8s unto him(which att the instance & request of this corporacon & for the use thereof hee had formerlie layed out & disbursed to the receavor of the rente due to the Kings Majestie from the towne of Grantham) was openlie read with his loveing kindness & respecte now & in other things for & towards the benefitt of this corporacon,this borough are & wilbe ever thankfull unto him,which this courte taking into consideracon ytt was ordered £65 part of the said £76 8s should by the chamberlins be paied out of such moneys as were in theire hands & as they were to receave of the mille masters what shoulde be then wanting of the said somme of £65 should by the said chamberlins be disbursed. And whereas there was yett £31 wanting of the money due to be payed Mr Bury,this court nott knowing well for presente how to raise the same by Mr Alderman & others well wishing this corporacon, ytt was propounded that some then in courte wold uppon this necessitie be pleased to lend unto this borough soe much money as shold make uppe the same, and thereuppon Mr Alderman lent £5 Mr More £iii, Mr Pearson £5, Mr Matkin £ii, Mr Hanson £ii, John Rawlinson £ii, John Bee £i, James Gibson £ii, George Wraye £i, George Hardakers £i, Edward Harden £i, John Fysher £i, John Knott £i, John Lenton £ii, & Nicholas Becke £ii in all £31 which said moneys this courte doth fullie order & agree that the same shall by this corporacon be againe be alle payed unto them att of before the second daye of Februarie nexte,comonlie called Candlemas daye. And soe the said somme of £76 8s was made good for the payemente of the said Mr Burye.

Att this courte Robert Ulliott the younger sonne John Ulliotte late of this borough cordwainer deceased being a free man borne did this court come in & desired to be incorporated & made a freeman of this corporacon, whereunto the courte was willing & did assente, and the said Robert Ulliott did paye to the chamberlins iis vid & to the Clarke & Sergeants xviiid tooke his oathe of allegiance & freedome & soe was admitted a freeman of this borough.

Att this courte likewise Michaell Taylor & Richard Nixe strangers borne haveing served theire apprentishippes,desired to be incorporated & made freemen of this borough: ytt was this courte assented & agreed unto that they should be admitted freemen,and thereuppon the said Michaell Tayler & Richard

Nixe did paye to the comon boxe vs a peece & xviiid to the Clarke & Sergeants tooke theire severall oathes of allegiance & freedom & soe were admitted free men of this borough.

Att this court likewise came in John Owen shoemaker being free borne & desired to be incorporated and made free of this borough, which this court did assent and the said John accordingly payed his iis vid to the boxe and to the Clarke & Sergeants xviiid and tooke his oath of a freeman according to anntient custome.

Fourth Court of John Mills 28 November 1645

Raphe Yardeley sonne of Thomas Yardeley being borne within this borough yett his father nott being free of this corporacon att such tyme as the said Raphe was borne hee did this courte as a stranger desired hee mighte be incorporated & made a free man of this borough and according to order & the anntiente custome of this borough brought into this courte ten poundes of lawfull English money which hee tendred for his freedome which this courte taking into consideracon hoping hee wold hereafter make a good member in this corporacon was willing & did agree hee shold be made free & that hee shold paye onely £iii vis viiid, and the rest to be given him backe againe of the said £x which £iii vis viiid was then payed to the chamberlins and the said Raphe Yardley tooke his oath of allegiance & freedome payed vs to the chamberlins & to the Clark & Sergeants theire due fees and was admitted a freeman of this corporacon.

Att this courte Thomas Smith sonne of Christopher Smith of this borough ioyner being a freeman borne did come in, and desired to be incorporated & made a freeman of this corporacon to which his request this courte did assente & agree unto, and the said Thomas Smith did thereuppon paye to the chamberlins iis vid to the Clerke & Sergeants xviiid tooke his oathes of allegiance & freedome and soe was admitted a freeman of this borough.

Ytt is this courte fullie concluded ordered & agreed uppon that whosoever hereafter shall come to Mr Aldermans courte for the tyme being to desire or challenge to be made free of this corporacon for or by reason of his birth being borne within this corporacon hee shall nott be admitted or made free of the same butt come in as other strangears doe, unlesse the father of the partie soe requesting & desiring the same was a freeman of this borough att such tyme as the said partie was borne.

Richard Pearson sonne of Mr Richard Pearson comburgesse was chossen & sworne constable for Castlegate & Edward Haddon sworne constable for the Markett Place.

Att this courte John Rawlinson late chamberline of this borough gave Mr Alderman & this courte to understand that hee had receaved for use of this borough of _____ Lane widow late weif of Thomas Lane deceased the somme of tenn poundes of lawfull money of Englande which the said Thomas Lane by his laste will bequeathed should be putt into the townes hands of Grantham for the use & benefitt of his child.

An assemblie holden att the Guylde Hall in Grantham by John Mills gen Alderman the comburgesses & burgesses the seventh daye of December Anno Dm 1645

Att this assemblie Wiiliam Fearine & John Newton are appoynted overseers for the well at Aple Crosse in Swinegate

Fifth Court of John Mills 16 January 1645

Att this courte Richard Elston late of Grantham draper,came & desired Mr Alderman & other the comburgesses & burgesses then in courte that they wold be pleased to graunt unto him the lease of a messuage or tenemente scyttuatte in the Markett Place of Grantham, wherein the said Richard Elston latelie dwelte butt now lette to others by his assignemente which this courte taking into consideracon did for the earnest of five shillings then payed to Mr Alderman by the said Richard Elston, as alsoe for & in consideracon of five & thirtie poundes of lawfull money of England for a fine to be payed unto them in maner following (viz) fiften poundes thereof to be payed the sealing the said lease with the comon seale of this borough which was to be sealed & done att or before the feaste daye of the Annuncyacon of the Blessed Virgin Mary next ensueing and the other twentie poundes to be payed att or before the feaste daye of Michaell the Archanngell nexte following for true payemente whereof accordinglie the said Richard Elston togeather with John Howett his wives father did both of them promise to become bounde to this corporacon, as alsoe for the yearlie rente of three pounds of lawfull Inglish money & a couple of capons to be likewise payed unto them, and to enter into such covenants as other the townes tenants usuallie doe & hee & his father Howett to be bound for performance of the said covenants which they did both promise to doe & lett unto the said Richard Elston the said messuage or tenemente for one & twentie yeares to comence after the expiracon of a former lease thereof to one Richard Gaule deceased.

This courte being now moved by Mr Alderman as touching certaine moneys to be paied by this corporacon which is now called for & demanded, this borough being unprovided for the payemente thereof, ytt was this courte againe desired that Mr William Clark the apothecarie yf hee were soe provided wold doe the curtesie as to lende unto this corporacon fiftie poundes for sixe monneths or soc longe as hee could spare ytt for which this borough promiseth to allow him use for the same & alsoe to have securitie for ytt under the comon seale of this borough as others in like casse use formerlie haveing lente money to this corporacon have had the same yf hee soe pleased. Uppon which mocon the said Mr Clarke answered hee wold be willing to doe the towne that kindness butt the towne alreadie ought him thirtie poundes due on the mills,and yf they wold be pleased to allow him that thirtie poundes hee wold lett them have fiftie poundes & soe make ytt uppe foure score poundes & soe lett the towne have ytt half a year or longer uppon use & under the comon seale as hee coulde spare ytt,to which his propositions this courte did condiscend & agree & thereuppon he payed the chamberlins fiftie poundes for which hee is to be allowed use for soe longe as the towne shall hold ytt.

Att this court ytt was ordered & agreed that Widowe Basse a pore woman being throwen out of her house & left harborles which this courte taking into consideracon & pittieing her extremitie did graunte unto her to pay the rente of a house for her yf she cold procure one soe ytt exceede nott above xls or be near.

Sixth Court of John Mills 27 February 1645

Att this courte came in Thomas Tomasman a stranger & a tayler by trade & desired to be admitted a free man of this borough, and according to the auntiente custome of this borough for such as strangers & forriners tendered downe in open courte to the use of this corporacon the somme of tenn pounds of lawfull money of Engeland, to which his request, this courte hoping hee wold prove a good member in this corporacon did condiscende & agree, and soe payeing the said somme of £10 to the chamberline of this borough taking his oath of alegiance & freedome the fees likewise to the officers being alsoe payed, hee was admitted a free man of this borough.

Att an assemblie holden in Corpus Christi Quiore within the Prebendarie Church of Grantham after the death & decease of John Mills late Alderman deceased for the election of a new Alderman in his place, the fifte daye of Maye in the twoe & twentith yeare of the raigne of King Charles Anno Dm 1646.

Att which electione Mr Arthure Rhoades & Mr Christopher Hanson did sitte uppon the cushion, soe then one being wanting to sitte uppon the cushion, three comburgesses more to goe downe into the church (viz) Mr Richard Cony, Mr Edward Rawlinson & Mr George Briggs.
Oute of which three one was chossen to sitte uppon the cushion or place of election (viz) Mr Richard Conye.
Then were there three comburgesses on the cushion or place of election (viz) Mr Arthure Rhoades, Mr Christopher Hanson, & Mr Richard Conye out of which there was one to be chossen Alderman for the residue of this yeare yett to come for the borough of Grantham in the place of John Mills late Alderman deceased.
And with a generall assente of this assembly Mr Christopher Hanson was chossen Alderman of this borough for the residue of the yeare yett to come. And the said Mr Christopher Hanson being elected Alderman as aforesaid for the remainder of this yeare, did att this assemblie take his oathe according to anntiente & laudable custome of this borough.

31 First Court of Christopher Hanson 15 May 1646.

At this courte by a generall consente & free agreement of the same Mr Richard Cony one of the comburgesses of this borough was nominated & appoynted to be elected Alderman of this borough att the nexte daye of electione, for one wholl yeare then nexte ensueing which office this courte hopeth hee will accordingly accept of.

Att this court the townes plate in Mr John Mills his custodie late Alderman deceased with the greater parte of the Statute seale was now delivered uppe in open courte by the inventorie thereof to Mr Christopher Hanson now Alderman viz twoe silver cannes, twoe beare bolls, one wine bolle, one guilte cuppe, twoe silver tunnes, one beaker, a silver salte & cover, the horse race cuppe & casse & thirteen silver spoones, with the greater parte of the said Statute seale.

Att this courte George Hardacres & Edward Still butcher were chossen colebuyers for this yeare following.

Second Court of Christopher Hanson 5 June 1646.

The names of	Alexander More esq comburg	jur	*Seconde xii*	
such of the	Richard Pearson comb	jur	John Bracewell	jur
first xii	Edward Christian comb	jur	John Bee	jur
whoe then	Thomas Mills comb	jur	Henrie Ferman	jur
tooke theire	Edward Rawlinson comb	jur	John Rawlinson	jur
oath to Mr	George Briggs comb	jur		
Alderman	Robert Clerk gen town clerk	jur		

Sergeants att	Mathew Whiting	jur	Gaoler Richard Poole jur
Mace	Richard Poole	jur	

The names of the Comoners then alsoe sworne.

Thomas Hansone	jur	Henrie Speedie	jur
Edward Hawden	jur	Thomas Baylie	jur
Robert Trevillian	jur	Edward Bristow	jur
William Clarke	jur	John Wythey	jur
James Gibson	jur	Thomas Marshall	jur
Thomas Graunt	jur	George Wraye	jur
Thomas Doughtie	jur	William Poole	jur
James Walker	jur	Robert Tompson	jur
John Kirk	jur	George Hardacres	jur
Edward Still tanner	jur	Nicholas Becke	jur
John Lenton	jur	Robert Smith	jur
Jeffrey Sher	jur	Thomas Knott	jur
Henrie Cole	jur	Richard Pearson	jur
William Grocock	jur		

Att this courte ytt is concluded & agreed uppon with John Lenton of Grantham barber & Robert Smith of the same towne & borough shoemaker by & with the consente of the wholl courte, that in consideracon of the somme of fortie poundes of lawfull money of Englande to be paied by them the said John Lenton & Robert Smith in maner following (viz) £xx uppon sealing a lease, and £xx next to be paied att or before Michaellmas next to the Alderman & burgesses of this borough a lease is graunted to them the said John Lenton & Robert Smith of a messuage or tenemente with the appurtenances in Markett Place of Grantham aforesaid & latelie in the tenure of Robert Clifton deceased. To have & to holde the said messuage or tenemente to them the said John Lenton & Robert Smith theire executors administrators or assignes from & after the exparacon of a former lease yett in being & unexpired of the premisses formerlie graunted to Marie Clifton widow deceased for during & to the ende of xxi yeares from thence next ensueing fullie to be complett & ended payeing therefore yearlie during the saide terme of xxi yeares the auntiente rent thereuppon formerlie reseaved and under such other covenants & agreements as other the towne tenants usuallie have theire leases,whereuppon they gave Mr Alderman earnest.

Att this courte William Newball a stranger borne haveing served his apprentishippe desired to be incorporated & made a free man of this borough whereunto this courte did condiscende & agree and thereuppon the said William Newball did paye to the comon boxe vs & to the Clarke & Sergeants theire due fees, tooke his oathe of alegiance & freedome & soe made a free man of this borough.

32 Att this courte alsoe William Frith sonne of Symon Frith one of the
comburgesses of this borough deceased and James Ferman sonne of Henrie
Ferman one other of the comburgesses of this borough deceased and Raphe
Osborne of other deceased being all free borne did this courte come in & desired
to be incorporated & made freemen of this borough whereunto this courte was
willing & did assente and thereuppon they paied to the chamberlins iis vid a
peece and to the Clark & Sergeants theire due fees tooke theire severall oathes of
allegiance & freedome, and soe were admitted free men of this borough.

Third Court of Christopher Hanson 12 June 1646

Att this courte ytt was agreed a letter shold be drawen & sente to Mrs Hester
Couham touching the buyeing of her lease which shee holdeth of the north
Prebendarie of Grantham and Robert Trevillian & William Clarke are appoynted
to be sente for the delivery of the said letter; and to bring an answere from the
said Mrs Couham what shee would doe therein which is likewise performed.

Att this courte alsoe the lease of a house & groundes in Manthorpe with a litle
closse in Tawthorpe in the parish of Londonthorpe late in the tenure of Marie
Clifton widowe deceased for £xxx fine seaven & thirtie shillings an yeare rente
& one couple of capons was demised & lett unto John Holland of Litle Gonerbie
for one & twentie yeares to begine after the expiracon of a former lease lett to the
said Marie Clifton which shalbe att the feast of St Michaell the Archanngell
which shalbe in the yeare of our Lord God The fine to be paide att the sealing &
deliverie of the said lease and to enter into such covenants as other the townes
tenants usuallie doe uppon theire leases.

Fourth Court of Christopher Hanson 3 July 1646

Att this courte Johnathan Parnum a stranger desired to be admitted a free man of
this borough and according to auntiente custome of this borough for such as are
strangers tendred downe in open courte to the use of this corporacon the somme
of tenn pounds of lawfull money of England to which this request this courte
taking into consideracon knowing a poore man and hoping he woldbe an honest
member in this corporacon was willing & did agree hee shold be made free and
that he should paye one £iii vi viiid the rest to be given him backe againe of the
said £x which £iii vis viiid was then paye into the chamberline and the said
Jonathan Parnum tooke his oath of aledgiance & freedome payed vs to the
chamberline & the Clark & Sergeants theire due fees and soe was admitted a free
man of this corporacon.

Att which courte alsoe the said Johnathan Parnum being a stranger borne desired
to be incorporated & made a free man of this corporacon, and according to the
auntiente order of this borough for such as are strangers & forriners tendered &
layed downe in open courte to the use of this corporacon the somme of tenn
poundes of lawfull money of Englande to which his request in regard hee was a
poore man & haveing noe trade whereby to preiudice or hinder other trad men
alreadie inhabiting within this borough this courte did condiscend & agree hee
shold be made free of this borough & gave him twentie nobles backe againe of
the said £x whereuppon he paied to the chamberline £iii vis viiid the Clarke &
Sergeants theire due fees tooke his oath of allegiance & freedome & soe was
admitted a free man of this borough.

Thomas Baylie was this court nominated & appoynted togeather with John Hutchine to be overseers for Westgate well & they to make a a leavie for the repaires thereof.

Fifth Court of Christopher Hanson 17 July 1646.

A lease graunted this courte to Gartrude Ingham widow of the house wherein shee dwelleth in Walkergate in Grantham for one & twentie yeares to begine att the feast of St Michaell the Archanngell nexte ensueing to paye five pounds fine att the sealing of her lease and a mark a yeare rente during the said terme a couple of good fatte hennes and to enter in to such covenants as other the towne tenants doe.

Att this courte George Lane a stranger & forriner being a tayler by trad desired to be incorporated & made a free man of this borough and according to the auntiente order of the said borough for such as are strangers & foriners tendered & laied downe in open courte to the use of this borough the somme of tenn poundes of lawfull money of England which this courte taking into consideracon hoping hee maye hereafter prove a good member of this corporacon did graunte him his freedome & agreed hee shoulde have fortie shillings given him backe of the said tenn poundes the remainder being £viii he paied to the chamberline tooke his oathe of allegiance & freedome paied the Clarke & Sergeants theire due fees and soe was made a freeman of this borough.

This courte Mr Alderman & his bretheren sente twoe constables (viz) Thomas Hanson & William Poole to Bryan Godleys for using & uttering malte in his house nott being ground att the Kings mills contrarie to order, and the said Brian Godley said unto them these words following (viz) Mr Alderman was a partiall fellow and that hee was a better townsman than Mr Alderman.

f. 133   Sixth Court of Christopher Hanson 3 August 1646.

Att this courte by the full consente of the same Bryan Godley was fined fortie shillings for scandalous & uncivill speeches formerlie uttered against Mr Alderman to Thomas Hanson & William Poole twoe pettie constables of this borough being sent unto him by this courte for a distresse.

Att this courte likewise Mr Hugh Asheley for & in regard this courte att his desire & request did readlie & freelie forgive unto him the arerages of rente due unto him by this borough for a house he late dwelte in Walkergate in Grantham. In consideracon thereof the said Mr Ashley did saye in open courte freelie clearlie & absoltelie yeld uppe & relinquish all his estates rights interest, tytles or domaunde whatsoever which hee the said Hugh Asheley now hath by reason of anie lease or graunte of anie lease to the said messuage or tenemente or otherwise howsoever.
Att which tyme alsoe the said Mr Ashley requested this courte that Edward Watson mighte be admitted the townes tennante for the said messuage which this courte was willing unto.
And thereuppon the said Edward Watson intreated Mr Alderman & his bretheren & the said courte to be pleased to graunte unto him the lease of the said messuage for xxi yeares which this courte considering was contented & did agree the said Edward Watson sholde have a lease for xxi yeares to begine att the feast of

St Michaell the Archanngell nexte ensueing for the rente of £iii xiiis iiiid per annum & a couple of fatte capons and entring in to such covenants as other the towne tennants doe uppon condicon alsoe that hee the said Edward Watson shall att his owne propper costs & charges satisfie & sette in a good & sufficyente repaires all the houses & fences in & aboute the premisses as formerlie they have bine & soe holde & continue them and thereuppon he gave to Mr Alderman for earnest.

Att this courte alsoe a lease was lette to John Courtebie of the houses yardes & grounde belonging unto the towne of Grantham which ioineth on the southe side of the houses & grounde of Thomas Loves in Castlegate in Grantham for eleavon pounds fine to be payed at the sealing of the said lease, the lease to be for xxi yeares payeing the olde yearlie rente of xs & a couple of fatt capons yearlie during the terme & entring into such other covenants as the reste of the townes tennants doe whereuppon he gave to Mr Alderman for earnest.The lease to comence att the feast of St Michaell the Archanngell nexte ensueing.

Att this courte Mr Blower of Leicester a Master of Arts & schoolemaster by profession att his earnest request & desire was by the aprobacon consente & good liking of this courte elected & chossen to supplie the place of cheife schoolemaster of this schoole of Grantham for one wholle yeare nexte ensueing and soe for longer tyme uppon the good liking of the Alderman & burgesses of the said towne of Grantham & theire successors and to have the schoolehouse to teach the children in, and alsoe to have the dwelling house & orchard with theire appurtenances belonging to the said schoolehouse and to have from the towne of Grantham for his yeares sallerie & stipend twentie pounds.

Att this courte alsoe a lease was lett to Thomas Shorte of twoe houses or tenements in Grantham one of which houses or tenements was situate in the High Street in Grantham the other in Markett Place late in the tenure of Buttler to hold from St Michaell the Archanngell next ensueing for one & twentie yeares yelding & payeing for the house in High Street yearlie during the said terme tenn shillings & a fatte hen to Mr Alderman & yelding & payeing for the house in the Markett Place xxs a yeare during the said terme & to Mr Alderman one fatte hen,and the said Thomas Shorte is presentlie after his entrye to reedefie & build uppe the said messuage & chamber the same over in & uppon the owne foundacone & cover the roofe with slate with other covenants for repaires & other things as in other the towne leases. This laste lease should have bine entred in the precedent court (viz) the fifte courte.

Seventh Court of Christopher Hanson 25 September 1646.

Att this courte ytt was fullie concluded & agreed that Edward Towne one of the auntientest of the second xii companie being a man able & fitt for the companie sholde hold & continue his said place & companie.

Att this courte ytt was likewise agreed uppon that an assessmente of twentie pounds should forthwith be made for & towards the repaire of the conduitt & the conduitte pipes for the conveyeing of the water to the conduitt in Grantham over & besides the gratuities of such as shall volluntrelie give & contribute towards this soe needfull a workes, and Mr Thomas Mills,Mr Edward Rawlinson, William Cole, Henrie Ferman, Thomas Graunt, Robert Trevillian, Edward

Bristow & Thomas Wallett are nominated & apointed assessors for the same and the said assessmente to be made before the seconde daye of October nexte.

And ytt was likewise further agreed that Mr Alderman & some of his bretheren with him shall agree as reasonable as they can of the making & performing the said worke.

Att this courte likewise Christopher Handley, John Foxe, Ashton Lorde & John Parker all strangers borne yett haveing served theire apprentishippe desired the favour of this courte that they mighte be incorporated & made free men of this borough uppon which theire intreatie ytt was assented & agreed unto that they should be admitted free men of this corporacon, and thereuppon the said Christopher Handley, John Foxe, Ashton Lord & John Parker did paye to the chamberlins vs a peece and to the Clarke & Sergeants theire due fees tooke theire severall oathes of alegiance & freedome and soe were admitted free men of this borough.

Eighth Court of Christopher Hanson 8 October 1646.

Att this courte John Fearon sonne of John Fearon late of Grantham in the Countie of Lincolne cordwainer deceased and James Gibson sonne of James Gibson aforesaid frublusher being both free borne did this courte come in & desired to be incorporated & made free men of this borough whereunto this courte was willing & did ascente and thereuppon they paied to the chamberlins iis vid a peece,and to the Clarke & Sergeants theire due fees tooke theire severall oathes of alleageance & freedome and soe were admitted free men of this borough.

f. 134 Ninth Court of Christopher Hanson 16 October 1646

Att this court ytt was ordered that the chamberlins should paye to Mr Blower the schoolemaster in parte of his sallerye for this yeare the somme of five pounds.

Whereas Edward Towne one of the second twelve companie hath long desired the courte wold be pleased to free & dismiss him of from the said companie this courte taking the same into further consideracon though willing hee shold have continued the same yett uppon his earnest desire have graunted his request & dismissed him from the said place & thereuppon was knocked of from the said companie.

Att this courte likewise for divers wanting in the first & second twelve companies soe that offices & buisnesses belonging to this borough could nott well be performed, ytt was this courte fullie concluded & agreed that those formerlie remaineing in the callender and of late left out, should according to auntiente custome againe be sente downe to the comoners & they to ad as manie to those in the callender as were wanting as they have formerlie usuallie done that they might proceed to the choyce of others. Whereuppon the names of James Gibson & John Phiper auntientlie in the callender were sente downe to whome the comoners added William Clarke & Thomas Doughtie out of whome was chossen James Gibson to be of the second twelve in the roome of Mr George Briggs and lefte remaining in the callender John Phiper,William Clarke & Thomas Doughtie to whome the comoners added Robert Trevellian out of which was chossen John Phiper to be of the second companie in the roome of Edward Towne, then remained in the callender William Clarke, Thomas Doughtie & Robert Trevillian to whome the comoners added John Wythey out of which was chosen William Clarke to be of the second twelve in the room Brian Newball & then remained in the callender Thomas Doughtie, Robert Trevillian & John Wythey to whome the comoners added Edward Bristow, out of which was chossen Thomas Doughtie to be of the second twelve in the room of Thomas Fysher, soe then remained in the callender Robert Trevillian John Wythey Edwarde Bristow all of which tooke theire oathes incidente to theire said places & paied the Clark & Sergeants theire due fees.

Att this courte likewise Gilbert Chauntler was elected & chossen one of the comburgesses of this borough in the roome of John Mills late Alderman deceased and took the severall oathes incydente & belonging to his place.

And att this court Robert Trevillian is elected one of the second twelve in the rome of the said Mr Chaunteler and tooke his oath incydent to the said place.

And ytt was then alsoe agreed that the persons hereafter named shall remaine in the callender or bill for the second twelve (viz) John Wythey
Edward Bristowe
Thomas Graunte

Tenth and Ultimate Court of Christopher Hanson 22 October 1646.

Att this court Thomas Secker formerlie chossen of the second twelve in the roometh of William Hodgkinson deceased came into the courte and there tooke his corporall oath incydente & propper to the said place & degree and paied the Clarke & Sergeants theire due fees & soe tooke his place.

Att this court Mr Robert Izacke a stranger
now inkeeper at the signe of the George in Grantham desired to be incorporated & made a free man of this borough, and according to the auntiente custome of this borough for such as are strangers & forainers tendered & layed downe in open courte to the use of this borough the somme of tenn poundes of lawfull money of Englande which this courte taking into consideracon the cariage & handsomeness of the said Mr Izacke hoping hereafter he may prove a good member of this corporacon did graunte him his freedome & agreed he shold have five poundes given him backe of the said tenn poundes the remainder being £v hee payed to the chamberline tooke his oath of alegiance & freedome paied the Clarke & Sergeants theire due fees & soe was admitted & made free man of this corporacon & borough.

Att this courte Beniamine Clarke sonne of Raphe Clarke one of the comburgesses of Grantham deceased haveing served his apprentishippe & being borne free did this courte come in & desired to be incorporated & made a free man of this borough whereunto this courte was willing & did assente and thereuppon hee paid to the chamberline according to anntiente custome iis vid & to the Clarke & Sergeants theire due fees & tooke his oath of alegiance & freedome & soe was admitted & made free of this borough.

The accounte of Richard Pearson comburgesse of the borough of Grantham & John Hutchine collectors for the schoolehouse rents.

Imprimis they charge themselves with a wholle yeares rears of the said landes due the laste

		£	s	d
Michaellmas rents amounting to the somme of		43	5	8
Item receaved of areares due in Mr Colcrofts tyme,Mr Christians tyme & Mr Thomas Mills his tyme of being Alderman viz of		9	10	9
Somme		52	16	5

Theire disbursements

This to be	Imprimis laid out about the new			
paied againe	house	3	6	8
by the	Laied out about Buttlers house	0	6	0
receaver of	Laid out aboute the Colledg			
the rents of	& Schoolehouse	8	15	0
Corpus	Paied to the schoolemaster for			
Christi	his quarters wages	5	0	0
Colledg	More paid to the chamberlins by			
	theire acquittances appeareth	26	0	0
		43	7	8

	£	s	d
Soe then resteth in his hands of all above	1	10	8
Received more of Robert Abott for parte of the new house	0	3	4
Of Francis Briggs for a yeare & quarters rent there	0	10	0
Of Foxe wief for the Colledg orchard	0	12	0
	1	5	0
Soe then resteth in his hands in all due to the towne which he hath mow paied to the Chamberlins	2	16	0

f. 135 The accounts of Thomas Mills coroner for the towne & soake of Grantham for the yeare 1645 & 1646.

	£	s	d
Imprimis receaved of the goodes of a man unknown founde drowned neare the new house in the River Whitam in Manthorpe feilde as the goodes were praised	0	13	10
Layed out for his bringing to Grantham buryall fees for executing the service	0	13	10

There was likewise a mans wief at Denton which drowned herself in a well haveing nothing butt her smocke one and being a mans wief haveing noe goodes there was noe benefitt did acrew to this corporacon soe there was nothing remaineing in his hands.

The accounte of John Bee churchwarden for one wholle yeare as followeth and first his receipts.

	£	s	d
Imprimis for the great bell ringing att severall tymes	4	1	4
Item att his (indecipherable)	17	10	7
Receipts of Church Rents	1	17	4
Of the assessemente	9	15	4
Of the last assessemente for Easter	3	00	10
Of Mr Christian att the sealing	1	9	11

Of Mr Christian	0	3	4
	37	18	8
His payements as by his charges apeareth			
Imprimis	13	13	10
Item	15	17	4
Item	7	4	10
	36	16	0
Soe remaineing in his hand	1	2	8

Att an assemblie helde by Christopher Hanson Alderman of the borough of Grantham aforesaid the comburgesses & burgesses of the same in Corpus Christi Quoire in the prebendarie Church of Grantham aforesaid the Fridaye nexte after St Lukes daye being the twoe & twentith daye of October Anno Regni R Caroli dei Anno Dm 1646.

First the said Mr Hanson Alderman did sitt downe in Corpus Christi Quoare in the Prebendaire Church aforesaid.

Then next to him being sick was to sitt uppon the cushion Mr Arthure Rhoades nexte to him did sitte Mr Richard Conye.

Then were there three comburgesses sente downe into the bodie of church (viz) Mr Edward Rawlinson, Mr George Briggs & Mr Alexander More.

Out of which three one was chossen to sitte uppon the cushione or place of electione (viz) Mr Edward Rawlinson.

Then there were three comburgesses uppon the cushion or place of election (viz) Mr Arthure Rhoades, Mr Richard Cony, Mr Edward Rawlinson out of which there was one to be chossen Alderman for the year to come for the borough of Grantham in the place of Mr Hanson.

And by a generall assente of this assemblie Mr Richard Conie was chossen Alderman of this borough for this yeare now next to come.

And the said Mr Richard Cony being elected Alderman as aforesaid for the yeare nexte to come did att this assemblie take his oath according to the anntiente & laudable custome of this borough.

137 First Court of Mr Richard Cony 30 October 1646

First twelve comburgesses comence		*Second xii*	
Alexander More esq comburgess	jur	William Clarke	cheiffe
Arthure Rhoades comb	jur	Thomas Doughtie	constables
Richard Pearson comb	jur	Thomas Shorte	jur
Thomas Matkine comb	jur	John Bracewell	jur
George Lloyd comb	jur	John Rawlinson	jur
Robert Colcroft comb	jur	John Bee	jur
Edward Christian comb	jur	William Cole	jur
Thomas Mills comb	jur	Henrie Ferman	jur
Christopher Hanson comb	jur	Thomas Secker	jur
Edward Rawlinson comb	jur	James Gibson	jur
George Briggs comb	jur	John Phiper	jur
Gilbert Chauntler comb	jur	Robert Trevillian	jur

Coroner	Mr Christopher Hanson	jur	Sergeants att Mace
Escheator	Mr Thomas Mills	jur	Mathew Whiting

Church	Robert Trevillian	jur	Richard Poole	
Wardens	John Wythey	jur	Gaoler & Bayliffe	
Chamber-	William Cole	jur	Richard Poole	
lins	William Parke	jur	Prisors of Corne	
Pettie Constables			John Fysher	jur
Markett	Richard Sheperdson	jur	George Wraye	jur
Place	Robert Izacke	jur	Markett Sayers	
High	William Fearon	ju	Edward Still	jur
Streete	John Symson	jur	Brian Godley	jur
West	Robert Kellam	jur	Millemasters for the Well Lane Mill	
gate	Beniamine Clarke	jur	John Bracewell	
Walker	Phillip Hollinworth	jur	William Grocock	
gate	Leonard Camocke	jur	Henrie Speedye	
Swine	Richard Elston	jur	William Poole	
gate	John Fearon	jur	For the Slatte Mill	
Castle	James More	jur	James Gibson	
gate	Thomas Fearon	jur	John Lenton	
Key	Mr Alderman	jur	Thomas Baylie	
Bearers	Willam Cole	jur	Leather searchers	
	Robert Trevillian	jur	Edward Ferman	jur
Collectors of the Schoolehouse			Thomas Knott	jur
Rents	Mr George Briggs	jur	Thomas Slater	jur
	Henrie Speedye	jur	Church Clarke	
Mr Robert Clerk Towne Clark		jur	Thomas Sommersall	jur
Bellman & Alexander Bothemley		jur	Bedle John Peak.	
& Sexton				

Nominated Commoners

Markett Place			Walkergate	
Edward Watson	jur		George Graye	jur
Thomas Graunte	jur		Robert Tompson	jur
Robert Wood	jur		George Hardaker	jur
James Walker	jur		William Bristow	jur
John Kirk	jur		Richard Pearson	jur
Edward Still butcher	jur		Swinegate	
Robert Smith	jur		William Graye	jur
High Street			Daniell Coddington	jur
William Grococke	jur		Nicholas Beck	jur
Thomas Wallett	jur		Castlegate	
Thomas Knott	jur		Edward Hawden	jur
Westgate				
Henrie Speedie	jur			
Thomas Baylie	jur			
Francis Bristow	jur			
William Parker	jur			
John Wythey	jur			
John Hutchine	jur			
Thomas Marshall	jur			
John Fysher	jur			

The wholle courte sworne to Mr Alderman.

The officers chossen & sworne.

The charter likewise delivered to Mr Alderman.

Att this courte alsoe Mr Christopher Hanson late Alderman delivered in open courte by the inventorie thereof all the townes plate to him Richard Conye now Alderman (viz) twoe silver cannes, twoe beare bolles, one wine bolle, one guilte cuppe, twoe silver tunnes, one beaker, a silver salte & cover, the horse race cuppe & casse, and thirteen silver spoones.

Hee likewise delivered uppe the greene deske with the writings haveing nott bine looked over this foure or five yeares and is agreed uppon to be perused & sorted att some conveniente tyme by Mr Alderman & some of his bretheren, second twelve & comoners and the inventorie thereof to be presented into the courte next after.

Att this courte Mr Alderman acquainted the courte with the contents of a letter by the consente of the first & second twelve to Mr Mold of Oneleape to desire to come over to preach to this congregacon, that soe yf ytt mighte be wee might talk with him to be our minister wee being in wante of one.

Att this courte Mr Alderman brought in a letter of the said Mr Mold in answere to the townes letter which was read in open courte and ytt was agreed uppon the letter should be sente to Mr William Burye now att Lincolne to advise in ytt & to intrete his assistance in procuring an able minister & meanes to maintaine him.

Att this courte ytt was ordered that a breviate of all the townes debts shalbe gathered togeather and what use money is owing to anie persons as soone as convenient maybe. And the same to be recorded in the courte booke, to the end wee may take care for the payemente thereof as soon as maybe.

Att this courte was taken into consideracon the order made in Mr Archers tyme in a courte holden the xith daye of November 1636 fol 44 that noo Alderman should keep a courte except at least six of his bretheren appeared att the said butt noe order taken for inioyning the said bretheren to attend att the occassione, whereby manie of the bretheren tooke libertie to come or nott to come as they pleased retarding the service of the corporacon for remedie whereof ytt was this courte agreed by the said courte, that for the tyme to come Mr Alderman shall sitt downe att nine of the clocke in the forenoone according to auntiente custome with such companie as doth then attend him, and call over the courte and whomsoever of the first twelve & second twelve doth nott appeare att theire call, nor before the tickett hath gone downe the stares for distresss according to auntiente custome shall forfeit (viz) xiid a man for everie one of the first twelve for offending and vid for every one of the second twelve & vid for every comoner to be leavied by distresse & sale of the offenders goods.

Att this courte ytt is now agreed that Mr Blowers now schoolemaster of this borough shall have the money which was made of the colledg orchard this last somer in regard hee was chossen schoolemaster before the fruit was ripe, and alsoe shall have the money from the state due for corne lyeing in his chambers since he was chossen schoolemaster.

Att this courte John Harford informed the courte that his wief was deade & left him four small children which hee was noe wayes able to maintaine being a verie poore man & children wanted necessaries. The court agreed hee shall have collectione throughout the towne for the same whereby they maye be fitter to be putt forth and for the presente appoynted the collectors to iis vid.

Att this courte Widow Blyeth brought in twoe children of Richard Brookes and informed the courte shee was behinde hand for paye for keping the children which Brookes agreed with her for Brookes being presente informed the courte hee was not able to mantaine his charge haveing twoc children more & wanting a house to follow the trade of cobbling. This court ordered Widow Blyeth to keepe the twoe children for xiid a weeke, & wait till that cold other wayes be provided for, and willed Brookes hearken out a house whereof hee might follow his trade for the maintenance of his charge & the towne wold pay his rente.

Att this courte was taken into consideracon the cole markett is soe noysomely kepte that there lis noe entrance onle passage that waye, thereuppon ytts ordered that the markett sweepers shall from tyme to tyme sweepe & keep ytt cleane weeklie and for theire upkeep to have 111s 1111d per annum payed by the chamberlins.

Second Court of Richard Cony 6 November 1646.

Att this courte ytt was ordered that the constables in everie ward shall against the next courte daye bring in theire severall bills of all strangers that have come to inhabitte within this towne for foure yeares last paste and what trades they use, nott being free men to the ende some speedie course may be taken with them to prevent charges that may ensue to the towne.

Att this courte was taken into consideracon the multitude of alehouses & victulers in this towne manie whereof have bine occassioned by reason of the late garison in the same to make provisione for the soldierye whilest ytt was a garisson which companie is now thought to numerous. Therefore the court doth order that against the next court the constables in theire severall wardes shall bring in theire bills of all victulers & alehousekeepers licensed & unlicensed, and withall whoe are licensed & who nott, to the end due consideracon may be had by Mr Alderman & his bretheren of a fitt number to be allowed & the reste to be discharged.

Att this court was agreed Mr Parkins shalbe retained Attorney for the towne to prevent anie damage to the towne by reason of the Escheator nott accounting those foure yeares since the tymes grew troublesome in regard they have receaved noe profitt by theire foure yeares office.

And this court ytt agreed that the house where Richard Poole dwelleth with the glass windowes shalbe sett in sufficyente repaire by the towne which done the said Poole his successors shall keep in good repaire from tyme to tyme at his or theire owne propper costes & charges.

Att this court ytt was agreed a tickett shalbe yssued out to distrean Nicholas Weymans goods att anie tyme when they can come by them for the somme of sixe poundes for his victuline in the towne for twelve moneths last paste nott being a free man.

Att this courte the good & laudable orders of this courte were reade & agreed uppon which are as followeth which for the presente are to be observed & the rest of the orders nott here expressed, ytt is agreed there shalbe consideracon taken of them by this courte & counsell yf need requires or the amendment & abrogating as need requireth.

142 Third Court of Richard Cony 27 November 1646

According to an order the laste courte made & agreed uppon the constables of this borough have delivered into this courte an note of all inmates, strangers, victulers & alehousekeepers which are & have come to dwell & inhabite within this borough for foure yeares now laste paste, as by the said order they were then inioyned.

Att this courte John Phiper being formerlie chossen one of the second twelve burgesses in the roometh of Brian Newball deceassed hath in open court taken his corporall oathes incydente & propper to the said place & degree & paied the Clarke & Sergeants theire due fees.

Att this courte Edward Watson for giving uncivile & unseemelie speeches in open courte against William Clarke one of the cheiffe constables of this borough (which words were that for sayeing that a lye.) was by the courte fined to paye iiis iiiid which he paied & was then & there putt into the boxe.

Ytt was likewise this courte ordered that the colebuyers, constables & others that were then in place & office should see what coales & other comodities laied out or disbursed to & for the use of Parliamente in such tymes as this towne was a garrison, that yf anie meanes could be used the same maye be a made good againe to this corporacon.

By reason of a caussualtie of fire which befell att the house of Widow Blyth in Castlegate, which house belongeth to this corporacon for preventing future danger, ytt is this courte ordered that Mr Rhoades, Mr Pearson, John Bracewell, John Simpson, & William Poole to veiwe the house of the said Widow Blieth & to direct & sett downe in what place in the said yard where shee shall erect & build an other house for her necessarie uses.

Ytt was likewise this courte ordered that all masons, carpenters, laboring servants, laborers & workmen dwelling & inhabiting in this borough shall from henceforth uppon anie breach of water made uppon the mille banckes belonging to this borough or other miscassualties happening in the said banckes att the comannde of Mr Alderman for the tym being & other of the towne offyceals or others as Mr Alderman and his bretheren shall appointe shall come & work for the amending the said banckes & cassualties they being allowed reasonable content for the same and yf anie laborer, mason, carpenter or servante faile therein to forfeit iis & the masters that detaines them to forfeit 5s.

Ytt is this courte alsoe ordered that the pettie constables in this borough shall nott walke the streets thereof without theire constables staves in theire hands butt for everie defalt that informacon shall thereof be given to forfeit xiid and yf they loose or breake theire staves to forfeit xviiid.

f. 143 Fourth Court of Richard Cony 4 December 1646

Att this courte Mr Alderman made a motion to the courte to have a weeklie lecture in this towne, as heretofore wee have had, by divers worthie & revered divines whereby there hath bine much comfort receaved by theire ministry att Grantham which lecture have discontinued above this foure yeares last past since these troublesome tymes of warres began in those parts and this courte taking Mr Aldermans motion into consideracon did verie willinglie & chearfullie condiscend thereunto, and did agree letters should be sente to the ministers to intreat theire paines withall convenient speed following for the keeping of the said lecture (viz)

Mr Robert Clark of Allington   Mr Northen of Harlaxton
Mr Dr Ramer of Lincolne   Mr Clerk of Rippingale
Mr Francis Browne of Colsterworth Mr John Taylor of Ropesly
Mr Lee of Burton   Mr Dr Drew of Barrowbye
Mr Ephallior Garthwait of Barkston.

Att this court was taken into consideracon the gifte of Bryan Godleys house to this corporacon for the use of the poore by Mr William Blyeth late of Oakham deceased whoe left the assurance latlie bequeathed by Mr William Blyeth of Strawson butt executors to the said Mr Blyeth the assurances being made as this court is informed according to the doctors guift, and was tendered by Mr Hanson late Alderman with there his bretheren to have them sealed by Mr Blyeth of Strawson, butt in regard hee being sicke & infirme, desired the buisnes might be respited till Mr Thorton his attorney cam home that hee might peruse the writings before hee did anything therein. The courte therefore desires Mr Alderman & some of his bretheren whome hee thinks good to call, to intreat Mr Thornton to be pleased to take the paines to goe over to Strawson to the said Mr Blyeth & be a means that the writings maye be sealed according to the intention of the doner.

Att this court Mr Alderman acquainted the court with Mr William Welby his desire which is that hee might have the remainder of his use money for three hundred poundes which hath bine longe due, being the some of fortie poundes & upwards, which the court ordered should be paied as soon as money comes in with as much speed as may bee, and that Richard Paxtons his clark should have xxs payed him by the chamberlaine forthwith for foure yeares allowance concerning the making of bonds for the said money.

Att this court these victulers following were discharged from brueing in regard they brewed nott being made free of this corporacon (viz) John Worth, Whyte, Lawrence Atkinson, Robert Gibson, William Dalby, Anthonie Roase, Richard Holley, John Drake, Jeffrie Warde, John Crawshaw. All these are to be discharged by the constables of each ward from brueing nott being freemen of this corporacon.

Att this courte Shertred being called in question for brueing in the towne he being a stranger answered that he maried Thomas Hands widowe desired that he might live in the towne and faithfullie promised hee wold putt in bonds nott to be chargeable to the town which the court tooke into consideracon he being a laborer & noe charg butt only himself & wief was contented he shold continue putting in good securitie before the first court in the new yeare nott to be chargeable to the towne.

Att this court Robert Gibson whoe haveing continued in this towne cam into the court & desired that hee might be admitted a free man of this corporacon which the court did agree unto hee comeing under the orders of the court, and gav him tyme to bring in his money the first court in the new yeare.

Att this court informacon was given by Thomas Hanson that Thomas Shorte, John Kirk, & William Broughton all of Grantham butchers did keep in the markett twoe stalls a peece of late on markett day att the least contrarie to anie order of the court for which the court appointed tycketts to be yssued out to the constables to distrean theire several goods for vs a peece according to the penaltie of the order.

Att this court James Gibson informed the court that Smith a pettye chapman in Grantham kept twoe stalls the last Satterdaye contrarie to the order of this court for which the court ordered that Phillippe Hollingworth should have a tickett delivered him to distreane of the goods of the said Smith for the breach of the said order the somme of five shilling.

144 Fifth Court of Richard Cony 11 December 1646.

Att this court Mathew Whiting & Richard Poole the sergeants at mace tooke theire oathes incydente to theire places and the said Richard Poole tooke his oath of Gaoler for the borough of Grantham & Baylie of the liberties thereof.

Att this court John Johnson late apprentice to Richard Saule haberdasher of hatts and being a stranger desired to be incorporated & made a free man of this borough, whereunto this courte was willing & did assente, and thereuppon he paied to the chamberline according to anntiente custome five shillings & to the Clark & Sergeants theire due fees took his oath of alegiance & freedome & soe was admitted & made a free man of this borough.

Att this court alsoe Godfrye Hanson a stranger borne late apprentice to John Hutchin cordwainer desired to be incorporated & made a free man of this borough whereunto this court was willing & did assente whereuppon he paied to the chamberline according to anntient custome vs & paid the the Clark & Sergeants theire due fees tooke his oath of alegiance & freedome and soe was admitted & made a free man of this borough.

Att this court came in John Worth a stranger & desired to be admitted a free man of this corporacon which this court did condescend unto hee submitting to the order of the same, there uppon he laid down his £x in open courte & tooke his oaths of alegiance & freedome paid the Clark & Sergeants theire due fees which done he humblie desired the faver of the court for mittigacon of the ten poundes whereuppon the court took into consideracon his great charge of children & the ympotency of his wives aged father maintained by him & the hopes of himself proving a good townes man were willing to accepte onelie fortie shillings which was delivered to the chamberline & gave him eight poundes the remainder thereof againe.

Att this court cam in Richard Hollie who maried the widow of Thomas Kidde & desired to be made a free man of this borough which the court taking into consideracon did condiscend he submitting himself to the order thereof, and thereuppon he paid ten poundes in open court being a stranger according to custome, took the oath of alegiance & freedom paid the Clark & Sergeants theire due fees and humblie desired the faver of the courte for the mittigacon of the ten poundes, whereuppon the court being trulie informed of his faithfull service to Parliamente for three yeares & upwards under the command of Collonell Fleetwood, and hoping he will make a good towns man were willing to accept onelie of six pounds xiiis iiiid which was paied into the chamberline & given him the other £iii vis viiid back againe.

Att this court cam in Thomas Robinson being free borne & desired to be admitted freeman of this borough which was graunted, thereuppon he tooke the oaths of alegiance & freedom paid to the chamberlaine iis vid to the Clarke & Sergeants vid a peece.

Att this court Phillippe Hollingworth paied in open court five shillings for a distresse taken of Robert Smith petty chapman for keeping twoe stalls in the markett contrarie to the order of this courte which was putt into the boxe.

Att this court came in Nicholas Weyman blacksmith & desired to be admitted a freeman of this corporacon which uppon consideracon had of the sufficyent number of smithes alreadie in the towne as alsoe in his being in armes against the Parliamente the court absolutlie refused to admitte him freeman of this corporacon and thereuppon discharged him of the towne.

Att this court Thomas Greene taylor sonne in law to William Todkill was called in question for using the trad of a taylor nott being freeman of this corporacon, what pleaded hee was bound apprentice to his father in law since or a litle before his mariage of Todkills daughter which answere did nott give sattisfaction to the court whereuppon hee desired tyme till the first courte after new yeares tyde to give better sattisfaction to the courte.

Att this court was taken into consideracon the illegall proceedings to the choyce of Henrie Ferman, Thomas Secker & William Cole, uppon the second twelve on the tenth court of Edward Christian then Alderman contrarie to the custome of this borough for that att a court held the eighteenth of October 1643 by Mr Rhoades then Deputie to Mr Colcrofte Alderman ytt was ordered James Gibson & John Phiper to remaine in the callender or bill for the next choyce uppon the seconde twelve and ytt was they by Mr Christian Alderman in his said tenth courte, in a most disgracefull maner cleare putt out of the callender, and clearlie made uncapable of being att that tyme chossen on the second twelve they being firme & faithfull men for the Parliamente and for that cause with other faithfull mene to the comon wealth were inforced to leave theire habitacons through the preveleneye of the enemie in & neare Grantham and putt the three above named (men disaffected to the Parliamente, and for which twoe of theire estates are alreadie sequestred in theire roomes, which this courte conceaves uppon good grounds was done to advance men dissafected & disgrace men well affected to the Parliamente, for that the said Mr Christian did nott in his tyme of being Alderman fill uppe the number of the second twelve neither did Mr

Thomas Mills the succeeding Alderman fill uppe the number in his tyme neither did Mr John Mills make uppe the wante in his tyme which ought nott to have bine neglected by them or anie of them) ytt haveing bine the auntiente custome of this Borough for everie Alderman respectivelie to fill uppe the number of the first & second twelve before the serarender of his office) which this court conceaves was omitted to prevent the bringing of anie well affected persons into the offices as hath appeared by the severall invectives of Mr Christian, (uppon insufficyent testimonie) against well affected men of severall ranckes in the said courte as alsoe to prevente the bringing uppon the second twelve James Gibson, John Phiper, William Clark, Thomas Doughtie & Robert Trevillian whoe all att the next choyer in the ninth courte of Mr Hanson late Alderman were in one daye brought uppe in the second twelve togeather (men all well affected to the Parliamente & imployed in the service of the comonwealth) and who this court conceaves ought to have had precedence of the other three above named for redresse whereof this court (taking the premisses into serious consideracon) doth fullie conclude order and agree that the said James Gibson, John Phiper, William Clarke, Thomas Doughtie and Robert Trevillian shall from henceforth proceed & take theire places as second twelve men & remaine above Henrie Ferman, Thomas Secker & William Coale anie order or agreemente formerlie made in this court in anie wise to the contrarie nottwithstanding.

Against this daye a courte was summoned according to the order of the clarke and there appeared of the first twelve Mr Richard Cony gen Alderman and the next unto him of the first twelve:–
Mr Richard Pearson
Mr George Briggs
Mr Gilbert Chauntler
of the seconde xii
William Clark
Thomas Shorte
John Bracewell
John Rawlinson
John Bee
James Gibsone
Robert Trevillian
William Coale
And by reason soe manie of the first twelve were wanting Mr Alderman held an assemblie or meeting and sent for distresses for those that were absent as by booke of distresses doth appeare.

Distresses solde by the chamberline or else redeemed att the assemblie.
Imprimis John Lenton redeemed a bason att Mr John Mills his third court for absence from courte vid.
Item he redeemed a brasse spoute potte taken att Mr Richard Cony his third court paid his vid.
Item John Mason redeemed a pewter platter taken the second courte of Mr Thomas Mills for swine going att random in the Markett Place paid iiiid putt in the boxe.
Item William Cole one of the chamberlins whoe should have solde the

distresses taken sicke sente word hee was nott able to stand to sell them soe ytt was left of till another tyme.

Item Mr Christopher Hanson & Mr Edward Rawlinson being both absent att this assemblie were sente to for distresses but non could be founde or taken of them.

f. 146 Sixth Court of Richard Cony 22 December 1646

Att this court ytt is agreed by a generall consente & desire of the wholle courte that Mr Thomas Redman shalbe vicar of the towne of Grantham in Mr Thomas Dilworthe his roometh latelie deceased. And alsoe ytt is agreed a petitione be made to the Parliamente and a letter be written to the burgesses of this borough for the establishing the said Mr Redman in the said vicarage.

Receaved of Mr Christian for Edward Watson his distresse taken the second courte held the vith daye of November 1646 the somme of vid and had his booke called the marow of martyrs

Att this court all the charter boxes were opened, and there were in them all the charters & writings according to the record, and there was in one of the boxes a charter graunted from King Edward the sixte of the schoolehouse lands & now putt into the new charter boxe.

Att this courte ytt was ordered that in regard the writings in the deske would take a longer tyme to sort, than this courte could spare, soe that ytt is agreed uppon by the wholle courte that Mr Alderman call att some convenient tyme to give notice by his sergeants that Mr More, Mr Colcroft, Mr Christian, Mr Thomas Mills & Mr Christopher Hanson, and of the second twelve William Clarke, Thomas Doughtie, John Bracewell & Robert Trevillian, Comoners, Francis Bristow, Thomas Graunte, William Poole, John Symson, Thomas Hanson & John Lenton, that they attend Mr Alderman att the tyme which they are warned to veiw the said writings,and yf they or anie of them faile to come then the first twelve to paye xiid the second twelve vid & the comoners vid a peece and the residue that doe appeare to proceed for effecting the buisnes.

Att this court was paied in open court by Richard Cony gen Alderman fortie shillings which hee receaved of Edward Wythers executor to Joanne Hutchinson late of Grantham deceased which is to be given to the poore of Grantham, and was receaved in court by Robert Trevillian churchwarden.

Att this courte Phillippe Hollingworth informeth that uppon Fryday laste hee being sent for a distresse to Edward Watson,for nott appearing att the Aldermans courte, hee told the said Phillippe that he wold come to the courte butt hee could have neither justice nor righte done there by Mr Alderman, and yf hee would doe him justice & right hee would come to the courte, for which this courte ordered him to be fined fortie shillings according to an order hb 5 fol 284 and gave him leave to bring in the said fine of fortie shillings against the nexte courte daye or else the same to be leavied by distresse.

Att this court came John Hutchine & complained to Mr Alderman against James Gibson for that hee gave him the lye in the court & proved ytt by twoe witnesses ytt being a breach of order & in the courte and therefore hee was fined iiis iiiid cald to the boxe & laied downe his iiis iiiid according to the order which is putt into the boxe.

Att this court there was complaint made to Mr Alderman that manie persons were gone out of the courte without leave & thereuppon Mr Alderman comannded to call the courte againe and there were wanting uppon the second calling Thomas Graunte, Edward Still, William Grococke, Edward Bristow, Thomas Baylie, John Fysher, Robert Tompson, William Bristow & Thomas Hanson which is by this court ordered that the constables of everie respective warde shall have ticketts & distrean the said persons & bring theire distresses into the Guyld Hall before the next courte daye and there deliver them to Richard Poole to be kept saffe.

147 Seventh Court of Richard Cony 8 January 1646.

Att this court Robert Kellam being distressed for his absence from the court this daye had the same delivered back in regard he was about the towne buisnes.

Att this courte was brought in twoe candlesticks the one distreaned of Edward Bristow & the other of John Fysher for departing the last courte daye without leave.

Att this courte Thomas Graunt, Edward Still, William Grococke, Robert Tompson, William Bristow, Thomas Hanson paied everie of them theire vid a peece for departing the courte the laste courte daye withoute leave which 3s was all putt into the boxe. And resteth for Thomas Baylye to paye vid for the like absence because noe distresse was to be founde.

Att this courte Mr Richard Pearson & John Bee appoynted overseers for the orphants goodes.

Att this courte was taken into consideracon the neglect of divers persons that have taken leases of this borough & neglect to putt in securite according to the covenants of theire leases whereby much damage may acrue to the towne thereby. Ytt is therefore ordered by a generall consente of this wholle court that all & everie person & persons whoe have taken anie lease or leases of the towne for anie land belonging to this borough shall before the xxvth daye of March nexte comeing take or accept theire leases, and therewithall to enter bond with theire sufficyente securities for payemente of the rente & performance of the usuall covenants in that behalf or else the towne forthwith to dispose of the said land & tenements in theire or anie of theire occupacons to anie other person or persons whatsoever, according to a former order in the xxiith court of Mr Alderman that now is when he was first Alderman.

Att this courte came in Robert Tompson & hath taken the toule of oatmeale & gritts & wheate meals belonging to this borough for one wholle yeare for which hee is to paye to the chamberlins for the use of this corporacon the somme of twentie shillings and paied to Mr Alderman in earnest of the said bargaine vid.

Att this courte alsoe came in Widow Scotte of the White Lyone & tooke a lease of one yeare of the toules of all wagons & pack horses which have resorted to her house since Michaellmas nexte, for which shee is to pay to the chamberlines for the use of this borough xiiis iiiid and she gave to Mr Alderman in earnest of the said bargain xiid.

Att this courte Mr Alderman desired the court to take into consideracon what was the fittest to be done with all the earnest money that shalbe taken for anie leases for the tyme to come declaring his opinion that hee thought ytt moste fitt ytt be putt into the boxe for the use of the corporacon although heretofore for the most parte Mr Alderman for tyme being tooke ytt for theire owne use. Which the courte taking into theire consideracons did declare & order for the tyme to come that whatsoever earnest money was given uppon anie bargaine for anie lease or leases or otherwise concerning the corporacon the same shold be putt into the boxe for the use of the towne.

Att this court Robert Gibson whoe victualls & brues nott being a freeman of this Borough & being latelie discharged from brueing & victualing desired the courte to respite untill the Ladie day next. And yf then hee continued anie longer in the towne hee wold desire of the courte to be admitted a freeman yf they pleased to accept of him & hee come into the orders of the courte for the paymente of his money to which motion of his this court did agree.

Att this court James Lambert nott being a freeman was discharged from brueing & victualing & to remove out of his house Widow Morrice which hee hath taken in as an innemate contrarie to the orders of this courte which hee hath promised to doe.

Att this court Humfry Hipworth being called in question for using the trade of a turner nott being a freeman came into the courte and did averre that hee had served his aprenticeshippe with John Funtance a freeman of this Borough & promised to give the courte full sattisfaccon there the next courte daye.

Att this court Humfry Hutt whoe maried Widow Walkers daughter being a stranger, Edward Enderby a ropemaker & Robert Lane sadler whoe useth theire trades in this Borough nott being freemen & being questioned by the court for the same desired respitt for giving theire answeres untill the Ladie daye nexte which the court condiscended unto.

Att this courte Edward Watson by waye of intreatie is respitted untill the next court day for payeing his fine for speeches which he used against Mr Alderman which was imposed uppon him the last court daye or else a distresse to be taken yf hee fayled to paye in his money according to the former order.

Att this court ytt was ordered that a tickett should be sent out to distreane William Calladine for using the trade of a carrier nott being made free vs. John Crawshaw for victualling nott being made free vs. And William Todkill for entertaineing a taylor nott being made free vs.

f. 148 Eighth Court of Richard Cony twenty-ninth of January 1646.

Att this courte Thomas Hanson being absente from the court paied vid which was putt into the boxe.

Att this courte search being made in the Court book concerning the coale monye which have bine wasted to the summes of £13 10 9 in all by delivering coales to the gards in Grantham when ytt was a garisone, an note whereof was made & Mr Alderman desired to deliver the same to Mr William Clarke treasurer for this countie to desire his furtherance that the said sume of £13 10 9 might be repayed which was delivered in coales for the use of the state, soe that hereafter the poore may nott loase the benefitte of ytt.

Att this court William Godhill laied downe vs for keeping Thomas Greene a taylor in his house nott being a freeman which was delivered to one of the chamberlines.

Att this court John Crawshawe had a panne distreaned for using victualing & selling ale nott being a freeman.

Att this court ytt was agred by the generall consente of the court that anie of the inhabitants within this borough may carye the manure out of anie of the streets or out of theire yardes att anie tyme before maye day nexte nottwthstanding a former order to the contrarie in regard of the extraordinarie wette which fell laste sumer soe that they could nott carie ytt out laste michaelmas.

Att this court Phillippe Hollingworth brought into the courte 3s a peece which hee distreaned of Thomas Shorte, John Kerke & William Broughton for keeping twoe stalls in the markett contrarie to order which money was delivered to Richard Poole to be kepte as distresses untill the court dispose of ytt.

Att this court John Fearone sadler late aprentice to Stephen Clemison cam into this court & desired to be admitted a freeman which this court condiscended unto paied iis vid being free borne which was delivered to the chamberlines and hee tooke his oathe of alegeance & the oath of a freeman of this borough & paied the clark & sergeants theire due fees.

Att this court Robert Greene felmonger late apprentice to Christopher Fysher cam & desired to be admitted a freeman of this borough which this courte condiscended unto & nott being a freeman borne hee paid 5s which was delivered unto the chamberlines tooke his oath of allegiance & freedome and paied the clark & sergeants xiid a peece for theire fees.

Att this court ytt was ordered that notice should be given to Robert Cooke of Sleaford that hee muste nott keepe in this towne on the markett daye hee dwelling oute of the towne which is contrarie to an order in this courte.

Att this court the churchwardens did complaine manie of the inhabitants of this towne & churchwardens parishe did refuse & delaye the paymente of theire assessments for the church, made in Mr Thomas Mills his tyme late Alderman and alsoe for the yearlie assessements for theire quartridge for theire seates in the church & for divers guifts which have bine given by well disposed people out of theire lands & tenements towards the repaires of the church whereby great losses have beene and likelye is to be yf some speedy course be nott taken to prevente the same. This court taking the premisses into serious consideracon & the libertie which divers persons be presented for neglecte thereof as theretofore they have beene. Itt is therefore ordered & agreed uppon by a generall consente of the wholle courte that what persone or persons whatsoever inhabiting within this borough of Grantham & parish thereof shall refuse or delaye the payemente of anie assessemente or assessements before made or hereafter to be made for or concerning the repaires of the said church or anie other dues thereto belonging being demanded by the now churchwardens or theire successors & payemente being nott made within one moneth next after anie such demande that then the said churchwardens or theire successors with the assistance of one constable or more shall distreane the goods of such persone or persons as shall refuse or delaye to paye theire assessmente or assessements, and alsoe to distreane the goods of anie the inhabitants which liveth in anie of the houses or tenements within the borough of Grantham for all such sume or sumes of money now due by anie guifte or bequeste formerlie given for & towards the repaire of the said church which heretofore hath beene payed,and what distresse or distresses shalbe taken by the churchwardens or theire assistance for neglecte of the payments aforesaid or anie of them shalbe aprised & forthwith solde and the overplus uppon the sale shalbe delivered to the partie or parties soe distreaned.

Att this court was taken into consideracon – the great abuse & hurte which heretofore hath beene comitted & done uppon the leads & other parts of the church belonging to this borough of Grantham by reason of the great concourse & innummerable companie of olde & younge people which uppon Shroove Tewsday have usuallie resorted to the said church, and often tymes abused the seats therein and by leave of the sextone have gott uppe into the ollyers ?louvres of the steeple of the said church whereby ytt doth manifestlie appeare there hath beene much hurte & iniurye done in those parts by breaking of the wyars belonging to the clocke & chymes and clangeling the bells & divers other misdemeanors. Ytt is now therefore fullie ordered concluded & agreed uppon by the wholle court that the now churchwardens & sexton or bellman & theire successors shall nott permitte or suffer anie concourse or number of people to have recourse into the said church or goe uppe into the steeple or the said ollyers uppon the daye comonlie called Shroave tewsday,butt shall keep the dores of the said church & steeple which goeth uppe the stares locked all the said daye except ytt be uppon other necessarie occassions then & there to be performed.

Att this courte Edward Watsone was called uppon for to laye downe his fine of fortie shillings according to an order made in for so abusing Mr Alderman in words uppon the informacon of Phillippe Hollingworth which words the said Edward Watson denyed att that tyme and being demanded yf anie were by save himself & Phillippe Hollingworth hee answered noe yett nottwthstanding hee now saith that hee can prove hee did nott speake the words wherewth hee is charged. The court being then uppon rysing ordered that hee should bring in his fine of fortie shillings the nexte courte daye or else a distresse to be taken for the same, and, in the meane tyme that his wittnesse should testefie under his hande before Mr Alderman & some of his bretherene what hee would saye in the buisnes and the sam to be considered of the nexte courte daye when hee brings in his money.

149 Ninth Court of Richard Coney 12 February 1646.

The said courte being then according to auntiente custome warned there appeared onelie of the first twelve comburgesses besides Mr Alderman, Mr Rhoades, Mr Pearson, Mr Briggs, Mr Chaunteler, and of the second twelve & comoners there appeared a full number for the keeping of a courte. And then Thomas Baylie being absente att a former courte & noe distresse could be then taken paid vid for his then absence & now putt into the boxe
And likewise John Wythey, John Fysher, Edward Bristowe & Thomas Secker hee being three tymes absente redeemed theire distresses which were taken before Mr Alderman came to his place which cam to iiis & was putt into the boxe.

Att the same tyme Mr Alderman declared divers buisnesses which hee then purposed to have proceeded (for the comon good of the towne) butt in regard there wanted twoe comburgesses to make uppe the other foure six besides Mr Alderman hee could nott proceed in anie of the buisnesses hee then intended to propounde unto the courte by reason of a former order made when Mr Thomas Archer was Alderman libro sexto fol 44 prohibiting anie Alderman that after should succeed nott to keepe anie courte or to doe aniething as att a courte except six comburgesses did at the leaste then appeare besides Mr Alderman for the tyme being whereuppon Mr Alderman was forced to respitte all his buisnes for this daye till a full courte should appeare.

Tenth Court of Richard Coney 19 February 1646.

150 Tenth Court of Richard Coney 19 February 1646.

Att this court appeared of the burgesses besides Mr Alderman (viz) Mr Rhoades, Mr Pearson, Mr Christian, Mr Mills, Mr Hanson, Mr Briggs,& Mr Chaunteler and alsoe a full companie of the second twelve & comoners which made a full court according to the order made in Mr Archers tyme libra sexto foll 44. Att this court was taken into serious consideracon the order made in the tyme of Mr Thomas Archer being Alderman Libro sexto foll 44 concerning the keeping of the Aldermans court,and haveing found the great inconveniences which have since growen by reason of the said order soe as the comon buisnes of this towne hath often bine retarded both in this Mr Aldermans tyme as formerlie which this court conceaves on good grounde hath bine by wilfull neglect of some of the comburgesses by reason of theire nott appearing att the Aldermans courts although warned according to auntiente custome. This courte desiring to settle all things for the comon good of the towne & peaceable government thereof have in open court used the charter graunted & confirmed by Kinge Charles which now is which followeth in [an extract from Charles I's charter]

Uppon the reading whereof & due consideracon thereuppon had ytt was fullie ordered concluded & agreed uppon that the order formerlie made in Mr Archers tyme libr sexto fol 44 concerning Mr Aldermans keeping of court shall & is hereby clearlie abrogated annulled & made voyde to all intents & purposes.

And ytt is further ordered & agreed by the said court the comburgesses the second twelve burgesses officers burgesses inhabatants within the said borough belonging to the said court being sumoned to apeare att Mr Aldermans court for the tyme being & his successors according to auntiente custome, whoe uppon theire meeting or the greater parte of them according to the charter shall have full power & authoritie in the said court to proceed in all buisnesses in theire said court as formerlie hath bine accustomed nottwthstanding anie order to the contrarie.

And the intent the courte may be alwayes furnished with a competente number of comburgesses ytt is fullie ordered by the wholle court that nether Mr Alderman for the tyme being, his successers noe anie of them shall nott hereafter give leave to anye of the comburgesses to be absente from the Aldermans court (except hee or they be well assured that there will appeare att the said court sixe comburgesses att the leaste besides Mr Alderman.

Att this court Mr Alderman acquainted the court with the debts which the town oweth for which they paye interest, and with the anuities where with the towne is charged, out of the towne mills & the wayes to the end the court may take notice in what casse the towne stands concerning theire debts that some good course may be taken for the payemente thereof in some conveniente tyme and in the meane tyme care to be had they goe noe further into debte; the debts which att presente the towne oweth with the anuities yearlie to be paied amounteth to the some of £1500 & upwards the payements which this yeare is to be paied before the accounte daye cometh to aboute £400 as appeareth by the particulars in writing which Mr Alderman hath gathered togeather the debate of the particulars was deferred till the nexte court daye in regard of the other great occassions of this court.

Att this court was taken into consideracon the debts & payements of the towne above mentioned,and for the preventing of goeing further into debt for the tyme to come: ytt was ordered by a generall consente of the wholle court that from henceforth noe money shalbe taken uppe att interest, butt onely for the paimente of such moneys which the towne now oweth uppon interest (yf the same be called for) and ytt is further ordered & agreed by the said court that what orphants money shall hereafter be brought into this court to be secured for & towards anie childe or childrens portions for which the terme is to pay interest the same shall forthwith be paied to some persone or persons for which the towne stands formerlie indebted uppon interest to the end that the towne may noe further goe into debt by receaving orphants portiones.

151 Att this court Mr Arthure Rhoades one of the comburgesses declaring his great age and infirmities and how unfitting hee was to undergoe the office & place of Alderman of this borough which hee desired this court that he might be excused from the cushion or place of election in which place he hath continued manie yeares shewing the court though he was nott elected Alderman since his being called uppon the cushion yett he hath bine made deputie Alderman during the tymes of troubles in the absence of Mr Colcrofte & Mr Christian for a longe tyme togeather the trouble of which place when he was deputie was such that he knows himself nott able to execute the Aldermans office and therefore desires the court when they please to nominate a man to sitt uppon the cushion in his place which motion the court taking into consideracon knowing his allegiance to

be true yelded to his request and ytt is by a generall consente of the wholle court ordered that hereafter annother comburgesse shalbe nominated & chossen to sitt uppon the cushion or place of election in the place of the said Mr Rhoades.

Att this court George Hardacker and Edward Still butcher being coale buyers for the poore were called uppon to know what coales they had boughte in this laste yeare for the use of the poore haveing had delivered unto them att the begineing of the Springe eleaven pounds odd money. Answere was made by George Hardacker that they had bought in butt one loade for which theire neglecte in theire office & dissapoynting the poore of coales ytt was then ordered by a generall consente of the courte that the said coalebuyers shall paye the rente due for the coalehouse being xvs iiiid for the laste yeare out of theire own purses in regard they did nott dissposse of the coale money as formerlie other coalebuyers have done and ytt is further ordered that the said coalebuyers before theire goeing out of theire offices laye out the money now in theire hands before such tyme as they shall give uppe theire accounte & the new coalebuyers chossen.

Att this court Edward Watson according to a former order came & laied downe his fine of fortie shillings ymposed uppon him for his uniuste charging Mr Alderman for nott doeing him iustice as apeareth by the court of Mr Alderman which fine of xls uppon the motion of the comburgesses then on the bench was then delivered to Richard Poole to be kept as a distresse till a bigger or greater number of the comburgesses doe apeare because there was now butt six comburgesses lefte besides Mr Alderman which is conceaved was to fewe in regard by former orders such fines are onelie left to the Alderman & his bretheren to mittigate yf they soe cause by an order mad libro 5 fol in Mr Wilsons tyme.

Att this court John Rawlinson brought into the court thirteen pounds tenn shillings being parte of the portion of Emma Welborne daughter of Welborne of Grantham a cooper deceased to remaine in the townes hands allowing interest according to her fathers will till shee accomplish lawfull age.

Att this court Thomas Doughtie likewise brought in tenn pounds for Anne Coddington daughter of William Coddington fellmonger deceased as a portion given her by William Everingham her uncle deceased to remaine in the towns hands uppon use for the said Anne Coddington till shee come to lawfull age.

Att this court ytt is agreed that thirtie pounds shold be taken uppe of Mrs Anne Walton widow for to make uppe the twoe somes receaved of orphans portions fiftie odde poundes for the payemente of Mr Wytheys principall debte & foure poundes use which was due laste Christmas to him as executor to Mr Hutchinson late of Grantham deceased which he now calls for which some of thirtie pounds was receaved by the chamberlins from Mrs Walton and ordered the said chamberlyne should forthwith paye the somme of foure & fiftie pounds due to Mr Wythey as aforesaid.

Att this courte the stones which came from the Crosse att the upper ende of the High Streete auntientlie called Queenes Crosse and the Crosse in Swinegate comonlie called Apple Crosse being throwen downe by soldiers in the late tyme of warre taken into consideracon and this consideracon and this courte being informed that manie of the said stones are taken awaye. Ytt is now ordered that the constables of everie warde shall make dil]igente inquirie & search to finde out in whose custodie anie of the said stones are remaineing and whoe hath taken anie of them & converted them to theire owne use and to certifie this courte thereof to the ende the towne may receave satisfactione of the offenders for those that are taken awaye and for the remainder of the stones of both crosses the constables are to see them to be removed to the church for the use of the corporacon.

Att this courte Henrie Rudkine a stranger and noe tradesman haveing maried one Margarett Pole born within this borough born a freemans daughter came and desired to be made a free man of this borough which the courte agreed unto hee submitting to the orders of this court, and thereupnon according to auntiente custome hee layed downe tenn pounds which this court taking into consideracon took al] his £x which was delivered to one of the chamberlins whereuppon hee tooke his oathe of allegiance payed the clerke & sergeants theire fees and soe was admitted a freeman of this corporacon

John Dawson a stranger borne whoe hath served his aprentishippe with Mr Pearsone came into the court & desired to be made a free man of this borough to which this court condescended whereuppon hee paied £x to the use of this borough tooke his oathe of allegiance paied the clarke & sergeants theire due fees and soe was admitted a free man of this corporacon.

f. 152   **Eleventh Court of Richard Coney 5 March 1646**

Att this court Mr Alderman brought in an note of particulars of the debts owing by the towne uppon interest or otherwise and likewise what anuities & other yearely payements is to be payed by the towne, and withall a particular of all the certaine rents & comeings in due to the corporacon to the intent speciall care maye be taken for the tyme to come that theire disbursements & expenses doe nott exceed theire comeings in to prevente the further going into debte which this court tooke into consideracon and ordered that a particular of all the towne debts anuities comeings in takeings out shalbe recorded att the foote of this order.

Att this court ytt was ordered & agreed upon by Mr Alderman his bretheren & the wholle court that the now towne clarke & his successors against everie courte daye shall make a particular of all the debts which shall then be due & owing by the towne & deliver the same to Mr Alderman for the tyme being and then Mr Alderman for the tyme being shall uppon the courte daye acquainte the court therewith and what debts are then owing by the towne to be recorded att the foote of the accountes made uppe for that daye.

Att this courte ytt was agreed that the chamberlines should forthwith cause the bucketts in the hall to be amended that they maye be serviceable yf anie occassion shall happen.

Att this courte ytt agreed that twoe constables should fetch a distresse from Mr Chauntelers for his absence from court in regarde Mrs Chaunteler shutt the dores on Mathew Whiteing the sergeante, & wold suffer him to take noe distresse being sente for one by the courte.

Att this court Richard Sentance had a graunt of that parte of Hoppes house wherein Robert Smith lived whoe is to paye rente to the collectors of schoole landes.

Att this court desired that the courte take into consideracon whether the letting of the towne mills or the keeping them in the townes hands was most conveniente for the profitte & benefitte of the corporacon, whereuppon ytt was concluded that the said mills shold be lette, yf they coulde lighte of a good chapman; and thereuppon James Gibsone one of the second twelve desired that hee mighte be admitted a tenannte to them which after much debate ytt was agreed by Mr Alderman his bretheren & the wholle courte that the said James Gibson sholde have a lease of the twoe water mills (viz) the well lane mille the slate mille & alsoe the horse mille for five yeares to begine the firste daye of this instant March, yelding & payeing therefore the some of eighteen pounds six shillings eighte pence of lawfull English money [viz] on the laste daye of this instante March eighteen pounds six shillings eighte pence and soe the laste daye of everie moneth during the terme of five yeares eighteen pounds six shillings eighte pence to be paied to the chamberlins of this borough for the tyme being for the use of this corporacon.

And ytt is agreed that the towne shall within some convenient tyme sett the twoe water mills & banckes thereunto belonging in good sufficyente repaires as by the iudgment of twoe sufficyente workemen chossen for all parties shalbe thought fitting: and the said James Gibsone doth promise to & with Mr Alderman his bretheren & the wholle court that hee the said James Gibsone will uppon demande give securitie of eighte hundred poundes for the true payement of the rent repairing the said mills & premisses in as good & sufficyente repaires as they shall bee when they are sett into repaire by the apoyntemente of Mr Alderman & the court. In earnest of which bargaine the said James Gibson gave to Mr Alderman tenn shillings which was putt into the boxe,and ytt is further agreed that the mille masters of both the said mills togeather with the chamberlins, Francis Bristow & William Graye shall veiwe & appraice the mille horses which the said James Gibson shall have yf he please payeing for them according to the praysemente: and they are alsoe to take an inventorie of all the goodes & implements belonging to the said mills which the said James Gibson is likewise to make good according to the schedule to his lease to be annexed.

153 Twelfth Court of Richard Coney 12 March 1646.

Att this court was taken into serious consideracon the great number of gentlemen & others whoe formerlie have bine made free of this corporacon uppon theire layeing downe tenn pounde a man according to an order for that purpose, and after they have taken theire oathes of freemen have had all theire money this given them againe by the Alderman for the tyme being the court nott onelie to the obstructing of the publicke profitte for the presente butt tending to the great damage of the corporacon for the future, by theire diminishing the tolles thereof which the respectivelie clayme his to have as freemen. Itt is therefore ordered agreed & concluded uppon by the Alderman his bretheren & the rest of the court, that for tyme to come noe persone or persons of what quallitie soever shall att anie tyme hereafter be made free of the same being strangers, except such as shalbe thought fitte by Mr Alderman for the tyme being his bretheren & the rest of the courte to be made free and shall alsoe respectively have paide theire severall somes of tenn poundes for theire freedomes to the use of the corporacon, which somes of tenn pounds for everie person soe made free is hereby ordered to be delivered to the then chamberlins without retorning the same or anie part thereof to the partie.or parties soe made free uppon anie pretence whatsoever, anie former order to the contrarie in anie wise nottwthstanding excepte onelie such person or persons being strangers as Mr Alderman & the reste of the courte shall thinke fitte to make Recorder deputie Recorder burgisse or burgisses of this borough to sitte in Parliamente for tyme to come, Towne clarke, sergeants or sergeants at mace, & such strangers as inhabitte att this presente within this towne & which Mr Alderman & his bretheren shall thinke fitt to make free, all which persons soe excepted shall alsoe laye downe theire severall somes of tenn pounds, for the use of this corporacon before they be made free which being done ytt shall be lawfull for the then Aldermane to propounde whether the said money or anie parte thereof shall be given them againe, and what shall then be agreed uppon by the maior parte of the courte shall stande.

Att this court was taken into consideracon the differente opinion & construction of an auntiente order in libro 4 foll 4 for prohibiting anie man in this court for them that breache orders which by some is taken litterallie that att the fine for the breach of anie order whatsoever as to be taken without mittigacon, and others ytt hold fitting that when the fine is laied downe the courte hath power to mittigate. This courte upon long debat thereof doth order & conclude that according to the anntient practise of this court everie such offender shall lay downe his fine,and then Mr Alderman for the tyme being & the court hath power to mittigate according as they in theire iudgement shall thinke most fitt & conveniente uppon hearing the allegacon of the offenders.

Att this court ytt is agreed that all the first twelve & second twelve which are behinde & have nott provided bucketts according to a former order shall bring in soe much money att the next court as shall buy them, & theire pay in the same, that ytt may be sente to London to buy bucketts of good neats leather for the securitie of the towne withall conveniente speed that may be, and the comoners to doe the like according to the number they are to provide,

Att this court, ytt was agreed that all those of the second twelve which have nott gownes shall provide against the nexte faire or against Easter att the furthest and those of the second twelve that have gownes shall weare them to the church on the Sabeth daye shall come in them to the court, to walke the faires in theire gownes as formerlie they have done.

Att this court ytt was alsoe agreed that there shalbe a booke provided for the service of the corporacon of all the ordinances that have bine since the begineing of this presente Parliamente.

Att this court ytt was agreed that everie inhabitante in everie street within this corporacon cause to be shoveled all the manure against theire severall houses in the street & cause the same to be caried awaye before the nexte faire,and alsoe anie person that has anie wood lyeing in the streets shall remove the same before the faire without anie further delaye

Att this court was taken into consideracon the great number of strangers that have latelie come to inhabite in this towne contrarie to the orders of this court which alsoe may in all likelhood prove preiudicall to the comon good of the corporacon ytt is ordered by a generall consente of this courte that ticketts shalbe given to the constables to distreane goods of all such landlords that have taken into theire houses such tenants to a value of twentie shillings uppon everie such offender according to the order of the court formerlie confirmed by the iudges of assize.

54 Thirteenth Court of Richard Coney 19 March 1646.

Att this courte was taken into consideracon the differente opinion & construction of an auntiente order in libro quarto for prohibiting anie man in this courte to speake for them that breake orders, which by some is taken litterallie that all the fine for the breach of anie order whatsoever is to be taken without mittigacon and others hold ytt fitting that when the fine is layd downe the courte hath power to mittigate. This courte uppon long debate thereof doth order & conclude that according to the auntiente practise of this courte everie such offender shall paye downe his fine, and then Mr Alderman for the tyme being & the courte hath power to mittigate according as they in theire iudgments shall thinke most fitte & conveniente uppon hearing the allegacon of the offenders.

Ytt was this courte ordered that true informacon & notes shalbe had & taken by _____ and other officers belonging to this borough of all such wood, candles, horse hyer & other charges that was laied onto & disbursed by anie the inhabitants within this borough during such tyme as this towne was continued a garrisone, that then such wayes & meanes may be had & used, that they maye in some sorte be satisfied towards theire losses & disbursement thereby had & sustained.

Ytt is this courte ordered & agreed that James Gibson whoe hath latelie taken a lease of the towne mills, shall according to the condicon & agreemente of his said lease uppon the last daye of everie monneth paye unto the chamberlins for the tyme being belonging to this borough such rente as uppon the concluding & taking of the said lease was agreed uppon.

Att this courte came in Robert Gibson a stranger borne & desired to be made a freeman of this corporacon which this courte did condiscend unto, he submitting to the order of the same and thereuppon he laied downe his tenn poundes in open courte tooke his oathes of allegiance freedome; paied the clark & sergeants theire due fees, which being done hee humblie desired the faver of the courte for mittigacon of the tenn pounds whereuppon the courte tooke into consideracon his charge & his orderlie kind of living & the hopes of himself to prove a good townesman, were willing to accepte of five poundes which was paid to the chamberlins & gave him £v backe being the remainder.

Att this courte William Dalbye whoe maried the wief of Robert Ulliott deceased a stranger & Thomas Bowes whoe maried Robert Tompsons daughter being likewise a stranger whoe useth a trad & the other selling of ale nott being free men & being questioned by the courte for the same desired respitte of the courte for giving in theire answers till the next courte which this courte condescended unto Thomas Greene,William Todkills sonne in lawe hath like respitte graunted him.

Att this courte William Man, Georg Mills his tenante being a stranger was absolutelie discharged for inhabiting anie longer in the towne, Laurence Attkinson whoe maried Seeleys daughter in Castlegat is alsoe discharged & hath tyme till maye daye next to departe the towne.

Joan Crawshawes panne which was formerlie taken by distresse for brueing without license & selling ale was this court lente her againe to use till the buisnes was further questioned.

Whereas complainte hath bine made in the eleaventh courte of Mr Alderman that now is by Thomas Hanson againste Thomas Shorte, John Kirke, William Broughton butchers for keeping twoe stalls a peece contrarie to order for which defalte they by the said order are to paye five shillings a peece & they was given till this courte to bring in theire moneys which they have accordinglie done and thereuppon ytt was ordered they shold have iis vid a peece given them back & the remainder being viis vid being payed ordered to the boxe.

Whereas Edward Watson hath bine formerlie fined for using & giveing Mr Alderman unseemlie & unsiville words,the some of fortie shillings which hee brought in this court, for which hee desired to submitte himself to the bench which being taken into consideracon uppon his submission that hee wold nott hereafter comitte anie such offence & maye hereafter proove a good townseman, gave him xxs backe of the said fine & the remainder being xxs was ordered to be putt into William Coles hands the chamberline & nott into the boxe.

Ytt was this courte ordered that the chamberlins shall paye unto Mr Alderman all such money as in his place hee hath disbursed for the townes use togeather with the £xx hee is to have for his sallerie as the use of this borough being Alderman.

Ytt was likewise ordered Henrie Ferman shall have the money due to him which hee hath disbursed for the use of the towne.

Apud curiam tentam in camera Aldermanni infra Guild aulam apud Grantham predicta vicessimo primo die Martii Anno Dm 1646 coram dicto Aldermano & sociis suis quorum nomina subscribuntur

Mr More	William Clarke
Mr Pearsone	John Rawlinson
Mr Colcroft	John Bee
Mr Mills	James Gibson
Mr Hanson	
Mr Rawlinson	
Mr Briggs	
Mr Chaunteler	

Att this assemblie the said Mr Richard Cony Alderman alledged his necessarie occassions of absence to travaile to London whereunto comburgesses & others there assembled did freely assente; and then likewise the said Mr Alderman did nominate & depute Mr Richard Pearson to execute the place of the deputie Alderman of this borough during the necessarie occassion of the Aldermans absence & the said Mr Pearson did then take his oathe incidente to the said office of the said deputie Alderman.

155 Whereas by order of this courte the nominacon of the succeeding Alderman for the yeare nexte ensueing is to be made in the first courte held by Mr Alderman next after Maye daye(this being the first courte after May daye held by Mr Alderman in regard of his necesscarie occassions att London) att this courte Mr Alderman moved the courte for the said nominacon of the succeeding Alderman which was then taken into serious consideracon and in regard there was butt on comburgesse uppon the cushion or place of electione ytt was agreed uppon, by a generall consente ot the wholle courte that the nominacon for this presente yeare shalbe deferred till some other courte held by Mr Alderman, and in the meane tyme Mr Alderman & his bretheren to take Mr Recorders advice in the premisses.

Att this courte ytt was ordered that George Hardakers & Edward Still for the yeare past shall continue colebuyers till the first courte after May Day nexte in regard they had the laste yeares colemoney in theire hands undistributed.

Att this courte the tanners constitution graunted in the tyme of Mr Browne Alderman [1605] was red & confirmed with some amendmente therein to be altered & amended in case the iudges of assize doe by writing under hands give allowance thereunto.

Att this court was taken into consideracon the great neglecte of Mr Thomas Milles Mr Edward Rawlinson, William Cole, Henrie Ferman, Robert Trevillian, Thomas Graunte, Edward Bristow & Thomas Wallett, assessers for the conduitt in the seaventh courte of Mr Hanson Alderman in nott making theire assessmente againste the seconde daye of October laste paste according to the said order by which meanes John Phiper is delayed his moneye whoe was agreed with Mr Alderman & others according to the order of that court to have the sume of twentie poundes for convayeing the water from the conduitte house in the feilde to the fryer walls finding twoe cocks payeing laborors wages & finding all materials & pipes yf anie wanted more then those, the towne were to furnish him oute of the Scalpe house. Ytt is therefore ordered by this courte that the said assessers shall assesse the summe of twentie poundes uppon the inhabitants of this borough within tenn dayes after this court, and yf anie of the said assessers shall faile to meet to assesse the said summe notice being given them everie one soe failing shall forfeite five shillings to the comon boxe to be levied by distresse & sale of theire goods according to order of this court, and soe manie of the assessers as doe meet to make the assessmente.

Att this court ytt was agreed the first & second twelve shall bring in all such moneys as is due by them to paye in theire places, and the comoners what is due by them to be payed according to a former order, that soe Mr Alderman may be discharged the money he paied for bucketts he bought att London for the use of the corporacon.

Att this court ytt was agreed that tycketts shalbe graunted forth. to distreane all such landlords as have taken anie strangers to inhabitte within this corporacon contrarie to a former order to that purpose.

Att this court ytt is ordered that Richard Elston draper paye into the nexte courte the summe of foure poundes which is yett behinde & unpaied being the remainder & parte of the money hee is to paye of the fine of the house where hee dwelleth.

Apud curiam tentam in camera Aldermanni infra Guildaulam apud Grantham predicta vicessimo sexto die August Anno Dm 1647 coram de Aldermano & sociis suls quorum nominae subscribuntur.

Mr Pearsone   Mr Mills
Mr Colcrofte   Mr Briggs
Mr Christian   Mr Chaunteler

Att this assemblie the said Mr Richard Cony Alderman alledged his necessarie occassions of absence to which the above named comburgesses there assembled freelie consente and then likewise the said Mr Alderman did nominate as deputie Mr Richard Pearson to exacute the office of deputie Alderman of this borough during the necessarie occassions of the Aldermans absence and the said Mr Pearson did then take his oath incydente to the said office of the said deputie Alderman.

f. 156   Fifteenth Court of Richard Coney 20 August 1647.

Att this court Richard Elston draper paid the foure pounds being the remainder of the fine he was to paye for the house where he the dwelleth, according to an order thereof made, and according to an order of the late court and this court att the request of the said Richard Elston, taking into further consideracon, the hardnes of the said Elstons bargaine with some other charges he did aleadge hee had bine att in getting possession of the said house is contente & agreed the said Richard Elston shall have fortie shillings of the foure pounds given him againe uppon condicon he putt in such securitie the next court for performance of the covenants in his lease as the courte shall then aprove & alowe of.

Att this same court cam Mr Blower M of Arts whoe the last yeare was admitted schoolmaster of the towne of Grantham & supplied the place for the yeare laste paste and craved the goodwill of the wholle courte to be established schoolemaster of Grantham during his lief. Whereuppon the wholle courte well considering & approveing of his cariage & demeanor in his place as alsoe his abilitie for the well performing thereof, unannimuslie condescende & graunte that hee should have & inioye the place of the cheiffe schoolemaster of Grantham during his lief,noe instante being given by him to the contrarie.

This courte was likewise moved by the said Mr Blower for inlarging the ushers sallaire & wages by reason the said Mr Blower could make no certaine agreement with his usher, till such tyme as hee was certefied what the courte would allow; which this courte taking into consideracon, ordered that Mr Thomas Armeson the usher should from the daye of the Annuncyacon of our Ladie laste paste have allowed him twentie pounds per annum during his continuance in his place excepte there shalbe instante cause for the contrarie.

Att this court Maurice Dalton a tanner whoe hath maried the wief of Thomas Fysher deceased came & desired to be incorporated & made a freeman of this borough and according to the auntiente order of the said borough for such as are strangers & forreniers tendred & laied downe in open courte to the use of this borough the some of tenn pounds of lawfull money of England which this courte taking into consideracon hopinge hee maye hereafter prove a good member of corporacon did graunte his freedome: and soe he paied the said sume of tenn poundes into the chamberlins hands,tooke his oathe of allegiance & freedome, paied the clarke & sergeants theire due fees & soe was made a freeman of this borough: hee had nothing given him againe of the tenn pounde by reason of an order made in the foureteenth courte of Mr Alderman that now is.

Att this courte complainte was made against Robert Lane a sadler for using the trade of sadler within this borough and as yett nott being a freeman of the same contrarie to the order of this corporacon: Whereuppon this courte doth order & agree that a tickett be granted out to the constables of the ward wherein hee dwelleth to distreane the goods of the said Lane for twentie shillings for using the said trade for the space of a fortnighte last past contrarie to the order of this courte.

157 Sixteenth Court of Richard Coney 14 September 1647.

Att this court Mr Alderman gave informacon to the court that there is a gentleman desirous to putt three hundred poundes into the townes handes, at the rate of sixe poundes per centum & to have the towne seale for his securitie which the wholle courte tooke into consideracon & desired that an answere may be returned to the gentleman that they are contente to accepte of the three hundred poundes payeing sixe pounds xiii iiii per centum soe longe as they keep the same, and ytt is further agreed uppon by the wholle court that the said three hundred pounds, when ytt is come in shall paye three hundred pounds of old debts for which the towne payees eight pounds p centu, and that the said three hundred pounds nor anie parte thereof shall be employed to anie other use else.

Att this court Mr Alexander More desired leave of the courte to assigne over a lease that hee hath of the towne of Grantham for meadowe & lande in Houghton feild belonging to the schoole in Grantham to Mr William Burie of this towne which this courte freelie condescended unto.

Att this court ytt was by a generall consente agreed that the constables of everie ward shall gather uppe the assessmente laterlie made for the conditte & whosoever refuseth to pay the money they are assessed the constables shall distreane theire severall goodes for the same, and bring the distresses to the court to be sold according to theire anntiente custome.

Att this courte George Lawe was sworne pettie constable in the roometh of Beniamine Clarke whoe has gone north of the towne to dwell.

Att this court Mr Edward Rawlinson promised to fetch a load of stones from Paunton pitts for the amending the water courses belonging to the well lane mills in lue of stones he fetched from the Queenes Crosse for his owne use.

Att this court ytt was agreed that the inhabitants of the Soake should be intreated to fetch the stones from the Congree [?Conygre] house for the paving of the streets in Grantham

Att this court James Gibson presented a noate of divers persons which grinde from the towne mills whereuppon the courte ordered that ticketts should be granted out to the constables for everie warde to take distresses of the offenders against the next courte & bring them into the court to be solde according to the order of the said courte.

Seventeenth Court of Richard Coney 17 September 1647

Att this court came in Widow Courtby late wief of John Courtby deceased & tendred in open courte Willam Coale & Henrie Coale for the securitie for the performance of the covenants in the lease which the towne latelie demised of the house & schoolehouse lands in Castlegate adioyneing to Thoms Loaves his house, late in the occupacon of George Arllis deceased

Att this court was taken into consideracon the greate neglecte of the first & second twelve & comoners in nott buyeing bucketts for the use of the corporacon according to former order whereby the corporacon hath nott bine furnished with bucketts as they oughte to have beene butt care being taken by this courte that all the first & seconde twelve & comoners being now bought & the money collecting for the same whereby to paye Mr Alderman for the sixtie bucketts he bought latelie att London for the preventing of future neglecte in that to paye kinde. Itt is ordered & agreed uppon by Mr Alderman & his bretheren & the wholle courte for the tyme to come that everie persone chossen uppon the first twelve shall paye iiis iiiid in open courte to the chamberline for the buyeing of one buckett for the use of the corporacon when hee takes his oathe to be of the first twelve and everie person chossen of the second twelve is to paye xxd to buy half a buckett to the use of the corporacon when he takes his oath to be one of the seconde twelve, and the comoners to pay as much money to the chamberlaine as the first & second twelve doth for buyeing of the said bucketts.

Att this court Mr Alderman acquainted the courte wth divers sumes of money amounting to above one hundred poundes which is made paied by the chamberlins in Mr Christian & Mr Thomas Mills tymes when they were Aldermen, in Mr Christiane there is divers sumes of money made paid for provisions of souldiers which is conceaved was for provision of souldiers that belonged to the enemie and there is three & twentie pounds to Mr Thomas Mills when hee was then Alderman and ytt appeares nott for what and they being both from the court consideracon of the buisnes is refered to some other court to be considered of.

Distresses

Att this court Daniell Coddington paied vid for being absent from the court which was putt into the boxe.
Thomas Shorte absente from the court distresse a bible.
John Howen for grinding from the mills a bible.
Henrie Rudkine for the like ii pewter dishes a seame of malte.
Henrie Humes the like ii pewter dishes.
Widow Walker for the like a brasse potte putt into the boxe 3s 4d
Of her for refusing to paye the conduitt assessemente a warmeing panne.
Of Edward Bristow for the like a pewter flagone.
Of William Sturley a stranger inhabiting in the towne a brasse panne.
Laurence Attkinson the like a pewter bason & a cuppe.
William Parker for wood lyeing before his dore in the streete a paire of shoes.
Edward Bristow for the like a pewter platter.

158 Eighteenth Court of Richard Coney 29 September 1647

Att this court ytt was agreed that everie inhabitante in the High Street soe farre as Christopher Smith's corner shall pave foure yards from his dore before the courte daye att the furthest uppon paine of five shillings according to former order & in the meane tyme to clense the olde pavemente unto the chanell & carrie away theire rubbish before Michaellmas.

Att this court is agreed that the chamberlins shall forthwith lead home the stones from the Conygree house to repaire the most needfull pavements in the markett place, cole markett hill, vine street before the nexte faire and that the inhabitants in vine street & swinegate doe sweep theire dores everie Satterday att nighte.

Att this court Thomas Shorte tendred Robert Tompson & Edward Watson to be his suerties for the performance of covenants in twoe leases hee hath taken of the towne which the court accepted of.

Att this court was ordered John Bracewell accounte as late collecter for the poore, to be reveiwed by Mr. Alderman & some of his bretheren and what money founde in his handes to be paied into the courte before the courte daye for the use of poore.

Att this court came in Mr John Dickinson & demanded George Woodruffe his son in law his portion of threescore pounds in the townes handes due to him in August laste past & the court promised to paye with conveniente speed.

Att courte William Gray being absent from court paid vid & putt into the boxe.

Att this court Mr Alderman desired the court to take into consideracon the nominacon of an Alderman for the yeare to come & with all informed them that Mr Rawlinson was onely on the quishion & place of electione to be Alderman for the next yeare which the courte takeing into serious consideracon in regard of a late ordinance of Parliamente dated the ixth of September past prohibiting the election of all such persons into the place of mayor, Alderman, justice of peace, constable or anie other office, in anie borough, towne corporate, as have bine in armes against the Parliamente, or haveing bine ayding or assisting the forces or hath bine or is sequestred as doth appeare by the said ordinance in hoc verbo called the said Mr Rawlinsone in questione by vertue of the said ordinance, for that hee had bine in armes against the Parliamente & had bine sequestred for his delinquencye which hee confest in open court, and likewise the court proceeded against Mr Edward Christian a comburgesse & justice of peace in the said borough for assisting the enemye against the Parliamente for which he was sequestred as himself confeste in open courte, the court further proceeded against Mr Robert Calcrofte annother comburgesse & justice of peace for ayding & assisting the enemy against the Parliamente as a captaine in the Kings armie for which he was sequestred which himself alsoe confessed this court considering the delinquencye of the said three members (viz) Mr Rawlinson Mr Christian & Mr Calcrofte & the force of this ordinance disabling them from being Alderman, justice of peace or anie other office in the corporacon did nott conceave them nor anie of them fitt members to continue in theire places, and therefore with a generall consente of the wholle court ordered, them to be dismissed of the first twelve & three others forthwith to be chossen in theire roomes in like maner the courte proceeded against Mr George Lloyde a comburgess & justice a peace aforesaid for ayding & assisting the enemye against the Parliament continueing in the enemies garisone above four yeares & comeing in hostile maner against this towne with the enemie when they tooke ytt, for which hee was sequestred and for that since then he hath bine of greate detriment to the corporacon contrarie to his oath & never to this day returned to his habitacon either to paye towne duties or doe towne service which the court taking into like consideracon did with a generall consente order him to be dismiste his place of the first twelve & annother forthwith to be chossen in his roome.

Att this court Thomas Short & William Cole being of the second twelve being by the said ordinance concerning delinquents & that by theire owne of confession (viz) Thomas Shorte for being an officer to the enemies garrisone & continuing there.a long tyme and William Cole for ayding the Kings garisons from tyme to tyme with provission were held by the iudgemente of the wholle courte nott fitt to be called uppon the first twelve nor fitt to beare anie office in the court, and therefore with a generall consent of this courte were dismist from the companie of the second twelve & twoe others ordered forthwith to be chossen in theire roomes.

Att this court Franncis Bristow, Edward Still & Robert Wood desired leave to be dismist the court, & the court holding them nott persons to beare anie office in the court in respect of theire delinquencye against the said ordinance dismist them the courte.

Then the court proceeded for the filling uppe of the second twelve & there was remaining in the callender att the last choyce   Thomas Graunt
                                                                John Wythey
                                                                Edward Bristowe
To which the comoners added a fourth man (viz) Richard Shepperdson

Out of which foure Mr Alderman his bretheren & the seconde twelve sente down to the comoners twoe names (viz) John Wythey & Edward Bristowe
Out of which the comoners made choyce of John Wythey to be of the second twelve in the roometh of Thomas Shorte, tooke his oath & paid the clerk & sergeants
And resteth in the callendar Thomas Graunte, Edward Bristowe & Richard Sheperdson
To which the comoners putt into the callender to make the other three a fourth man Thomas Baylie out of these foure Mr Alderman his bretheren sent downe to the comoners Edward Bristowe, Richard Sheperdson

Out of which the comoners made choice of Edward Bristowe to be of of the second xii in the roometh of William Cole, tooke his oath & paied the clarke & sergeants theire fees

Att this court John Rawlinson was chossen of the first twelve by a general] consente of the court in the roometh of Mr George Lloyde & tooke the oath incidente to his place, the oathe of supremacye & the oathe of justice of peace & paid the clark & sergeants theire fees.

Then left in the callender Thomas Baylie
To which the comoners putt into the callender to make uppe the other three a
fourth man Henrie Speedye

Out of these four Mr Alderman his bretheren & the second twelve sent downe to
the comoners Thomas Baylie. Out of which twoe was chossen Richard
Sheperdson of the second twelve in the roometh of Mr John Rawlinson tooke his
oathe paied the clarke & sergeants theire fees

Att this court John Bee was chossen of the first twelve by a generall consente of
the court in the roometh of Robert Colcrofte tooke the oath incydente to his place
the oathe of justice of peace, & the oathe of supremacy & paid the clark &
sergeants theire fees.

Then rests in the callender Thomas Graunte & Thomas Baylie
To which the comoners putt into the callender Henry Cole to make the other
three a fourth man.

159 Out of which was sent downe to the comoners by Mr Alderman his brethren &
the second twelve (viz). Thomas Baylie, Henrie Speedye

Out of which twoe was chossen Thomas Baylie in the roometh of John Bee tooke
his oathe & paied the clarke & sergeants theire fees

Att this court James Gibson was chossen of the first twelve by a generall
consente of the court in the roometh of Mr Edward Christian tooke the oath
incydente to his place, the oath of justice of peace & the oath of supremacy &
payed the clark & sergeants theire fees.
Then rests in the callender Thomas Graunte, Henrie Speedie & William Poole

To which the comoners putt into the callender to make the other three a fourth
man Thomas Graunte, Henrie Speedie, William Poole, John Symson

Out of which was sente downe to the comoners by Mr Alderman his bretheren &
the second twelve (viz) William Poole, Henrie Speedie

Out of which twoe was chossen Henrie Speedye of the seconde twelve in the
roometh of James Gibson, tooke his oath paide the clark & sergeants theire fees

Att this court William Clark was chossen of the first twelve by a generall
consente of the courte in the roometh of Mr Edward Rawlinson tooke his oath
incydente to his place, the oathe of justice of peace & the oath of supremacye,
paid the clarke & sergeants theire fees.

Rests in the callender Thomas Graunte, William Poole, John Sympson

To which the comoners putt into the callender to make the other three a fourth
man Henrie Cole
Out of which was sente downe to the comoners by Mr Alderman & his bretheren
& the seconde twelve William Poole, John Sympson

Out of which twoe was chossen of the second twelve William Poole in the
roometh of William Clarke tooke his oathe & paid the clarke and sergeants theire
due fees

Att this courte John Phypher was chossen cheiffe constable in the roometh of Mr William Clarke tooke the oath incydent. to the place of cheiffe constable.

Nineteenth Court of Richard Coney 28 September 1647.

Att this court Alexander More Esquier one of the comburgesses of this borough came into the courte & acquainted Mr Alderman, his bretheren & the rest of the courte that there being a late ordinance made by the Lords & Comons in Parliamente for the dissabling of all persons whatsoever that have bine in armes againste the Parliamente or hath bine ayding or assisting the force of the enemye or hath bine or is sequestred as appeareth more att large by the said ordinance bearing date the ninthe of September laste by which he conceaves he cannott continue a member of the courte hee being a member of the courte & one of the first twelve & justice of peace. Therefore in obedience to the ordinance of Parliamente he came & yelded uppe his place which the court taking into serious consideracon dismissed him of his place & ordered that one of the second twelve shold be chossen in his roometh.

Att this court Mr Alderman acquainted the court that the mille banckes was much decayed & inn great danger of breaking yf anie suddaine floods came & that there wanted willowes & oysers to be sett in the banckes side for the savegard thereof for the tyme to come, which the court tooke into consideracon & ordered that three dayes shalbe appointed next weeke for mending the said banckes (viz) Mondaye, Tewsdaye & Wednesdaye, against which tyme the constables of everie warde are to give notice to everie householder & inhabitante that be free of the corporacon shall finde a sufficient laborer one of the dayes aforesaid. The Markett place & Walkergate on Monday, High street & Castlegate Tewesdaye & Westgate & Swinegate for Wednesdaye, Mr Pearson for furthering the worke was contente to be overseer for Monday, Mr Mills for Tewesday & Mr Hanson for Wednesdaye. And ytt was ordered that the constable of everie ward should attend the gentlemen aforesaid uppon theire severall dayes with a bill for the calling of all those that ought to send laborers & whosoever of abilitie did nott send able laborers there to paye twelve pence for theire neglect to be leavied by distresse as hath bine accustomed.

And ytt is further ordered that there shalbe att least five hundred perre good willow setts provided against the spring by those that shall have the oversight of the mills & care to be taken for the preserving of the said setts: and likewise there is to bee provided oziers to be sett for preserving the said banckes those to be boughte att the charge of the towne.

Att this courte William Bristow was censured for using unseemerlie words in open courte against Mr Gibson (whoe is now farmer of the towne mills) sayeing ytt was not fitt for Mr Gibson to have the mills and used these words (viz) as good a sow & eleaven pigs come into the mills as Mr Gibson & his wief which words were proved by John Fysher. The courte thereupon thought fitt & ordered he should paye iiis iiiid for a fine due for a breach of an order heretofore made & likewise ordered that a tickett be sente to distrean his goods.

Distreaned of the said William Bristowe for his fine of iiis foure pence a great pewter dish & a frute dish.

Att this courte ytt was ordered that Mr William Clarke & John Wythey goe to Sir Robert Thorold of the heath Mr Audley & the inhabitants of Spittlegate to give them notice that the River is landed in everie place betwixte Spittlegate & the towne of Grantham which is a great obstruction to the water course; and to desire them that the same maye be forthwith scoured to prevent inditemente at Folkingham sessions.

160 Att this court Mr Alderman moved the court that the chancell is much decayed & in danger of falling yf nott tymely prevented, which the court being sensible of desired Mr Alderman to move Mr Burie to take veiwe of ytt with the churchwardens & workmen to estimate what the charge wilbe for the repaire thereof, & to intreate Mr Burie to ioyne with the corporacon for the sending to the prebende for the speedye repairing of ytt.

Att this courte was taken into consideracon that manie strangers being tradesmen come into this towne, under pretence of living in theire owne houses, & others pretending leases doe use mixsture in divers trades secrettlie in theire houses selling silke wares, haberdasher wares, lining, draperie, stockins, gloves, grocerie & other things belonging to the trades of freemen of this corporacon, whereuppon the court by a generall consent ordered & agreed, that from henceforth noe persone or persons whatsoever inhabiting in this towne or that hereafter shall inhabitte shall sell or putt to sale anie silke wares, haberdasher wares, lining, draperie, stockings, gloves, grocerie or anie other thing belonging to the trade of anie freeman of this corporacon shall for soe doeing forfeit the some of five shillings for everie tyme soe offending, and for everie tyme that they or anie of them shall carye anie wares a broad to putt in sale in the towne in the weeke daye (except in open faire or markett) shall forfeite for soe doeing the some of vis viiid to the use of the corporacon to be leavied by way of distresse, according to the custome of this borough.

Att this court was taken into consideracon that manie of the second twelve doe nott come to take theire place in the church as they ought to doe, and that they doe nott provide gownes in conveniente tyme, after they be chossen, as heretofore theire predecessors have done; whereuppon ytt was ordered by the consent of the court that everie person latelie chossen uppon the second twelve shall the nexte Sabeth daye after theire choyce take theire places in the church sub pena iiis iiiid and they are likewise to provide themselves of gownes within six weeks after theybe chossen, uppon penaltie of five shillings to be leavied by way of distresse according to auntient custome.

Att this court John Braunston tanner formerlie apprentice to Thomas Baylie senior deceased desired to be admitted freeman of this corporacon which was graunted & hee payed vs being a stranger & iiis to the clarke & sergeants & tooke his oathe of aleigiance & freeman.

Att this courte was agreed that the first & second twelve shall from henceforth paye for theire owne dinners att the sessions.

Thomas Graunte
Rests in the callender the laste court John Sympson
Henrie Cole

This court ytt was thought fitt to fill uppe the second companie of twelve, there wanting one soe the comoners putt into the callender to make the other three foure Robert Izacke

Out of which was sent downe to the comoners by Mr Alderman his bretheren & the second twelve John Sympson, Henrie Coale

Out of which was chossen of the second twelve John Sympson in the roometh of John Bracewell tooke his oath & paid the clarke & sergeants theire fees

Att this court John Braunston was chossen constable for the high street in the roometh of John Sympson & hee nott being in court when he was chossen itt was ordered he shold take his oath before the Alderman att his owne house.

Twentieth Court of Richard Coney 1 October 1647.

Att this court Thomas Doughtie was chossen of the first twelve in the roometh of Mr Alexander More tooke his oathe incydente to his place of justice of peace & the oath of supremacie paied the clerk & sergeants theire fees. Thomas Doughtie of the first xii

Att this court John Wythey was chossen cheiffe constable in the roometh of Mr Doughtie & tooke the oath incydente to the place of cheiffe constable.

Att this court Mr Georg Briggs one of the comburgesses of this borough was by a.generall consente of the courte nominated to be Alderman for the yeare nexte ensueing. Mr Briggs nominated Alderman.

Att this court was taken into consideracon the feast that Mr Alderman usuallie hath made after his choyce day for his bretheren & others whome Mr Alderman pleaseth to invite and because ytt falleth on a Satterdaye when all tradesmen have occassion to looke after theire owne buisnes. Itt was moved by Mr Alderman that ytt might be putt of till some other day when Mr Alderman shall thinke convenient to make ytt, whereuppon ytt was agreed by a generall consent of the courte that Mr Alderman shall have libertie to make his feaste when hee pleaseth.

f. 161 Twenty first court of Richard Coney 8 October 1647.

Att this court were taken into consideracon the debt of £300 principall & the interest £54 15s which this towne oweth to Mr Welby of Denton & the death of parte of his securitie, & desire of disingagemente of the rest, & therefore what new securitie shalbe propounded to him that the olde bonds may be taken in: and ytt was agreed that Mr Alderman should give him thankes for his longe forbearance both of principall & interest, & desire him to make up what we owe £500 at seaven pounds per centum as wee paye him for the £300 for the discharging of moneys now called for, for which wee paye £8p cent & for his securitie desire him to aocepte of the comon seale, which the towne conceaves to be better then that privatte securitie.

Att this court was taken into serious consideracon the worth of Mr William Ellis a member of the house of comons & the relacon betwiste him & us in regard of his birth in this towne, & hee being our Recorder for this five yeares past of whose faithfullness and abilities wee have had sufficyente testimonies and for the further expression of our hartie affections towards him, & the future ingaging him still & continue to be our noble Recorder this court doth order that a pattente of the Recordershippe shalbe presented him under the comon seale, in full & ample maner as ytt was formerlie to the Right Honorable George late Earle of Ruttand our late Recorder a coppie whereof is extante.

Att this court was openlie read the ordinance of Parliamente dated October the 4th 1647 disabling malignants to beare office or to have anie voate or voyce in chussing anie maior, alderman, justice of peace, constable or anie corporacon in hac verba the consideracon whereof was referred to the next courte.

Att this court Thoms Hanson distreaned a litle pewter flaggon for his absence from court.
Mrs Porter distreaned a pewter dish for nott paye her assessment for the conduitt.

Att this court was taken into consideracon the order made as appeares in libro 5 fol for the chusing of Mr Pellam to be of the towne councell & to have a patente thereof during his lief was by the generall consente of this court made null & voyd to all intents & purposes, in regard Mr Pellam never was imployed by the corporacon since the order was made being about eight yeares paste, he continueing att London during the said tyme.

Att this court Mr Thomas Secker desired to be dismissed from the court in regard hee had bine sequestred for his delinquencye which the court taking into considercon that the ordinances of Parliamente doth dissable him from bearing anie office in the corporacon with a generall consente dismissed him.

Att this court Mr Izack was chossen on of the second twelve in the roometh of Mr Doughtie took his oath of a second twelve man & paid all due fees & there rests in the callender Thomas Graunt William Grocock Leonard Camocke

Att this court the overseers of the High Street well presented into the court an assessment of twoe pounds one shilling vid formerlie agreed on to be made for the repaireing of the said well, & the payement of areares due for the same well which the court appointed to be delivered to the constables the High Street & Castlegate & for non payment to distreane.

162 Att this courte the ordinance of Parliamente of the fourth of October laste was againe read by vertue whereof Mr Gilbert Chauntler one of the comburgesses of this borough, was called in question for assisting the enemy against the Parliamente (viz) for haveing corespondencye with the enemye att Lincolne, & provideing prohibited materialls as apeared by his letter to Mr Lloyde master of the enemies magazine att Lincolne, and founde in that magazeene when the Earle of Manchester tooke Lincolne, with another letter from Mr Lloyds sonne to his father, for providinge brimestone for powder for the said garisone: as alsoe for makeing Belvoyre his refuge from the Parliamente forces, where by his owne confessione (in open courte) hee was dyeted att the Governors owne table, as alsoe for releiving that garisone with comodities and for rebuking John Kirke & others butchers, whoe had seaven horses loaden with meate goeing to Sleeford markette taken from them & driven to Belvoyre and they adressing them selves to hime for releiffe tauntingly replyed nay they were instantlie served for

sending theire meate to the Parliamente quarters and therefore would nott indeavore theire releiffe both which was proved in open courte by all which the court conceaved him to be within the compasse of the said ordinance & nott meet to continue on the first twelve Therefore with a generall consente dismissed him his place and ordered that another forthwith should be chosen in his roometh.

Att this courte Mr John Phiper by the generall concent of the courte was chosen uppon the first twelve & tooke the oathe incydente to that place, & the oathes of a Justice of Peace and supremacye & paied the clarke & sergeants theire due fees and soc tooke his place.

Att this courte Richard Sheperdson was chosen cheiffe constable in the roometh of Mr. John Phiper & tooke the oathe incydente constable to his place

Att this courte Henrye Ferman had a small pewter dishe distreaned for beinge absente from courte

f. 164 Att this court the ordinance of Parliament bearing the date the fourth of October laste was the seconde tyme reade & the whole courte generallie agreed Twesdaye next to be the daye appointed to receave further informacon againste all such as by vertue of the said ordinance are excluded from offices & voates in corporacon, against which tymes the constables are inioyned to bring in the names of all free men of theire respective wards, that the courte maye further proceed against delinquents according to the said ordinance & noe man to faile his attendance att that courte sub pena for everie first twelve man vs everie second xii man iiis everie comoner iis to be leavied by way of distresse & sale of the offenders goodes without anie mittigacon.

Att this courte Edward Watsone was distreaned one paire of stirrups for his absence from courte

Att this court Thomas Hanson paid vid for his absence this daye & vid to redeeme a flaggon for his absence laste daye which xiid was putt into the boxe.

Att this court Phillippe Hollingworth was appointed constable for the markett place in the roometh of Mr Izacke

Att this courte Robert Greene was chossen constable for Walkergate in the roometh of Phillippe Hollingworth & being absente was appoynted to take his oath att master Aldermans house.

Att this court was openlie read the lease which Mr Gibson is to have of the mills belonging to the towne, according to former agreemente and ytt was agreed to be sealed on the courte daye with the comon seale in the revestrie and att the same court the said Mr Gibson tendred Mr William Clark & Thomas Baylie for his securitie which the court willinglie accepted of.

Att this court those persons following were appoynted overseers for the mills demised to Mr Gibson that they veiw them foure tymes by the yeare & oftner yf need require, as alsoe to procure willowes & osiers to be sett about the bankes and carefullie preserved (viz) Mr Alderman Mr Richard Pearson Mr Christopheer Hanson, Mr John Rawlinson of the first twelve Richard Sheppardson, William Poole, John Symson & Robert Izack of the second xii.

John Hutchine, William Grococke, William Gray, John Lenton, Morice Dalton, Edward Hawden of the comoners or anie foure of them and yf anie defects be to informe the court thereof that corse may be taken for speedy repaire of what shalbe founde amisse.

Att this court was agreed Monday next to be a comon daye for the finishing the repaires about the mille banckes and is agreed eveare free man of abilitie to pay to the same vid to the constables or send a sufficyente laboror, and for defect thereof to be fined xiid to be taken by way of distresse without mittigacon, & the porer sort to come themselves or send one in theire roomes.

Att this court was agreed that Sir Robert Thorold & the rest adioyning uppon Wytham River betwixt Grantham & Spittlegate shall have present notice to clenge the River from all annoyances within this fortnight & those that faile to be presented att the nexte sessions held att Folkingham.

Att this court Mr Alderman confirmed that William Cole one of the chamberlines wold nott bring to Mr Alderman his accompte to be examined & recorded as ytt ought to be. Thereuppon the court ordered the said William Cole shall give to Mr Alderman a coppy of his booke formerlie written of his receipts & disbursements, before the court on Tewsdaye nexte to be perfected & ingrossed, least by anie mistakes be by sooden passing his accompte on the courte daye, & for defect thereof to paye xxs in the said court without mittigacon, & for non paymente to leavie his goodes by way of distresse according to anntiente custome.

Att this court was agreed that the constables in the High Street & Walkergate shall give notice to clense theire streets before the faire in paine of vid according to former order.

Att this court is agreed the Vine Street pavements be perfectlie repaired by the overseers of that street (viz) Henrie Ferman & William Graye att the charges of the inhabitants foure yardes from theire dores & the porer sort that be nott able & whose landlords live out of towne to deduct the charge out of the next Ladie daye rente

Att this court ytt is agreed that uppon next Tuesday all the distresses that is remaining shalbe sold (except redeemed by the owners) after the buisnes of the court be over.

Att this court was taken into consideracon the six pounds Mr Parkins claymeth in the marieing Mr John Mills his widow,which he said Mr John Mills lente to paye parte of an assessemente for the towne when General Hotham, my Lord Willoughby & Collonell Cromewell was here att the beginning of the warre in consideracon whereof this court is contente, that the five poundes Mr John Mills late Alderman had of Henrie Ferman then chamberline more than his half yeares allowance before his death shalbe allowed Mr Parkins towards the six pounds above mentioned.

Att this court ytt was ordered that Mr William Clark & Mr Doughtie late cheiffe constables shold bring in the bill of all the charge that was expended when Captaine Grymes companie laye here as gard uppon the souldiers sente hither by his excellencye Sir Thomas Fairefaxe to be tryed by a councell of warr,and alsoe the bills of charges layed forth for the quartering of sixteen of Collonell Thorne his men that laye here one nighte that care may be taken att the next court for the raising of money to discharge the same.

Att this court ytt was agreed that forasmuch as hollidayes are putt downe by the Parliament on which dayes the first & second xii are by an order of this court inioyned to ware theire gownes made libr quinto fol which order att this court is made voyde & null, and ytt is this daye ordered by a generall consente of the courte that from henceforth the first & second twelve onelie be inioyned to weare theire gownes to the church everic sabeth daye & everie court daye & faire daye the fifte of November and everie sessions daye, and whosoever shall offend herein pay xiid for to be leavied by waye of distresse as heretofore hath bine accustomed.

Att this court ytt was agreed the first twelve shall nott walke abroad in the towne without their cloakes uppon paine to forfeit for everie offence xiid to be leavied by waye of distresse as hath bine accustomed.

Att this court ytt was agreed that Mr Alderman for the tyme being shall nott henceforth walke into the towne without his gowne as heretofore hath bine accustomed before these late tymes of distractions.

f. 165 Att this court informacon was given that divers tennants have late yeares refused to paye rente capons & hens to the Alderman for the tyme being according to the covennants in theire leases whereuppon the court did order that whosoever is behinde for anie capons or hens ytt shalbe lawfull for the Alderman to sue the parties either in his tyme of being Alderman or after his tyme be expired

Att this court was taken into consideracon the great abuse that is in Innes & Alehouses within this towne in selling theire beare & ale in small juggs & other measures contrarie to the statute in that casse provided whereby the poore people & others are much wronged thereby for remedie whereof ytt is agreed by generall consente of the court that noe Innekepper Alehousekeeper or victuler shall after the first daye of December next sell or suffer to be sold in anie of their Innes Alehouses or victuline houses or other places anie beare or ale butt in measures sealed by Mr Alderman's order whereby the poore & others maye be suer they have a full quarte for a pennye or nott soe they maye complaine to the Alderman for the tyme being or his bretheren or anie of them that the offenders maye be punished according to lawe,a farthing a quarte being allowed (the sellers besides the pennie a quarte) according to the ordinance of Parliamente.

Att this court Mr Alderman againe acquainted the courte this being the third tyme that there was twoe small tenements out of lease the one of them being without a tennante & late in the tenure of Mr Greenwood & the other in the tenure of Mr Archer & both of them goeing to decaye for wante of repaire desired yf anie one wold take them might provided that whosoever wold give the most money shold have them, butt there was anie man att that court or the courte before wold offer anie money for them whereuppon Mr Alderman offered to give sixe pounds xiiis iiiid for a fine & to paye the antiente rente, nottwithstanding the house late in the tenure of Mr Archer was gone much to decaye,and alsoe a fence wall was taken awaye in the tyme of the garrison for paveing the great barne in the parsonidge yard for stabling for horses which repaires & making uppe of the fence wall, will coste att least twentie nobles making good againe which the courte perceaving, & that neither nowe or heretofore anie man had anie desire for the said twoe tenements with the appurtennances thereto belonging, for the terme of twentie yeares from Michaellmas last paste for the some of sixe pounds xiiis iiiid fine to be presentlie paied unto the chamberline for the use of the corporacon and the yearlie rente of sixteen shillinges per annum for them both to be paied quarterlie, to the collectors of the schoolehouse landes, and to enter into such covennants as other the townes tennants doe whereuppon ytt was agreed by a generall consente the said Mr Cony shall have a lease of the twoe tenements sealed with the comon seale uppon demande of the said Richard Cony or his assignes as soone as the leases can be drawen in earnest whereof he gave unto the chamberline xiid which was putt into the boxe

Agreed the cheiffe constables to bring in the bills what money is owing to divers persons for wood & candles & for the guard when the prisoners were tryed. Agreed alsoe that a locke be made for the hutch with three keyes to be sett one by the courte daye yf ytt maye bee.

166 Twenty fourth Court of Richard Coney 19 October 1647

At this court it was agreed by a generall consent of the court that a ticket shall forthwith be sent, for to distraine the goodes of William Coale one of the chamberlaines for breaking the order made by this court the thirteenth day of this instant October, for the not bringinge his accompte to Mr Alderman to be perfected accordinge to the said order.

At this court it was agreed by a generall consent that William Welbie Esq shall have covenants drawne for the payment of three hundred pounds principall debt which the towne oweth him, with twentie one pound use for the same for one yeare to come to be sealed with the comon seale of this corporacon for the discharge of a bond wherein Mr Calcroft, William Hodgson Robert Trevillian and Francis Bristowe stand bound for the use of this Borrough, and for the interest which is allready due to the said Mr Welby comeinge to £54 10s he is to be satisfied it on the count day next day.

It was agreed at this court that noe accountante shall pay in any clipt money uppon the count day next excepting William Parker one of the chamberlines for what moneys he receaved for toales the last faire day.

At this court it was agreed by a generall consent of the same that fourteene halberts shalbe bought at London with twoe faire halberts for the cheife constables and twelve other halberts for each constable (and theire successors) against the next faire day, for which every one of the first twelve promised to give 18d a peece and every second twelve xiid a peece and the comoners belonging to the court and the key bearers to pay the remainder of what the halberts shall come to.

At this court informacon was given that the brassiers was deprived of theire ancient standings against Mr Sackers house the last faire day which the court takeing into consideracon it was ordered by a generall consent of the same that accordinge to ancient custome twoe of the stalls for the braissiers shalbe set the one against the Angell kitching window and the other against the parlour windowe and the rest of the stalls against them on the other side of the way and the coale market sill as conveniently as they may.

At this court it was agreed by a generall consent that those persons that sell woollen and lininge cloth haveing noe halls shalbe removed from standing before Richard Elston his shopp doore,and they are to stande both on faire dayes & market dayes in the corner betwixt Richard Elstons his shopp and Robert Trevillians house.

At this court Thomas Smith and his wife came into the court and informed the court that there was a bastard childe sent to there house that was borne at Folkingham he being reputed father of the said child which he denieth and alsoe saith that if he keepe it the town must keepe his son he affirmeth he is not able to maintaine his owne; which the court takeing into consideration ordered that the collectors of the poore shall forthwith send the child back againe to Folkingham where it was borne there to be maintained according to lawe.

At this court it was agreed by a generall consent of the same that George Hardackers & Edward Still the now coalebuyers shall make their accompts for what coales they have bought this last summer and the yeare before uppon the count day next, and what money shalbe remaineing in their or either of their hands to paye the same in open court on the count day.

At this court it was agreed that a ticket shalbe forthwith sent out by the towne clerke to distraine the goods of Robert Lane for useing the trade of sadler in this Borough contrary to the order of this court which distresse is to be taken by the constables of that ward against the next court day.

At this court it was agreed that an assessment of tenn pounds shall be made uppon the inhabitants of this Borrough for the payments of the moneys due for the wood and candles for the guarde when Captaine Grime and his souldiers was guard over the souldiers that was tryed by a councell of warr and other charges then expended.The assessors agreed uppon is Mr Clarke Mr Doughtie Thomas Bayley Henry Speedy John Hutching William Gray Thomas Knott and John Fisher, and if any person refuse to pay there assessment the goods of the said persons to be distrained & sould according to ancient custome.

p. 167 Twenty-fifth Court of Richard Coney 21 October 1647

At this court it was agreed by a generall consent of the court that the assessment of tenn pounds concluded uppon the last court be made for twentie pounds for the defrayeinge of billett for fireinge and candle at the court of guard when Captaine Grimes his souldiers was guard over the souldiers that was to be tryed by a councell of warre and alsoe for the paying of the constables bills for passengers and the like and for other necessary charges this yeare and this assessmente to be made by the assessors appointed the last court and forthwith to be gathered by the constables of every respective warde and if any refuse to pay the same they are assessed then the constables to distraine the goods of the delinquents accordinge to ancient custome.

At this court Mr Alderman acquainted the court that Mr Rhoades one of the comburgesses being aged and infirme and not able to proceed for the managinge the affaires of the corporacon desired to be dismist of his place and that Mr Bury might succeed him if he pleased to accept of it, whereuppon the court proceeded the nominacon of a second twelve man in the roometh of John Phiper lately chosen on the first twelve: And there being remaind in the callender at the last choyce of the second twelve man Thomas Graunte William Grocock Leonard Camocke which was sent downe to the comoners to put in a fourth man Mr William Bury out of which Mr Alderman his bretheren and the second twelve sent downe Mr William Bury and Leanard Camocke and the comoners made choyce of Mr William Bury to be of the second twelve who being absent his oath was deferd giving him untill another tyme. Remaineing in the Callender

> Thomas Graunt
> William Grococke
> Leonard Camocke

At this court the ordinance of parliament dated the fifth of October 1647 was againe read,for the disableinge of those that had beene aiding or assisting the enemy or hath beene or is liable of sequestracon for haveing any vote or the electing any Alderman as appeared more at large in the said ordinance whereuppon William Gray William Bristow Edward Watson Thomas Hanson who was proved delinquents in assisting the enemy contrary to the said ordinance of parliament and therefore by a generall consent was dismist from the court and bearing any office in the corporacon

At this court was agreed by a generall consent that noe person whatsoever that hath beene dismist this court by virtue of the ordinances of parliament the one bearing the date the ninth of September and the other the fourth of October 1647 or any other person which is in the compace of the said ordinances shall hereafter be brought into court uppon any pretence whatsoever during the five yeares exprest in the said ordinances nor after without the consent of the court, or by ordinance of parliament. And in the meane tyme noe person or persons that hath beene in armes against the Parliament or is within the compasse of the ordinances shall have any vote in the chusing the Alderman as is exprest in the ordinance bearing date the fourth of October 1647.

At this court was taken into consideracon the great want that the corporacon hath of a learned councell to advise with the great and weighty affaires of the towne, and knowing that John Archer Esq councell at law is a very eminent able man for that place hath with a generall consent of the whole courte made choyce of him to be of the townes councell and doth order that he shall have a pattent of the said place under the comon seale of the corporacon and a standing fee of xls per annum duering his residence in the countie or any place adiacent.

At this court was taken in to consideracon the order made in fol in the now Aldermans his tyme concerning the gatheringe in of the arreares rents and assessments belonginge to the church which hath not beene prosecuted according to the said order. It is therefore now indented by a generall consent of the whole court that from henceforth what churchwarden or churchwardens whatsoever shall neglect the executinge of their office in not gathering the arreares rents assessments and other dutyes accordingly as is exprest in the said order shall pay for their neglect therein xls a peece to be leavyed uppon their goods according to the custome of this Borough.

At this court Thomas Chilvester of Barkston payed his fine of xxs that was imposed uppon him the last sessions which payed in open court to William Parker chamberline.

At this court Richard Brooke paid in open court to William Parker chamberline the some of nine shillings which was lately lent the said Richard Brooke by the appointment of Mr Alderman and his breetheren to buy leather for the setting of himself on worke.

At this court the tanners payd to William Parker chamberline for the use of the Hall for sealinge of leather according to order of the court the some of six shillings eight pence for this last yeare.

f. 168 At this court Mr Christopher Hanson coroner certified to the court that he neither receaved money nor payed money soe that he hath nothing in his hand to accounte for.

At this court Mr Thomas Mills Escheator alsoe certified the court that he neither received nor payed money this last yeare therefore hath nothing to accompt for.

At this court Mr George Briggs & Henry Speedy collectors for the schoolehouse lands for this last yeare made their accompte, the whole charge of their accompte is fortie six pounds eleaven shillings and foure pence of which received fortie pound thirteene shillings twoe pence the rest uncollected five pound eighteene shillings twoe pence paid to the schoolemaster usher & other charges £34 13s 8d more – received of Mr Courtice which was paid to William Cole chamberlaine fifteene pound seaventeene shillings soe then rest in the collectors hands six pound three shillings and six pence.

Received more of Thomas Mills for a shoppe rent		00	01	00d
received more of the chamberlaines		06	06	08
rests in the collectors hands		06	11	02

At this court Mr Alderman brought in a note of arreares of the schoolehouse lands amountinge to the some of twentie nine pounds nine shillings and foure pence as appears by the booke ever since he was collector & amongst which appeareth that Thomas Shorte is behinde for a house in the High Street for divers yeares and Mr Matkine many yeares for a meadow near the new house and the said Thomas Shorte being in court was demanded the rent due and he answered the towne was in his debt formerly layd out for the townes use; which the court not knowing of desired him to produce his accompte and they would take order to pay him his money if due for them to pay, in the mean tyme it is ordered that the succeeding collectors shall distreane for the arreares against the next quarter day and if he doe not give securitie to the town according to former order then the town to lett the houses before Lady Day.

At this court uppon debate of the accompte which Thomas Shorte demanded he said there is money in some mens hands which was formerly collected out of which he should have beene paid, and being earnestly asked by Mr Alderman to acquaint the court in whose hands the money conteynneth he notwithstandinge refused to declare the same to the court whereuppon it is ordered by a generall consent of the court that diligent enquiries be made what assessments have beene made and whoe hath beene collectors of them, and if it doe appeare that the collectors or any of them have any money remaineing in their hands of the said assessments that they forthwith pay the same to the chamberleines in open court uppon notice given by the succeeding Alderman or whom he shalbe pleased to appointe and them to remaine untill the court shall dispose of the same.

At this court the widowe of Tobias Platt came in to court and informed them that her late husband had bestowed a great deale of money in repairing the house where she now liveth and desired to be acquited of the rent that was oweing in respect of the said charge which the court did condisend unto. And it ordered she shall pay xiiis iiiid per annum from Michaelmas last at foure usuall fees as in the yeare as formerly hath beene accustomed.

At this court was taken in to consideracon the great occassion of the townes buisnes from tyme to tyme to be such that in respect thereof it wilbe needfull for Mr Alderman for the tyme being to keepe divers courts according as he shall finde occassion and to the end that the great affaires of the towne may be proceed in with effect, yf it thought meete and soe ordered by the whole court that the Alderman of this Borough constantly shall hold a court the first fryday in every moneth (if he be well and at home) and at any other tyme as of tyme as often as he shall thinke good.

At this court Mr Alderman called for all the distresses to be brought forth, that saile might be made of them if not borrowed at which tyme was delivered back by a generall consent of the court John Hickson his distresses that was long since taken,from grinding from the towne milles (viz) a bible, & a coverlead, because there was no proof made of his offence.

At this court John Kirk an ancient comoner in respect of his age and infirmities desired to dismist of the courte which was granted.

At this court William Cole one of the chamberlaines made his accounte and it appeared by the casting upp of the same that his receipts was twoe hundred nineteene pounds eleaven shillings and a penny and his disbursments twoe hundred fifteene pounds eighteene shillings and eight pence as they was then cast upp soe there remaineth due to the towne from the said William Cole three pounds twelve shillings five pence which he tendred downe in clipt money affirminge that he tooke it for the townes use after prohibited by the Ordinance of Parliament not to goe uppon long debate in the court, it was ordered that his flax lately taken for a distresse for xxs should be delivered him with the said money after which he promised to pay three pounds in good money to William Parker uppon Satterday morninge next or else be liable to the order formerly made for not payinge in his money uppon the court day.

At this court William Parker the other chamberlaine . . . [Incomplete]

169 At this court the chamberlaine payd towards the repaires of the foure wells,which was Greys guift (viz) Phillippe Hollingworth & John Fearon overseers for the pumpe in the Market Place (late well) iis vid To Thomas Knott

one of the overseers for the High Streete well iis vid To Robert Kellam for the overseers of the Westgate well iis vid To William Gray one of the overseers of Swinegate well iis vid.

At this court Mr John Phiper brought in an accompte of money that have beene long oweing him for repaires of the church comeing to _____.

At this court the comon box was opened and there was in it three pound sixteene shillings & eleavene pence whereof by a generall consent of the court was given to Richard Blacke, who had his right arm laymed in defending Mr Alderman in the mutiny of Captaine Gryme his souldiers the sume of fiftie shillings. And the other six shillings eleavene pence was delivered to Thomas Borvel for work he hath done for the corporacon.

At this court it was agreed that Mrs Walton shall have tenn pounds parte of the eighteene pounds six shillings & eight pence take, payed for his next months payment for the mills.

At this court it was agreed that Mr William Clarke shall have his money in areare which is due of the mill & likewise his interest money payd out of the money payd by Mr Gibson or other moneys that shall come in with as much speed as may be.

At this court Thomas Hanson for being absent from court was distreaned a litle pewter flagon which was borrowed by William Poole who payd vid and it was put in the box.

At this court was taken in to consideracon how Mr William Welbie might have his use money payd that is in areare for the loane of three hundred pounds which cometh to £54 15s 00d of which some of £54 15s out of his love he beareth to the corporacon is content to abate £15 15s and desired that £39 might be payd him presently whereuppon Mr Alderman moved for the speedy payment of Mr Welby that the first & second twelve would lend soe much money for the use of this corporacon to be payd unto them the first of January next out of the money that is to be received of the mills or some other way as thee court hearafter shall agree uppon whereuppon Mr Alderman certified the court he would lend £3 6s 8d towards the payment of the said debt

	£03	06s	08d
Mr Richard Pearson the like	03	06	08
Mr Thomas Mills ye like	03	06	08
Mr Christopher Hanson	02	00	00
Mr George Briggs	02	00	00
Mr James Gibson	02	00	00
Mr John Phiper	03	06	08
Mr William Clarke	03	06	08
Mr Thomas Doughty	03	06	08
	26	00	00
Second xii			
Mr Trevillon	02	00	00
Henry Ferman	02	00	00
John Wythey	01	00	00
Edward Bristow	01	00	00

Thomas Bayley	01	00	00
Henry Speedy	02	00	00
William Poole	01	00	00
John Simpson	01	00	00
Robert Izacke	01	00	00
Henry Coale	01	00	00
	13	00	00

And att this court it was further agreed that those severall somes of money above named shalbe payd to William Parker one of the chamberlaines and that he pay the same to Mr Welby on Satterday next and bring the same in his accompt the next court.

And at this court it is agreed by a generall consent of the same that the £39 lent for thee payment of Mr Welby shalbe payed to the aforesaid recited parties at or uppon the first of January next either out of the rent of the mills or some other way as the court hereafter shall thinke most fitting.

170 At this court uppon a motion made by Mr Alderman concerninge the putting downe into the church and the bringing upp on the chushion such persons as the courte shall thinke most meete, in regard there was none uppon the cushion nor any in the Church save Mr George Briggs whereuppon the court by a generall consent agreed that for the most peaceable and quiett proceedings for the election of the succeeding Alderman forthwith there should be a nominacon of such persons as the court should agree uppon to be put downe in to the Church that soe they might proceed for the settling three uppon the cushion out of which they are to chuse the succeeding Alderman whereuppon the court agreed that Mr Pearson should be first sent into the Church to Mr Briggs and that Mr Thomas Mills shalbe sent into the Church to make the other twoe three out of which it was agreed by a generall consent of the court that Mr George Briggs should be first chosen uppon the chushion. Then it was agreed that Mr Christopher Hanson should be sent into the body of the Church to make the other twoe a third man out of which it was agreed that Mr Mills should be a third man uppon the chushion

At this court it was agreed by a generall consent for the more orderly and quiet proceeding for the nominacon of the Alderman for the tyme to come that before the Alderman be hereafter nominated the court by a generall consent shall fill upp the number out of those that shalbe put downe in the Church and to proceed to call soe many uppon the chushion or place of eleccon as occassionly hath beene before the eleccon out of which the Alderman for the yeare following is to be nominated.

At this court uppon the motion of Mr Alderman it was agreed by a generall consent that Mr Alderman that now is shall see that all the proceedings of this court be entered in the court booke accordinge to the agreement of this and the late courts and that the debts that the towne oweth shalbe entered in particulars into the courte booke before the succeeding Alderman take place.

An assemblie holden by Richard Conye gen Alderman of the Borough & Soake of Grantham in the said countie of Lincolne the comburgesses & burgesses of the same in Corpus Christi Quire within the Prebendarie Churche of Grantham aforesaid uppon Friday next after St Luks daye being the twoe & twentith daye of October Anno Dm 1648 _____

Att the said assemblie Mr Richard Conye Alderman did sitt downe in Corpus Christi Quire within the Prebendarie Church.

And then none other being uppon the cushion Mr Rhoades being removed att his owne intreatie by order of the courte Mr George Briggs being then onlie in the Church there was sente downe unto him in the bodye of the Church Mr Richard Pearson & Mr Thomas Mills out of which three the said Mr Briggs was first chossen to sitt uppon the cushion.

Then was sent downe into the bodye of the Church to make uppe the other twoe a third man Mr Christopher Hanson out of which three Mr Richard Pearson was chossen to sitt uppon the cushione.

Then was sent downe into the Church to Mr Thomas Mills & Mr Hanson Mr Edwarde Rawlinson to make uppe the third man out of which three Mr Thomas Mills was chossen to sitt uppon the cushion or place of electione.

Out of which three now being uppon the cushion or place of election one was to be chossen Alderman of the towne & Borough of Grantham for this yeare now to come.

And by a general consent of this assemblie Mr George Briggs was chossen Alderman for this yeare to come.

Whereuppon the said Mr Richard Cony discharged himself from the place & office of Alderman according to antiente custome,and the said Mr George Briggs being elected Alderman as aforesaid for the yeare to come did att this assemblie take his oath according to the auntiente & laudable custome of this Borough.

p. 174 First Court of George Briggs 30 October 1647

Mr George Briggs Alderman.

Mr Richard Cony gen *comburgesse*	*Second twelve*
Mr Richard Pearson comb	Robert Trevillian cheife cons.
Mr Thomas Matkine comb	Henrie Cole chieffe constable
Mr Thomas Mills comb	Henrie Ferman
Mr Christopher Hanson comb	John Wythey
Mr John Rawlinson comb	Edward Bristowe
Mr John Bee comb	Thomas Baylie
Mr James Gibsone comb	Henrie Speedie
Mr John Phiper comb	William Poole
Mr William Clark comb	John Sympsone
Mr Thomas Doughtie comb	Roberte Izarke

Nominated Officials

Coroner	Mr Richard Conye	Sergeants att Mace	
Escheator	Mr John Bee	Matthew Whiteing	jur.
Church	John Wythey	Richard Poole	jur.
wardens	Phillippe Hollingworth	Gaoler & Bayliff	
Chamber-	Richard Sheperdson	Richard Poole	
lins	Richard Gibson	Prisors of Corne	
		John Fisher	

Pettie Constables

Markett	Morice Dalton	Markett Sayers	
Place	John Fearon	John Kirke	jur.
High	Leonard Camocke	John Peeke	jur.
Streete	Richard Halley	Robert Nidd	jur.
West	George Lowe	Leather Searchers	
gate	Robert Greene	William Haskerd	jur.
Walker	George Wraye	Robert Ulliott	jur.
gate	John Johnsone	Henrie Wrighte	jur.
Swine	John Braunston	Thomas Slater	jur.
gate	Edward Charles	Church Clark	
Key	Mr Alderman	Thomas Somersall	jur.
Bearers	John Wythey	Bellman & Sexton	
	Richard Sheperdsone	Alexander Bothomley	jur.
Collectors for the Schoolehouse		Bedle	
Rents	Mr Thomas Doughtie	John Peake	
	William Fearon	Mr Aldermans Clarke	
Nominated Commoners		Robert Clerke gen	jur.

Markett Place   Phillippe Hollingworth,John Lenton,Robert Smith
High Street   William Grococke,Thomas Knotte
Westgate   Robert Kellam, John Hutchine, Thomas Marshall, William Parker, John Fisher.

Att this court Mr Richard Cony late Alderman delivered uppe in open courte by the inventorie thereof, all the towns plate unto the said Mr George Briggs now Alderman (viz) twoe silver cannes, twoe beare bolles, one wine bole, one gilte cuppe, three silver tunnes, one beaker, a silver salte & cover, the horse race cuppe & case & thirteen silver spoones.

175 Second Court of George Briggs 5 November 1647

Att this court ytt was ordered that a tyckett to be sent out to distreane William Parker being chamberline & nott making his accounte as chamberline uppon the courte daye according to an order for that purpose formerlie made and offering to paye money due to this borough as chamberline the same nott being lawfull nor allowable.

Att this court Daniell Coddington for giving uncivill & unseemlie speeches to Mr Richard Conye late Alderman which speeches & words (were that Mr Cony was a partiall man) was by this courte fined fortie shillings according to auntiente order & custome for which a distresse was taken (viz) three pewter dishes, a pewter flaggon, and twoe brass potts whereof one was lente him againe.

The tolles of packhorses & waggoners being this courte moved to be hired was putt of to the next courte to be lett, and in the meane tyme ytt is ordered that Richard Tomlinson & Richard Johnsone shall receave & take the said tolles for the use of the towne and the nexte courte to yeld an accounte thereof.

Att this court Francis Bristow, William Bristow & Thomas Hanson doe all iustifie & afirme the words they spoke in the church one the church daye (viz) noe voate noe charter.

Thomas Hanson and William Kirk afirme in open court that the charter is broken.

Mr James Gibsons disbursements and layeings out about the mills was this court openlie read and he then propounded for his securite Mr William Clarke, John Fisher, & Thomas Gibson.

Att this court ytt was ordered to goe from thence to the vestrie to take out the comon seale for sealing Mr Gibsons lease of the mills and Mr Welbies assurance for moneys lente the towne,Mr Recorders Patentte and Mr John Archer the townes councells patente.

Third Court of George Briggs 12 November 1647

Att this court Mr Gibson bills of layeings & disbursements about the mills was now againe read & allowed.

Att this court ytt was ordered & agreed that the constables of everie ward shall the nexte courte daye bring into the courte all theire bills uppon the assessments of twentie pounds with the moneys by them collected & gathered & alsoe what is uncollected and what moneys they have receaved uppon anie other assessemente.

Att this court the tolles auntientelie due for packe horses & waggons passing tax free through this Borough was lett to Thomas Knotte of this said Borough cordwainer to have & to holde the said tolles of packe horses & waggoners from the daye of the date of this presente court untill the daye called the courte daye belonging to this Borough which is aboute three weekes after the feaste of St Michaell nexte ensueing yelding & payeing therefore during the said terme to the Alderman & Burgesses of the said Borough the some of three pounds of lawfull money of Englande to be paied in manner following (viz) thirtie shillings of lawfull money of England in & uppon the feaste day of the Annunciacon of the Blessed Virgine Marye nexte ensewing and thirtie shillings more of lawfull English money in & uppon the courte daye of Grantham above specified. In earnest whereof the said Thomas Knotte has given to Mr Alderman xiid which was putt into the boxe

Att this court Leonard Camocke was censured for using uncivill words in open court against Phillippe Hollingworth in saying Phillippe Hollingworth tonge was to bigg for his mouth which words were proved by ____ The court thereuppon thought fitt & ordered hee shold pay iiis iiiid as a fine due for the breach of an order heretofore made and for some occassions he had tyme given him till the next court to bring in the said fine

Att this court William Cole late chamberline was sente for to paye in three pounds remaining in his hands & due by him as chamberline to be paied into this borough which £iii at a courte formerlie holden by Richard Cony gen late Alderman the said William Cole promised to paye accordinglie all reckonings & accounts being then sett straight & allowed between him and this borough uppon his accounte as chamberline. The said William Cole being in court uppon his sending for refused to paye the said £iii according to his former promise & agreement whereuppon this court ordered hee should paye in the said three pounds as he formerlie did agree without anie more alledgmente or witholdinge.

176 Fourth Court of George Briggs 19 November 1647

This courte being moved by Mr Alderman as concerning the paymente of certen money due to ＿＿＿ Woddruffe sonne late of Denton deceased. And earnestly demanded Mr Alderman withall shewing the divers payments & great occassions this Borough hath the presente use of money, which being taken into consideracon and nott knowing well for presente how to paye & discharge the same. Ytt were by those whose are underwritten & hereafter mentioned wishing the welfare & good of this corporacon concluded & agreed yf this borough wold soe be pleased and that they might have theire moneys paied unto them againe, by this corporacon, att or before the feast daye of the Annuncyacon of the Blessed Virgin Marye next ensewing. They for the presente wold laye downe in manner following (viz)

John Hutchine	xxs	Daniell Coddington	£5
James More	xxs	William Grococke	xxs
George Wraye	xxs	Robert Greene	xxs
Edward Charles	xxs	Thomas Knott	xxs
Morrice Dalton	xxs	George Hardacker	xxs
Richard Halley	xxs	John Fearon	xxs
Edwarde Hawden	xxs	Thomas Fearon	xxs
Thomas Wallett	xls	Robert Smith	xxs

Uppon which theire offer & paymente this court doth order the said parties shall have theire severall moneys soe by them lente repaid unto them againe att or before the Annuncyacon of the Blessed Ladie Marie the Virgin above mentioned according to theire desires, whereuppon they paied to the chamberline theire said money towards the sattisfaction of the said Woodruffs debte.

Att this court by the appoynement thereof was borowed of Suzanna Courtby the relicte of John Courteby deceased the some of twentie pounds of lawfull English money for the use of this corporacon which is to be repaied att Mr Burye his comeing home for the which Richard Sheperdson & John Sympson have given an noate under theire hands for the payemente of the same, and the court hath promised to save them harmeles.

Att this court alsoe William Poole promised to lend tenn poundes to the towne for one fortnighte & then to be repaied. And the constables are inioyned to bring in the assessmente of £xx & conduitt & to veiw the defects of the mille banckes against the nexte courte.

177 Fifth Court of George Briggs 3 December 1647

Att this court Richard Braunston baker was chossen & sworn constable of Swinegate.

Att this court Thomas Knotte who had formerlie taken a lease of this borough of the tolle of packe horses & waggons desired libertie to make a deputie to demande & receave the said tolles according to the lease graunted unto him, butt he to remaine tenante & to stand chargeable for the paymente of the rente & performance of the covenants in the lease to be demised.

Att this court Thomas Greene a stranger desired hee might be incorporated &

made a free man of this borough, and according to the order & auntiente custome of this borough brought into this court tenn poundes of lawfull English money, which hee tendred for his freedome which this court taking into consideracon, hoping hereafter hee wold make a good member of this corporacon was willing & did agree hee should bee made free, and that he should paye onelie five pounds and the rest to be given him backe againe of the said £x which £v was then paied to the chamberlins and the said Thomas Greene tooke his oath of alledgiance & freedome paied £v to the chamberlins and the Clarke & Sergeants theire due & soe was admitted a free man of this corporacon.

Att this court ytt was ordered & agreed the constables of everie warde to bring in all theire assessments the nexte courte uppon everie bille according to a former order & penaltie or else to forfeit xxs a man according to the said order.

Att this courte Mr Richard Conye, Mr Mills, Edward Bristowe, William Poole, Morice Dalton, & Thomas Wallett are appointed overseers for the markett for the remainder of this yeare that non forestall the markett or buye anie corne or graine before the markett begine or use anie other course of buyeing or selling corne or graine contrarie to lawe.

Att this court came in Willian Knewstubbs & Richard Sentance and desired to be retained & continued the townes waites againe whereunto Mr Alderman & this court doth assente to begin att Christide next & in the meane tyme to take the parishioners benevolence & good wills this next Christ tyde & att the faire.

Att this court Daniell Coddington was fined xls for using uncivill speeches against Mr Richard Cony late Alderman. And thereuppon a distresse sent for, butt uppon his submission & paieing downe xs in open court had his distresse againe.

Ytt this court likewise concluded & agreed Leonard Camocke to be fined xls for speaking uncivill words againste the second twelve viz

A distress alsoe now sent for to Leonarde Camockes for using other uncivill words & thereuppon a brasse morter was brought into courte.

f. 178 Sixth Court of George Briggs 21 January 1647.

Att this court the tolles auntientlie due & belonging to this borough of oatmeale & gritts was lett unto Robert Tompson of this borough from the eighte daye of this instante Januarie for four yeares yelding & payeing tharefore yearlie during the saide terme of foure yeares the some of twentie shillings of lawfull English money to the Alderman & Burgesses of this Borough att foure feasts in the yeare (viz) the feaste of the Annuncyacon of the Blessed Virgine Marie, St John the Baptiste, St Michaell the Archaungel & St Thomas the Apostle by eaven & equall portions in earnest whereof the said Robert Tompson gave in earnest to Mr Alderman which was putt into the boxe.

Att this courte Daniell Prime a stranger borne & carrier by trade, being come into this borough with certen children with him and using the trade of a carrier nott being a free man of this corporacon ytt being contrarie to the orders & auntiente custome of this borough had this courte warning to departe the towne with his children before the nexte courte or else to endure the penaltie of the order for strangers inhabiting & using a trade within this borough nott being thereof made a free man which for everytyme offending contrarie to that order xs.

Att this court Thomas Tomason had a distresse of foure pewter dishes sente for & broughte into this courte for setting one Edward Leake a stranger on worke contrarie to the foresaid order, and had warning to discharge the said Leake his iorneman before the nexte courte.

Att this court Thomas Shorte & Thomas Hanson were distreaned either of them a pewter dishe for refusing to paye the £xx assessemente according to a former order to that purpose made.

Ytt is this court agreed a new assessemente of twentie poundes to be made for the payemente of souldiers quartering and alsoe what allowance should be allowed them, and ytt was concluded the horsemen to be allowed eight pence a meale & foure pence a nighte eache and the foote souldiers to be allowed vid a meale and Mr John Rawlinson, Mr William Clarke, Thomas Baylie, Henrie Speedy, Richard Elston, John Lenton, Leonard Camocke & Richard Pearsone ar nominated & apointed assessors for the said assessmente Agreed further that an assessemente likewise be hereafter made to paye for the quartering of anie other souldiers which shall hereafter come to be quartered in this boroughe.

Agreed this court that they that heretofore lente money to this borough towards the dischardge of Woodruffs soones money shalbe payed them againe as speedlie as anie money can be gott.

A motione now made by Mr Trevillian & John Symson & others toutching the getting this corporacon out of debt to be considered uppon against next courte.

Seventh Court of George Briggs 28 January 1647

Att this court Edward Charles, Edward Lemon Thomas Fearon & John Johnson being foure pettie constables of this borough were by Mr Alderman & this court inioyned to distreane Leonard Camocke for uncivile wordes which he had formerlie uttered & spoken, and yf they doe neglecte to doe the same they are to forfeite xs a man to the use of this borough.

Att this court Mr Robert Trevillian of this borough promised to lend unto this borough one hundred pounds after the rate of vii per cent uppon condicon Mrs Waltons household then be paied the use money due unto her for her money in the townes handes being twoe & twentie poundes to which this court did agree and thereuppon he had daye to bring in the £100.

Att this court the fine of fortie shillings formerlie ymposed uppon Leonard Camocke for uncivile wordes uttered againste the second xii uppon some consideracons mittigated & lessoned to iiis iiiid which was then paied in to courte.

Thomas Tomason a tayler & freeman of this borough having hired a iorneman like to be chargeable to this borough & nott being a free man of this borough is this court forthwith inioyned to discharge him or else to suffer the penaltie of the order formerlie made touching the same.

Att this courte James Hodgkine late apprentice to Symon Frith of this borough came & desired his freedome butt uppon speeches & allegacons had in court toutching the same he had day given him till next courte to come about ytt againe.

Att this court the constables of everie ward are ordered & inioyned to bring in the next court the assessements formerlie to them delivered (viz) the £xx assessmente, conduit assessmente & fortie marke assessment, or else to forfeite to this borough xxs a peece according to a former order.

Leave this court graunted to Mr Alderman to lead out certaine manor which hath annoy him in his yard nott withstanding anie former order to the contrarie.

f. 179   Eighth Court of George Briggs 25 February 1647

Att this court ytt was ordered & agreed that Mrs Walton & Robert Trevillian att Mr Aldermans courte held the xviiith of Januarie last did for the good of this borough lend unto this borough one hundred pounds for a yeare, after the rate of vii per cent that they shold have securitie for the said money to be repaied att the yeares ende from this daye under the comon seale belonging to this borough.

Att this courte ytt was ordered & inioyned that the constables of everie ward shall att Mr Aldermans nexte court bring in the names of all innemates, forinors & strangers inhabiting within theire severall wards within this borough that some speedie redresse maye be had & taken for the reforming & avoyding of the same.

Distresses this court brought in by Morice Dalton one of the constables for the fortie mark assessmente and the money then paied to Mr Robert Trevillian.

Att this courte Thomas Tomason had warning once more to avoyd his iorneman being a stranger & noe freeman & soe to have his distresse againe or else his distresse to remain.
Ytt was this court likewise ordered & appointed that the constables of Westgat shall give warning to Widow Goodwine of Westgate that shee putt away her iorneman before the next court otherwise the penaltie for the order for that purpose made wilbe laide uppon her.

Att this court James Hodgkine late servante & aprentice unto Symon Frith of this borough came & desired hee might be incorporated & made free of this borough, butt in regard ytt cold nott then apeare that he had instantlie served his seaven yeares aprenticeshippe ytt was nott this court graunted unto him.

Att this court ytt was ordered & agreed that ticketts for distresses shalbe graunted out against all such as Mr Gibson shall give informacon of that grinde from the towne mills contrarie to order.

At this courte Edward Enderby a roper & a stranger borne haveing a longe tyme inhabited within this borough desired Mr Alderman & the courte that they wold be pleased he might be incorporated & made a free man of this corporacon which the court taking into consideracon knowing of his longe continuance in this towne haveing a weif & three or foure children being a poore man in consideracon that he shall maintain & keep all the bell ropes & other roapes belonging to the Church of Grantham for seaven yeares next ensueing at all tymes as need shall require, his freedome was graunted unto him whereuppon he tooke his oathe of alegiance & freedome paid the Clarke & Sergeants theire due fees & soe was admitted a free man of this borough.

The vestry agreed to be gone unto in the afternoone to seal Mrs Waltons & Mr Trevillians securities.

Ninth Court of George Briggs 21 April 1648

Att this court Leonard Camocke one of the pettye constables of the High Street in Grantham was fined xxs for being negligente in his office in nott gathering upp assessments & such taxacons as have bine latelie made within this borough nor brought in distresses for the same nor given an accounte in performance of his said office according to the auntiente order formerlie made & confirmed in the eighte court of Mr Edward Christian late Alderman of this borough wherein ytt was then ordered that anie constable that shalbe faltie in the exorcucone of his said office accordinge to the former & the then order agreed uppon shall forfeit xxs.
He was likewise this courte againe fined xxs more for his uncivill & abusive behavior att this court according to anntiente custome but uppon his submission in open courte the court was contente to forgive him both the said fines all butt for five shillings which hee then paied to the chamberline and was then discharged the courte.

And Thomas Knotte was this court chossen constable in his roome for the High Streete for the remainder of his yeare & tooke his oathe accordinglie.

Agreed this court that John Trigge shall have his liverie provided for him against the nexte faire in Grantham.

Att this court Walkergate constables & High Street constables promised to paye in the moneys they have collected & gathered uppon assessemente to the cheiffe constables tomorow being Satterdaye.

Att this court a litle close in Tanthorpe in the precincts of Londonthorpe in the countie of Lincolne in the possession of Henrie Johnson of Manthorpe was lette to the said Henrie Johnson to have & to holde the said close or inclossed peece of ground from the feast of the Annuncyacon of the Blessed Virgine Marie last before the date of this courte for & during the residue & remainder of yeares which he hath yett to come in the farme in Manthorpe wherein he dwelleth & holdeth from this borough yelding & payeing therefore yearlie during the said terme the some of twentie shillings of lawfull money of Englande viz xs uppon the feast day of St Michaell the Archaungell & xs uppon the feast day of the Annuncyacon of the Blessed Virgine Marie or within tenn dayes after either of the said feast dayes yearlie, and to maintaine & keep the fences in good & sufficyente repaire & soe leave them att the end & expuracon of his said terme. In earnest whereof the said Henrie Johnson hath given to Mr Alderman xiid which was putt into the boxe

Ytt was this court ordered & agreed that ticketts shold be sent out to the constables of everie ward to distreane all innemates strangers & forinors which inhabitte within theire severall wards contrarie to the order thereof formerlie made & by the court confirmed.The names of which inemates forinors &

strangers were now given in by the constables viz in Castlegate Lawrence Attkinson, Thomas Jarett, Christopher Marks & William Newball; in Westgate Edward Woolley; in the High Street Robert Pattison, William Man, William Wager, William Sturley & Thomas Clarke; in Walkergate George Holeswert & William Sharpine; in Swinegate Cornett Hodgkine, John Cooper, Richard Davis & William Spur.

f. 180 Tenth Court of George Briggs 28 April 1648

Att this courte Mr Alderman moved the same touching the towns debts showing them to be manie & greate & unless some speedie course were taken for the settling of them they wold prove verie preiudicall to this corporacon which this courte taking into serious consideracone ytt was ordered & agreed that Mr Thomas Mills, Mr William Clarke, Mr Doughtie the twoe cheife constables, Richard Shepperdsone, Thomas Graunte, Richard Elston, Morice Dalton, John Fearone, William Parker & John Lenton shold be appointed to meet togeather for the settling some speedie course for the getting this towne out of debts and to certifie the nexte courte what they have done in the buisnes.

According to an order made the last court for the avoyding forinors & strangers inhabitine within this borough the parties here named viz George Holdworth, Charpins Walkergate & Robert Lewins sonne in Swinegate being all strangers & foriners inhabiting within this borough contrarie to order, were by this courte absolutilie discharged for inhabiting anie longer within this borough other the penaltie of the said order to be inflicted uppon them.

Att this courte uppon a motion made by Mr Alderman toutching a petitione by Mr William Buries meanes to be preferred for the procuring some moneys which Mr Burie informeth Mr Alderman & his bretheren that alreadie is bequeathed & given by _____ deceased to be bestowed uppon pious uses, parte whereof he hopeth may uppon the petitione delivering be graunted to this corporacon towards the buyeing of the impropracon of the vicarage of Grantham towards the maintenance of an able minister to recyde & be constantlie within this borough, which petitione was this courte openlie read and thereuppon apsolutlie & fullie consented unto. In performance whereof ytt was this courte ordered & agreed forthwith to goe to the vestrie to have the comon seale to be putt to the said petitione and soe the same to be delivered to Mr Burie to be pursued in as he shall thinke fitt with manie thanks for his care & kindnes to this corporacon.
And thereuppon Phillippe Hollingworth one of the churchwardens being absente & forth of the town soe that the Alderman could nott goe & open the vestrie without twoe churchwardens ytt was by this courte agreed that William Grocock shold be sworne churchwarden during the absence of Phillippe Hollingworth & till he came which said oath the said William Grococke tooke accoringlie.

Ytt was this court likewise ordered & agreed uppon that uppon Wednesday next att one of the clocke in the afternoone the chamberlins & constables shold meet at hall & to sell all the distresses remaineing in the town hall & then to sell them yf they be nott borowed, and Alexander Bothomley to give notice in everie street to everie one to come in to borow theire distresses.

This courte being moved by Richard Nixe, mason for money due unto him for paveing in Vine Street ytt was ordered that Mr Mills, Henrie Ferman and the said Richard Nixe shold meet togeather & soe ende the same yf they can.

Eleventh Court of George Briggs 26 May 1648

The nominacone of Mr Alderman for the nexte yeare being this courte moved according to an order thereof formerlie made, being now taken into consideracon for some speceall occassions, was att this court ordered, shold be respitted for the said nominacon, till such tyme as Mr Alderman & other of his bretheren shall have conveniente tyme to speake with Mr Recorder aboute the same.

Att this court William Poole & Nicholas Beck are nominated & appoynted colebuyers for this yeare to come & have been payed & receaved of & from the old colebuyers the some of fifteen poundes of currante English money.

Att this court the leases of certaine houses & tenements heretofore demised & lett to Marye Clifton widow deceased which after her decease came to the hands & disposure of Mr Hacley clerk her said father whoe hath since suffered the said messuages, houses & tenementes to goe into great ruines & decaye contrarie to the covenantes in the said Widow Cliftons lease to the great hurt & damage of this corporacon. Ytt is therefore this _____ ordered & agreed that a writt should speedlie be sent for, & the said Mr Hackey to be sued for making good the repaires of the said messuages & houses.

Att this court Mr Doctor Hurst his motione as concerning the letting & disposing of certaine houses & tenements in Grantham to & for the good & benefitte of this corporacon, was this court freelie accepted & aproved of, with thankes for his great kindnes graunted & agreed unto now shewed to this corporacon.

Distresses this court sent out concerning Mr Gibson for such as grinde from the towne mills contrarie to order.

Ytt was this court ordered & agreed that an assessmente of twentie shillings forthwith be made towards the maintenance & repaire of the pumpe & well in the Markett Place and Phillippe Hollingworth & John Fearon to be assessors of the same.

Corker now weif of _____ is by this court appoynted to looke unto old Clark & order him & in regard thereof her husband & she are admitted to inhabit within this corporacon till Mr Alderman & his bretherens further pleasure.

Att this court Mr Doughtie & Mr Trevillian were intreated to bestow theire labour to goe to Mrs Everatt at Boothby to see yf they caulde procure of her to lend money to this corporacion.

81 Twelfth Court of George Briggs 9 June 1648

Att this courte speeches being moved by Mr Alderman toutching the keeping of the nighte watch within this borough & now taken into consideracon, and thereuppon some reasons shewed, in regard there are divers inhabitants within this borough which denye to perform the said service as namelie such as have bine justices of the peace & of the first twelve, being by ordinance of Parliament dismissed theire said places doe now refuse to watch & ward. Ytt is therefore this courte ordered & agreed that all such justices as according to the said ordinance have bine dismissed theire places, shall perform theire severall watch & ward as other the inhabitants within the said borough.

Att this courte was taken into consideracon of the continuance of the musicians for this borough, and for the providing them with liveries, and after much debate thereof had, considering the troublesommes of these tymes, and other occassions wherewith this court was then made acquainted. Ytt was this court fullie ordered & agreed that the said musicians shold for presente be dismissed theire places till other & better opportunities & occassions shall serve.

Ytt was this court ordered that John Corker shold have five shillings payed him for certaine haye this borough had of him for the furnishing some soldiers horses then in towne

Att this courte on _____ whoe maried Robert t Lewins daughter, was this courte distreaned six ioyners plainers, twoe pewter dishes for inhabiting within this borough being a stranger contrarie to order.

Thirteenth Court of George Briggs 14 July 1648

At this court was brought in William Palmer a fatherlesse & motherlesse childe & late apprentice unto Richard Braxer whoe having turned him away nott being able to maintaine & keep him the said apprentice was by the consente of this court placed with Nathaniell Whitehead to serve out the remainder of the yeares hee was to serve the said Richard Braxer.

Ytt was this courte likewise ordered & agreed that the colebuyers now being shall after this courte ended repaire to Mr Aldermans house theire to make & perfect theire laste yeares accounte,and to pay in such money is remaineing in theire hands to the town uppon theire said accounts.

Mr Alderman likewise moved that the court wold take into consideracon the greate debt this borough stood ingaged to paye especiallie a debte presentlie growing due to be paid owing to Mr Greenwood, and desired some course mighte be speedlie taken for the procuring money whereby the same might be sattisfied & paied.

Att this courte came in Doctor Hurste, and he related to the courte the names of certaine pore people to whome he had given waye to inhabitte & dwell in certen houses & tenements in this borough (which hee porposseth & promiseth to bestow & conferre uppon this corporacon) yf this courte & corporacon shall thereof like & aprove otherwise nott.

f. 182 Fourteenth Court of George Briggs 18 August 1648

Att this court ytt was agreed by a generall consente of the same that George Hardackers & Edward Still the now colebuyers shall forthwith make theire accounts to Mr Alderman & some other of his bretheren for what coales they have boughte this laste somer, to paye in what money shalbe in theire or other of theire hands for this yeare or before.

Uppon a motione this courte made by Mr Alderman for the procuering of money due to borough to be paid to Mr Greenwood & others to whom this corporacon stands indebted. In answer to which motion Mr William Clarke then presente & desiring the good of this corporacon made answere that he hoped by a friend of his to procure a hundred pounds presentlie to be lente to this borough for a yeare, att the rate of seaven pounds per cent and promised to helpe this borough presentlie therewith, uppon such securitie under theire comon seale as usuallie they give to others for such like debts.

Att this court Phillippe Hollingworth being charged by Mr Richard Cony one of the comburgesses for uncivill words spoken in open court against the said Mr Cony he was fined by the courte to pay iiis iiiid which he laied downe & uppon his submission was restored to him againe.

The said Phillippe Hollingworth was againe charged by William Clarke one other of the comburgesses for some scandalous & uncivill words formerlie spoken against the said Mr Clarke, butt by reason of some other urgent occassions in this court theire to be proceeded in the buisnes for presente was then remitted & a distreeane of fortie shillings to be sent against for the same.

Att this court Mr Richard Pearsone one of the comburgesses of this borough was twoe or three tymes sente for, and being as ytt seemeth verie ill & nott able to come, sente word by his sonne that in regard of the late Ordinance of Parliamente made by the Lords & Comons for the disabling of all persons whatsoever that have bine in armes against the Parliamente or have bine ayding or assisting the force of the enemye or hath bine or is sequestred, as appeareth more att large by the said ordinance bering the date the ninthe of September 1646 by which he conceurs he cannot continue a member of the courte, he being a member thereof & one of the first twelve, therefore in obedience to this said Ordinance of Parliamente he had yelded his said place which this court taking into consideracone dismissed him of his place.

183 Fifteenth Court of George Briggs 20 August 1648

Att this court Robert Trevillian was chossen of the first twelve in the roometh of Mr Richard Pearsone tooke his oathe incydente to his place of Justice of the Peace & his oathe of supremacye and paied the Clarke & Sergeants theire fees.

Att this courte Thomas Graunte was chossen one of the second twelve in the roometh of Mr Robert Trevillian tooke his oathe of a seconde twelve man & paied all due fees.   William Grococke
And there rests in the callender   William Parker &
                                   Richard Elston

And the said Thomas Graunt was alsoe this courte chossen cheiffe constable in the roometh of the said Mr Robert Trevillian to serve for the remainder of this yeare, and tooke his oathe incydente to the place of cheiffe constable.

And thereuppon Mr Henrie Cole that was cheiffe constable was nominated to be one of chamberlines for the yeare next followinge.

Att this courte uppon a motione made by Mr Alderman,and theruppon some speeches had concerninge the putting downe into the church & the bringing uppe of the cushion such persons as the courte shall thinke most meete for the avoyding oppositions in the church, and for the pecable & quiett proceedings of the choyce & election of succeeding Alderman, there should this presente courte, be an nominacone of such persons as the courte shall agree uppon, to putt downe into the church that they might proceed for the settling three uppon the cushion, out of which they are to chuse theire succeeding Alderman. Whereuppon the courte agreed that Mr Bee should be sent downe into the church to Mr Hanson & Mr John Rawlinsone, out of which three ytt was agreed that Mr John Rawlinson should be on the cushion or place of electione in regard Mr Pearsone being gone of from the companie & being one of the cushione and thereuppon Mr Gibsone is putt downe into the church to Mr Bee out of which former three Mr Hanson was chosen to sitt uppon the cushion or place of election & Mr Rawlinson now to be nominated Alderman for the next yeare which this court taking into serious consideracon did then by a generall consente of this courte then nominate the said Mr Rawlinson to be Alderman for the yeare next ensewinge.

f. 184 Sixteenth Court of George Briggs 1 September 1648

Att this courte was taken uppe at use by this borough of one Raphe Taylor of Weson in the countie of Stafford gentleman the some of twoe hundred poundes after the rate of sixe pounds per cent for a yeare to be paied the firste daye of September next for which payemente hee had the towns securite under the comon seale which twoe hundred was this courte disposed of to be paid by the chamberline to those this towne are formerlie indebted in manner following (viz)

To Mr Rowlande Greenwood   £133
To Mr William Clarke   50
To John Wytheys sonne   20
To Mr Fermans daughter   7
To Widow Courtby   20
To Mrs Porter   10

Whereas Mr John Rawlinsone according to the auntient custome of this borough by a full consente of the laste courte holden by Mr Alderman & his bretheren was fullie and clearlie nominated to be Alderman for the borough & soake of Grantham for the yeare next following he then partelie denieing the same,he being this courte three or foure tymes sente for, to give his absolute answere hee wolde accept his said nominacon & place of Alderman for the nexte yeare or nott butt he then absenteing himself & nott comeing into the court to give his absolute answere thereunto according to auntiente order & custome of this borough, ytt is this courte fullie ordered & agreed that yf the said Mr Rawlinson doe nott the nexte courte come in & accept & acknowledg & alow his said nominacon a distresse of tenn pouns shalbe sent out against him for refusing his said nominacon according to the anntiente order & custome of this borough.

Seventeenth Court of George Briggs 10 September 1648

Att this court Mr John Rawlinson was fined tenn pounds for refusing his office of being Alderman for the nexte yeare, and likewise putt of from being one of the cushione.

Ytt was likewise by the courte ordered & agreed that Mr John Phiper of the first twelve notwithstanding his absence shold still hold his place of the said companie & that he shold be in the bodie of the church with Mr Bee & Mr Gibson att the next election.

Eighteenth Court of George Briggs 8 October 1648

Att this court Mr John Rawlinson one of the first twelve comburgesses according to an order made the laste courte before this being then fined tenn pounds for refusing to take uppon him the place of Alderman the next yeare according to his former nominacon for this borough & according to the anntient & laudable orders of this borough did att this court accordinglie tender & pay in his tenn pounds fine for his said refusall alledging manie occassions why hee shold have bine spared the office of Alderman for this nexte yeare, & that his fine might be mittigated which being putt unto the voate of this courte ytt was fullie concluded & agreed the said Mr Rawlinson shold pay five pounds part of the fine of £x to the chamberline for the use of this borough without anie mittigacon and the other £v due by the said order to the succeeeding Alderman to be left alsoe in the chamberlins hands for the succeeding Alderman to doe with ytt as he pleases.

Att this courte uppon the motions of Mr Thomas Mills & Mr Christopher Hansone twoe of the comburgesses of this borough from being putt of from being Alderman for the nexte yeare in regard they have latelie bine Alderman, Mr Rawlinson refusing his nominacon of being Alderman which this court taking into consideracon & weighing the burthen thereof, did thereuppon nominate Mr John Bee to be Alderman for the next yeare.

Att this courte Robert Colcrofte sonne of Robert Colcrofte of this borough a freeman, John Still sonne of Bey Still butcher & George Short sonne of Thomas Shorte being formerlie apprentice did now all of them desire to be incorporated & made free men of this borough. Whereunto this court did freely assente & tooke theire oathes of allegiance & were sworne free burgesses of this borough & being free borne paid vid a peece to the boxe & the due fees to the Clark & Sergeants.

An assemblie holden by George Briggs Alderman of the borough & soake of Grantham in the said countie of Lincolne the comburgesses & burgesses of the same in Corpus Christie Quoare within the Prebendarie Church of Grantham aforesaid upon Fridaye nexte after St Lukes daye being the twentith daye of October Anno Dni. 1648.
Att the said assemblie Mr George Briggs did sitte downe in Corpus Christi Quoare in the Prebendarie Church aforesaid. Then nexte unto him did sitt Mr Thomas Mills upon the cushione & Mr Christopher Hanson.
Then were sente downe into the body of the churche three comburgesses viz Mr John Bee,Mr James Gibson & Mr John Phiper butt absente.
Out of which three Mr John Bee was chossen to sitt upon the cushion or place of electione & Mr Gibsone & Mr Phiper lefte in the bodie of the church.
Soe then there were three comburgesses upon the cushione or place of electione (viz) Mr Thomas Mills, Mr Christopher Hanson & Mr John Bee.
Out of which three now being upon the cushione or place of electione one was to be chossen Alderman of the towne & borough of Grantham for this yeare now to

come: and by a generall consente of this assemblie Mr John Bee was chossen Alderman for this yeare to come.

Whereupon the said Mr George Briggs discharged himselfe from the place & office of the Alderman according to auntiente custome, and the said Mr John Bee being elected Alderman as aforesaid for the yeare to come did att this assemblie take his oathe according to the anntiente & laudable custome of this borough.

f. 189   First Court of John Bee 27 October 1648

John Bee Alderman

The first 12 comburgesses			*The second 12 burgesses*	
Mr Arthur Rhodes comb	jur		Henry Ferman	jur
Mr Richard Cony comb	jur		John Whythey	jur
Mr Thomas Mattkine comb	jur		Richard Sheperson	jur
Mr Thomas Mills comb	jur		Henry Speedy	jur
Mr Christopher Hanson comb	jur		Henry Cole	jur
Mr George Briggs comb	jur			
Mr John Rawlinson comb	jur		William Poole	jur
Mr James Gibson comb	jur		John Simpson	jur
Mr John Phiper comb	jur		Robert Izacke	jur
Mr William Clarke comb	jur		Thomas Graunt	jur
Mr Thomas Doughtie comb	jur			
Mr Robert Trevillian comb	jur			

Nominated Officials

Coroner	Mr George Briggs	jur	Sergeants at Mace	
Escheator	Mr Robert Trevillian	jur	Mathew Whitinge	jur
Church	Henry Ferman	jur	Richard Poole	jur
Wardens	Phillipp Hollingworth	jur	Prisers of corne	
Chamb-	Henry Cole	jur	John Peeke	jur
erlins	Maurice Dalton	jur	Robert Greene	jur
High	Edward Bristow	jur	Markett Sayers	
Constables	Thomas Bayley	jur	William Broughton	jur
Markett	John Fearon	jur	Christopher Browne	jur
Place	Hugh Wilkinson	jur	John Still	jur
High	Thomas Knott	jur	Leather Sealers	
Street	Richard Holley	jur	Edward Ferman	jur
West	Richard Braunston	jur	William Jorden	jur
gate	Michaell Taylor	jur	Parish Clerke	
Walker	Richard Pearson	jur	Thomas Somersall	jur
gate	Thomas Barnes	jur	Sexton Alexander Botham	
Swine	Edward Charles	jur	Scavengers John Peeke	
gate	John Johnson	jur	Richard Poole	
Castle	Edward Kemmian	jur		
gate	Ashton Lord	jur		
Keeper of	Mr Alderman	jur		
the Comon	Henry Ferman	jur		
Hutch	Henry Cole	jur		

Collectors of	William Clarke	jur
the School	John Fisher	jur
house rents		

Mr Aldermans Clarke
Mr Robert Clerke

Att this court Mr George Briggs late Alderman delivered upp in open court by the inventorie there of all the townes plate unto the said Mr John Bee now Alderman (viz) twoe silver cannes, twoe beare bolles, one wine bolle, one guilt cupp, twoe silver tunnes, one beaker, a silver salt and cover, the horse race cuppe & casse and thirteene silver spoones.

Att this court itt is ordered that Richard Elston one of the chamberlins shall att the next court bring in a true & perfect accompt of all such some & somes of money as he hath received and acquittances or other discharges of all such moneys as he hath paid in the yere last past for the use of this corporacon. And if he faile herein then he shalbe fined according to auntient order and custome of this borough.

Att this court Hugh Wilkinson a stranger desired he might be incorporated and made a freeman of this borough and according to order and the auntient custome of this borough brought into this court tenn pounds of lawfull English money which he tendered for his freedome which this court taking into consideracon hoping hereafter he will make a good member in this corporacon was willinge & did agree he should be made free and that hee should pay onely fortie shillings and the rest to be given him back againe of the said tenn pounds which fortie shillings was then paid to the chamberlins and the said Hugh Wilkinson tooke his oath of alledgance & freedome paid vs to the chamberline and the Clarke & Sergeants their due and soe was admitted a freeman of this corporacon.

Att this court Thomas Barnes a stranger borne late apprentice to Robert Colcrofte chandler desired to be incorporated and made a freeman of this borough which this court did agree unto and the said Thomas Barnes tooke his oath of alledgance & freedome payed to the chamberlins according to auntient custome vs and the Clarke & Sergeants their fees and soe was admitted a freeman of this corporacon.

90 Second Court of John Bee 3 November 1648.

Mr Robert Trevillian sworne escheator for the towne & soake of Grantham for the yeare to come.
Henrie Ferman sworne churchwarden.
Christopher Browne & John Still sworne Markett Sayers.

Att this courte John Ireland sonne of John Irelande a freeman of this borough, desired to be incorporated & made a freeman of this borough, which this courte taking into consideracon and hoping he would prove a good member thereof did graunt unto him his freedome whereuppon he tooke his oathes of supremacy & freedome paied the Clarke & Sergeants theire due fees & soe was made a freeman of this corporacon.

Att this courte all orders formerlie made for the good govermente of this corporacone were now reade & ordered to stand good & be in force which are nott either expired, vaccated or altered by anie latter order agreed uppon in courte.

Thomas Fearone sworne constable for Westgate for the yeare to come.

Att this courte ytt was ordered & agreed that Master William Clarke togeather with the chamberlins shold doe theire endeavors to take uppe fiftie poundes att use for the payemente of certaine moneys due from the towne to the Ladie Ellis.

Att this courte ytt was likewise ordered & agreed that the use money due to Mr William Welby should first be paid out of Mr Gibson's first moneth rente following to be due for the mills and Mr Richard Sheperdson the chamberline to be paid the next monneth out of the said rents such moneys as uppon his accompte he hath made appeare is due unto him from the corporacon and in the meane tyme he is to have such moneys as is now in the chamberlins hands towards the payment thereof.

Att this court ytt was ordered & agreed that Richard Elston one of the chamberlins of this borough for the laste yeare by reason he hath nott brought in a true & perfect accompt & acquittances of all such some & somes of money as he hath receaved & paide the last yeare for the use of this corporacon according to an order made the laste court toutching the same ytt is therefore this court ordered & agreed the said Richard Elston to be fined twentie shillings for his said neglect which said fine of xxs hee is likewise ordered to bring & paye in the next courte or else a distresse to be sente oute for the same.

Third Court of John Bee 24 November 1648.

Ytt was this courte ordered & agreed that Mr Alderman with some of his bretheren & workemen shold take a veiwe of Robert Smiths house where he dwelleth & see what defects the houses are in for wante of repaires that some speedy course may be taken for redresse thereof.

Whereas there is a scrivener latelie come to inhabite within this borough being a stranger & hath brought his wief with him whoe was this courte sente for & uppon speeches with him ytt was ordered he himself mighte continue a quarter of a yeare in the towne butt his wief shold goe elsewhere.

Att this courte Henrie Cole was complained uppon for speakeing scandalous wordes in open courte against Thomas Baylie one of the cheiffe constables (viz) in sayeing that he durst nott looke out of his dores & that he hide himself under a tubbe & did oppresse people in quartering soldiers for which hee is censured by the courte & fined fortie shillings which the said Henrie Cole promised to bring in the next courte & to abide the censure of the said courte as concerning the same.

Att this courte likewise Mr Thomas Doughtie to be questioned for speaking scandalous speeches against the said Thomas Baylie cheiffe constable in sayeing that the cheiffe constable Mr Baylie was chossen to opresse & order men & that the cheiffe constable dealt knavishlie & foolishlie for which he was this courte censured & fined fortie shillings which he refusing to laye downe ytt was ordered a distresse to be sent out to the Markett Place constables to distreane for the same against the next courte.

Richard Elston late chamberline brought & paid in his fine of xxs as he was ordered the laste courte for the neglecte of finishing his accounte whereof viis vid was clipped money.

Wordes spoken by Mr Baylie against Henrie Cole was by this court thought nott to be finable.

Att this courte Mr Gibson was contented & did offer to resigne uppe his lease of the towne mills into the townes hands againe uppon condicon the towne wold allow him such money as hee had trusted for corne solde & they to take ytt (from) those where hee had trusted.

Tewsday next appoynted to veiwe the mills (viz) by Mr Alderman. Mr Cony, Mr Mills, Mr Hanson, Henry Ferman, William Poole, Henrie Speedy, Phillippe Hollingworth, William Parker, William Grococke & Hugh Wilkinson, to meet att hall at one of the clocke & then likewise to treat with Mr Gibson further aboute the lease.

91 Fourth Court of John Bee 1 December 1648.

Articles of Agreement indented for Mr Gibsons lease of the mills concluded & agreed uppon & now sealed & delivered by & betweene Mr Alderman & the burgesses of the one parte, and the said Mr Gibsone of the other parte.

Att this courte Widow Blacke being caste out of her house & wanting harbour made her casse knowen to this courte which Mr Alderman & his bretheren taking into consideracon pittyeing her necessitie are pleased yf Richard Poole will lett her his house in Swinegate yf ytt exceed nott above Ls a yeare rente the towne contente & doe promise to paye half the rente & shee to paye the other half the same to be paied quarterlie and this towne to repaire the said house for her & to paye the other half of the rente yf shee faile till such tyme as shee shalbe otherwise provided.

Ytt was this courte alsoe ordered to goe to the vestrie uppon Tewsdaye next att twoe of the clocke to seale an assurance to Mr Doctor Asheton for £50 this corporacon have borowed of him for a twelve monneth.

Att this courte Richard Davie a stranger borne being a ioyner by trade came in & desired to be incorporated & made a free man of this borough which this courte taking into consideracon & understanding he was a good workeman in his trade of a ioyner did graunte unto him his freedome uppon condicon nottwithstanding that from this courte he should keepe & maintaine all the wainsecoate belonging to the pues & seates in the church with workmanshippe for seaven yeares which he promised to performe and thereuppon tooke his oathe of allegiance & freedome paid the Clarke & Sergeants theire due fees,and soe was admitted a freeman of this borough.

Att this courte Mr Richard Cony, Thomas Graunte, William Grococke & Hugh Wilkinson were nominated & chossen mille masters for the towne mills for this yeare next ensueing and Mr Hanson, _____, Thomas Knott & John Fearone were then likewise chossen mille masters for the Slate mille for this yeare next ensueing.

William Parker & Richard Elston were by this courte ordered & inioyned to veiwe the repaires of Doctor Hursts Almes houses & yf they wanted anie repaires to gett them forthwith amended & to yeld an accounte thereof to Mr Alderman.

Fifth Court of John Bee 29 December 1648.

Att this courte ytt was ordered & agreed that the towne wold paye for Widow Basse the laste quarters owing for her house & likewise to helpe to putt oute twoe of her children the next spring soe soon as they can.

Att this courte Mr Briggs, Mr Rawlinson, Mr Gibson, Phillipp Hollingworth & Maurice Dalton were all fined iiid a peece for speaking without leave in disturbance of this court according to an auntient order formerlie made which fines they all paied was putt into the comon boxe.

Att this courte a distresse of fortie shillings was brought in by John Fearon & Hugh Wilkinson constables of the Markett Place from Mr Thomas Doughtie one of the comburgesses being a peece of mingled stuffe containeing 24 yards & a quarter being taken of him for a fine imposed formerlie uppon him by the court for scandalous & uncivill words & speeches by him uttered against Thomas Baylie one of the cheiffe constables.

Att this court likewise Henrie Cole tendered in xls which hee was formerlie fined by the court for scandalous & uncivill speeches by him uttered which being taken into consideracon by Mr Alderman the first & second twelve which uppon his submission they gave him all againe butt iiis iiiid which Mr Dalton the chamberline receaved & putt in the boxe.

Att this court ordered & agreed an assessemente of xxs to be presentlie made for repairing Swinegate well and Henrie Ferman & Daniell Coddington are by this courte apointed assessors.

Att this courte the order made in Mr Wilsons tyme touching mille masters was abrogated & made voyde & the mille masters laste courte chossen to stand, William Poole onelie in Mr Shepherdsons roome.

Agreed this courte Goodwief Holte late Courtebyes wief to make uppe £xx shee hath in the townes handes £xxx shee is to have the chamberlins bonde for securitie for her money.

Assessors apoynted to make an assessmente of xxs for the repaire of the Markett Place well Richard Sheperdson, Nicholas Becke.

Agreed this courte that the money formerlie lent to the townes use by anie belonging to this court shalbe forthwith paied to the chamberline & hee to receave ytt & pay ytt againe to those that lente the same.

Agreed this courte that twoe shold be sent to inquire of the ableness & sufficyency of Richard Sheperdsons brother for being the towne schoolmaster (viz)

f. 192   Sixth Court of John Bee 6 January 1648

Att this courte ytt was ordered & agreed that Phillipp Hollingworth should bring in to Mr Alderman his accompt for money receaved uppon an assessment for the wells & hee to see what money is in anie of theire before the now assessemente be made & gathered and then an assessemente of xls a well be made.

Att this court ytt was ordered & agreed that Mr John Archer of Great Paunton esq the towne councell should be made acquainted with a certifficate the towne hath drawen to be preferred to gentlemen of the countie & others for procuring money to sett the poore people on work in Grantham towards theire releiff, and Mr Archer to approve & ad to ytt what he shall thinke fitte.

Ytt was adiudged by this courte that Richard Sheperdson hath broken the auntiente order of speaking withoute leave in disturbance of the courte for which hee was fined iiid & paied & putt into the boxe.

Att this courte came Mr Birkett Batchelor of Artes att his earnest request & desire was by the approbacon & consente of this courte was for the presente elected & chossen to supplie the place of the cheiffe schoolemaster of the scholle belonging to this borough for this yeare to come yett to yeld uppe the same againe yf the towne shall provide themselves of Mr Kempe or some other of better abilities than himself.

Att this courte ytt was agreed an assessemente of £xx to be made for payemente of the charges of the soldiers when Colonel Rainesboroughs corps wente through the towne towards London. Assessors apoynted for the same Mr John Rawlinson, John Sympson, Maurice Dalton & Richard Pearson.

A letter agreed uppon this court to be sente to Mr Hackeley to come over & sattisfie Mr Alderman aboute the repaires of Cliftons houses noe in the tenure of Robert Smith.

Att this courte alsoe ytt was agreed that Phillipp Hollingworth with some others to be ioyned with him shold receave the tithes & annuities due & belonging to the viccarage late Mr Dilworth & the same to be paied to Mr Redman.

Agreed this courte that Widow Courteby now Holts wief to have the comon seale for the securitie of her childrens money when shee hath made uppe her £xx £xxx & shee to lett ytt to the towne untill her children come to age.

Seventh Court of John Bee 26 January 1648

Ytt was this courte agreed that the constables of everye warde shall distreane all that are behinde & in areare for anie moneys due uppon anie assessments for anie of the wells.

Ytt was this courte likewise agreed that Mr Alderman, Mr Skipwith, Mr William Burye, Mr William Parkins & Mr Wyatte Parkins shold agree uppon the forme of a certifficate to be preferred to gentlemen of the countie & others for the procuring money for setting the poore in Grantham on worke for theire releiffe & maintenance.

Ytt was this courte adiudged that the order in speaking without leave in disturbance of the courte was the last court broken by Richard Sheperdson for which the iiid fine was paied & putt into the boxe.

Att this courte the order made the laste courte for Mr Berketts being cheiffe schoolemaster of Grantham schoole was now againe reade & ordered & confirmed to abide & continue as then ytt was drawen uppe & nott otherwise.

Ytt was this courte ordered & agreed that yf the collectors of the areares of tythes faile in payeing Mr Redman his nexte quarters allowance the towne doth then promise to paye him for the next quarter.

Agreed this courte that Mr Alderman, Mr Mills, Mr Trevillian, William Poole & Thomas Graunte to peruse the laste yeare chamberlins & colebuyers accompts & to perfecte them against the nexte court yf they can.

f. 193 Eighth Court of John Bee 23 February 1648.

There being nothing done by the constables since the laste courte for gathering the assessmente for the wells as they were then inioyned ytt was this courte ordered they should have tyme to gather & bring in the same against master Aldermans nexte courte.

The accounts of the chamberlins & colebuyers was likewise unperfomed to be taken as ytt was laste court ordered by reason Thomas Graunte & Richard Elston were both from home & some other occassions.

Ytt is this courte ordered that the constables shall the nexte courte bring in the names of all strangers & inemates inhabiting in theire severall wards and likewise theire landlords names that some course maye be taken for a speedye reformacon thereof.

Widow Cliftons leases to be veiwed as concerning her covenants for repaires of the houses shee holdeth of this borough that a sute may be comenced against Mr Harley her suertie for the same.

Ytt was this courte ordered that Mr Alderman, Mr Cony & Edward Bristowe to take accounte of the mille masters,chamberlins & others with anie other in theire absence whoe Mr Alderman name.

The constables to give Mr Alderman notice every tyme how they quarter anie soldiers that Mr Alderman maye nott be opressed.

Agreed this courte that a petitione should be drawen & delivered & Mr William Bury to see yf he can procure allowance to be had & allowed for free quartering of soldiers.And that hee wold be pleased to inquire after Mr Kempe for bein this towne schoolemaster.

f. 194 Ninth Court of John Bee 23 March 1648.

The constables according to former order were this courte againe inioyned to bring in the names of all strangers & innemates inhabiting within this borough & alsoe theire landlords names againste the nexte courte att theire perills.

Ytt is this courte ordered & agreed that Mr Doctor Hurste maye have libertie to assigne over three poundes per annum given by his father to this borough & other places to them to whome ytt is given to be payed them by this borough and his name to be lefte oute for the assessmente iiis per annum.

Ytt is this courte likewise ordered that Mr Gibson, Mr William Clarke, John

Wythey, Henrie Speedye, Morice Dalton & William Grococke amended shall veiwe the River banckes & see whoe are defective therein on Tewsdaye nexte and then to give them warning forthwith to amend them or else to be indited att the nexte Countie Sessions.

Att this courte Mr Thomas Mills & Thomas Graunte are apointed overseers for merchants goods hapening or falling within this borough.

Agreed likewise that the constables of everie ward shall distreane for the twentie pounde assessemente and they to be borne oute by the courte yf anie trouble arises thereupon.

The order formerlie made that Mr Alderman & others (viz) Mr Conye & Edward Bristow to take the accounts of the chamberlins & other accountants the Fridaye nexte after every monnethlie courte, and they that refuse then to give uppe theire acconts to forfeite vs and the collectors & overseers for the poore for theire neglecte to forfeite xs.

Att this courte ytt was concluded & agreed that Mr Richard Conye one of the comburgesses shoulde goe uppe to London for the soliceting of the townes buisnes att Parliamente for an equall divisione to be made betweene the towne & soake in assessments & other things. And the towne is to allow Mr Conye his owne charges & expenses onely butt yf he have anie with him besides himself to attende him he is to beare theire charges & expenses himself.

195 Tenth Court of John Bee 20 April 1649.

Ytt was againe this courte ordered & decreed that the constables of everye warde shall bring in the names of strangers & innemates & theire landlords to Mr Aldermans owne house uppon Frydaye nexte coming or else they are to forfeite five shillings a man severallie.

Agreed likewise this court that according to former order made the laste courte shold againe be reveiwed & thereuppon notice to be given to those that are anie wayes defective that they gett them amended att or before this daye fortnighte nexte otherwise they wilbe presented the nexte Sessions.

A motione made this courte by Mr William Clarke & Mr Thomas Doughtie for a testimoniall to be graunted by this courte concerning Mr William Parkins aboute a presentment graunted againste them for nott summoning all the residents in Grantham to apeare att the Courte Leete according to his warrante formerlie sente to them when they were cheiffe constables which was putt off to be considered uppon till the nexte courte.

Agreed this courte that a letter shalbe sente to Mr Harley toutching the repaires of certaine houses late Cliftons.

Ytt was this courte ordered & apoynted that the distresses taken uppon the £20 assessemente shold be solde att or before Frydaye nexte and likewise the distresses taken for quartering soldiers.

Mr Hanson & Henrie Ferman apoynted likewise this court to apeare att Mr Aldermans house this daye sennite to take accounts of the collecons for the poore millemasters & others.

Ytt is this courte ordered that all that are in areare for payeing schoolehouse rents to have notice given them to come the nexte courte & to give theire answeres why they paye nott theire said areares or else to be putt in sute.

Ytt was this courte likewise ordered that a letter be drawen & sente the nexte weeke by Morice Dalton to Mr Kempe a schoolemaster to see yf hee will come to be schoolemaster of the towne of Grantham.

Ytt this courte alsoe ordered that foure of Grantham viz Mr Doughtie, Mr Trevillian, Thomas Graunte & Phillipp Hollingworth & foure of Gonnerby to veiwe the lande in difference belonging to the schoole in Grantham betweene Goodman Threaves & Robert Wilcocke for incroaching & sett out yf they can.

Agreed this court that the moneys due to Mr John Phiper for worke by this towne be paied unto him by the now churchwardens att or before the nexte courte, Mr Phiper allowing all assessements due by him to this borough for the church & poore.

Ytt is further alsoe this courte ordered that Henrye Cole now chamberline paye such money due to be paied by this borough as are due in his halfe yeare & the same to be paid before Maye Daye nexte.

Eleventh Court of John Bee 18 May 1649.

Att this courte Castlegate constables & Westgate constables brought in bills of strangers & innemates, the Markett Place constables brought in a bill butt have neither stranger nor innemates, the rest of the constables that brought in noe bills to be fined according to order of the laste courte.

Ytt is this courte ordered & agreed that the distresses taken uppon the £20 assessmente shall presentlie be solde.

Att this courte ytt was ordered that Richard Butler of Braceby with others forthwith enter bonds for the performance of the articles & covenants in the lease graunted unto him of the schoolehouse lands & then he hath libertie to assigne & lette the same.

Att this courte Mr Harley according to a letter formerlie sente unto him for compounding aboute the repaires of Cliftons houses in Grantham butt although hee was in courte, yett he did nott yeld himself to the censure of the courte as hee formerlie promissed and soe ytt was agreed the sute should proceed againste him.

This courte agreed that the nominacon of the nexte yeares Alderman be putt off till the nexte courte & then to be nominated.

Mr Izacke of Gonnerby by order of this courte is to have a sighte of the writtings in a litle truncke in the press in the olde shoppe lefte by Mr Thomas Conye & Mr Sharpe.

Whereas Morice Daltone by the apoyntmente of of the laste courte was sente with a letter to Mr Kempe dwelling at Hitchine to desire him to be our schoolemaster att Grantham in the roometh of Mr Birkett whoe now bringing answere that Mr Kempe now being settled is nott willing to remove. Whereuppon this courte ordered that an inquiry should be made by anie belonging to this courte that yf they coulde finde oute a more fitter & abler man in the iudgmente of the courte for performance of the schoolemasters place than Mr Birkett is, the courte is then to proceed to a new choyce.

Att this courte William Poole & Nicholas Beck ar chossen colebuyers for this nexte yeare towards which they already have ten poundes in theire hands, and the chamberlins are to paye then xiis more for coales the poore had, and ten poundes more the courte promiseth to allow them

196 Tenth Court of John Bee 18 June 1649.

Ytt is this courte ordered & agreed that the constables of everie warde give warning to the landlords for to oute theire tennants being innemates against the nexte courte day yf the constables neglecte theire office herein then inmates to be fined.

Ytt is this courte likewise ordered & agreed that the collectors of the schoolehouse lands lett Thomas Shorte know that yf he doe nott give good bonds for the performance of his rente & covenants in the leases graunted unto him from this borough from the nexte courte daye & paye his arears then the courte will reenter of the same. And likewise that the said collectors give notice & warning to the reste of the tenants of the said lands whoe are behinde with theire rents, that they alsoe paye them in att or before the nexte courte daye otherwise the towne will either enter or otherwise sue them.

William Man discharged being a stranger & to depart the towne before nexte daye or else a distresse to be taken. James Hande alsoe to departe the towne before Auguste or to be distreaned.

Ytt is ordered that the chamberlins for the tyme being shall sell all the distresses formerly taken, againste the nexte courte daye according to an order formerly made in that casse.

Uppon Mr Hacketts noate made to this courte wherein hee is contente to submitte to the courte for the repayering of the houses he holdeth of this borough to paye what the courte shall thinke fitte: Att this courte ytt was then ordered & agreed that Mr Hackeley shall paye to the towne tenn pounds towards the repaire of the said houses in Grantham and that a letter be sente unto him to acquainte him with the decree of the courte, and that he give bonde to paye the money betwixte this & the first of August nexte or else sute to proceede.

Att this courte ytt is agreed uppon that inquirye be made for a head schoolemaster against the nexte courte daye, and that a letter be sente into Essex to _____ or _____ and that Mr Wrighte be spoken to whether he will accepte of the schoole yf hee be chossen and ytt is further agreed uppon that Mr Joseph Clarke shalbe usher of the said schoole.

Att this courte ytt was agreed Mr William Clarke shalbe putt downe into the church uppon the electione daye, to make uppe Mr Phiper & Mr Gibsone three out of which Mr Gibsone is to be brought uppon the cushione to make uppe Mr Mills & Mr Hansone three uppon the cushione and in the mean tyme Mr Gibson is nominated to be Alderman for the nexte yeare.

Ytt is likewise this courte ordered & agreed that the chamberlins & other officers belonging to this borough shall show Mr Alderman his or theire particular accompte every Fridaye after Mr Aldermans courte yf Mr Alderman doe sende for him or them, or att anie other tyme when Mr Alderman shall send for him or them, and yf hee or they doe refuse to come then he or they shall paye xs for his defalte.

Att this courte Phillippe Hollingworth one of the churchwardens was ordered to paye Thomas Somersall his wages betwixte this & the nexte courte daye.

Ytt was likewise ordered that Mr John Rawlinsone & Mr Richard Sheperdsone doe attend Mr Alderman the nexte Fridaye to take the accompte of the towne officers & yf anie of them refuse to bring in theire said accompts then to paye theire said fine.

Asheton Lorde & Christopher Handeley are appointed overseers for the Highe Street well.

Hugh Wilkinsone appoynted overseers for Westgate well.

f. 197 Thirteenth Court of John Bee 6 July 1649.

Att this courte Mr Hanson, Edward Clarke & & Thomas Fearone paid theire vid a peece instead of xiid for being absente from walking the faire all of which was putt into the boxe.

Ytt was this courte concluded & agreed uppon that an assessmente of £30 should be made for the paymente of Mr Robert Colcrofte for pease hee delivered to the constables to furnish Sir Thomas Fairefaxe his souldiers when he was at Grantham and alsoe for the quartering of souldiers in Grantham and first the comittee to be noved to have theire allowance for approving the same.

Agreed likewise this courte that the distresses taken uppon the twentie pounde assessment shall this afternoone by the constables and yf they neglecte to perform the same they are to forfeit vs a peece to the peece use of this borough.

Att this courte ytt is agreed that yf Mr Hackley shall neglecte or refuse to pay to this borough £x for the repare of the houses late Cliftons then the towne is to paye John Lenton £x (viz) £v before Auguste nexte & £v more uppon the courte daye nexte in consideracone whereof the said John Lenton is to repaire that parte of the house late Cliftons which he hath hired of this borough in good & sufficyente repaire as anie twoe men whence Mr Alderman & his bretheren shall appoynte to veiwe shall approve & allow the same.

The assessemente of 30s for the High Streete well agreed to be made & assessed & accounte thereof to be made by Richard Halley & Thomas Knotte on Frydaye nexte: assessors apoynted for the same Mr Hansone & John Bracewell & the now overseers.

Att this courte ytt is concluded & agreed Mr Berkett to continue schoolemaster till the breaking uppe befor Christide and then yf the courte thinke him a fitting man for the place to continue him otherwise the courte are att libertie to chuse whome they will.

Att this courte the comoners have fully & openlye promised the taxes laide uppon poore men in Grantham according to theire donors guifte as Mr Alderman & his bretheren shall hereafter thinke fitte.

Ytt was this courte ordered that uppon Frydaye nexte the leases belonging to this borough of Grantham shalbe veiwed att Mr Aldermans house to see what leases are almost expired that they may be lett againe to raise money for the use of the towne.

Ytt is further ordered & agreed that Mr Gibson & William Poole meet att Mr Aldermans house one Frydaye nexte to take accounts howe assessements have bine paied & what is in areare & ungathered.

Agreed that twoe or three shalbe sente to Mr William Burye to knowe his approbacon & allowance concerning Mr Redmans wages.

Att this courte Mr James Gibson one of the comburgesses of this borough being formerly nominated to be Alderman for the next yeare did willingly & freely allow & approve his said nominacon and saith he shalbe willing to doe the towne that service as ytt shall please God to inable him.

Ytt is this courte graunted & agreed thatt Phillippe Hollingworth & Morice Dalton bestowe theire paines to gather good mens charities & devocons for the releiffe & behoofs of John Handley a needful & poore creature.

Att this courte Wednesday next is appoynted a comon daye for mending the banckes belonging to the Slate mille & ordered that every householder within this borough send a sufficiente persone to worke aboute or else be distreaned by the overseers of the worke whoe are inioynte to be there alsoe.

Lastely ytt is ordered & agreed that those that shall refuse to doe theire services of watch & ward according to an order thereof formerly made libro 5 185 shall for every such neglecte forfeit vid to be leavied & distreaned by the constables of the said warde.

198 Fourteenth Court of John Bee 3 August 1649.

Whereas there hath bine divers complaints made for the quartering of souldiers uppon free coste for ease of which burthen ytt was this courte ordered & agreed that an assessemente of thirtie pounds shalbe made after the £xx assessemente formerlie agreed uppon towards the discharging as suffered therein.
Assessors appoynted to assesse the same Mr Hanson, Richard Sheperdsone, William Parker and John Lenton.

Ytt is likewise this courte agreed that the distresses alreadie taken uppon the twentie pounde assessmente shalbe forthwith praised & sold by the said constables att or before Fryday nexte or else the said constables to forfeite xs a peece & distresses to be taken uppon them for the same.

Att this courte Mr Alderman giving the courte to understand that Mr Harley had nott paied in his tenn pounds towards the repaires of the houses late Cliftons according to a former order hereuppon ytt was this courte ordered that the sute alreadye comenced against him by this borough shall againe proceed againste him.

The assessemente alreadie made for the repaires of the Highe Streete well was this courte againe confirmed, and the constables of the said streete inioyned to gather the said assessemente, & to give an accounte thereof the Fryday nexte after the nexte courte.

Ytt is this courte ordered & agreed that the schoolemaster now of Grantham for the tyme being yf hee please to have coppie of parte of the schoolehouse orders concerning the admittance & taking schollers into the schoole or otherwise and the order as concerning Mr Beckette for his continuing to be here schoolemaster was this courte made & according to the latter order thereof formerlye made now confirmed.

Att this courte came in Richard Paxtons of Sommerbye a tenante belonging to this borough for a messuage in Gonnerby being to live in Denton neare Mr William Welbye his master whome he now serveth desired this courte that they wold be pleased to graunte him leave to assigne over the lease of the said messuage & premisses to one Denice Burde of Gonnerby aforesaid which this courte taking into consideracon desireing the welfare & good of the said Richard Paxtons nott preiudicing this corporacon did graunte him libertie to assigne over his said lease unto the said Denice Burde uppon condicon nottwithsatnding that he the said Richard Paxtons enter bonde with the said Denice Burde to the Alderman & burgesses of this corporacon for performance of the covenants contained in the said lease.

Att this courte ytt was alsoe ordered & agreed that Mr William Clarke & William Poole should meete att Mr Aldermans house on Frydaye nexte to take & see the accounts how assessements have bine gathered & paid in, and what is in areare & uncollected & gathered.

Att this

Att this courte ytt was ordered & fullie agreed that Mr Thomas Redman now minister of Grantham shalbe paid five & twentic pounds parte of his sallery & wages att Christide nexte by Phillippe Hollingworth for which ytt is this courte ordered that the said Phillippe Hollingworth shall this daye give bonde to Mr Alderman & this corporacon for payemente of the said money to the said Mr Redman according to his Articles of agreemente & his promise now in open courte made to performe the same. Butt in casse he faile in the preformance thereof the courte & corporacon doe promise to see the said Mr Redman sattisfied accordinglie

Att this courte Timothye Mattkine of the High Street & John Dawson of Walkergate cam in aboute taking theire leases of this borough and had daye given them till nexte courte to come & compounde for the same.

Somme speeches being this courte by Mr Alderman moved touching the taking order about the towne debts. Ytt was this courte fully concluded & agreed by the wholle courte butte onely Mr Doughtie & Mr Trevillian that uppon anie needfull occassions for the good of this borough anie of them wilbe contente to become bounde for the towne debts soe they maye againe be secured for saveing them harmeles by the towne under the comon seale.

Att this courte came Henrye Rudkine, whoe haveing formerlye used violence &

affronted the constables & collectors of assessements in the collecting & gathering theire said assessements & other duties and desired Mr Alderman and the courte wold be pleased to remitte his said offence which this courte taking into consideracon hee then in open courte never to remitte the like againe & hereafter to paye his assessemente & other duties uppon which his submissione the courte hath pardoned his said offence.

Att this courte Phillippe Hollingworth was fined iiis iiiid for speaking uncivill words in open courte, butt uppon his submission ytt was all given him backe butt iiiid which was putt into the boxe.

Att this courte Jeffery Hinde a stranger & tayler nott being free was by Mr Alderman & the courte discharged for inhabiting anie longer in this borough & for using his trade in the same.

Ytt was this courte uppon request made by the Comoners graunted by Mr Alderman that yf they wolde they maye keepe a comon house some daye the next weeke.

Uppon complainte now made by John Litles wief for money owing them for certen scones this (court) promised hereafter to consider of the buisnes.

199 Fifteenth Court of John Bee 31 August 1649.

Ytt was this courte ordered & agreed that the chamberlins shall call uppon Richard Buttler of Braceby for sealinge bonds for performing covenants of the lease graunted unto him of the schoole house lands & Doctor Saunderson to be bounde with him the said lease being graunted unto him att the requeste of Doctor Saundersone.

Agreed this courte that Mr Blowers sister to have her brothers full quarteridg for his laste quarters wages for the tyme of his being schoolemaster of Grantham.

Att this courte ytt was concluded & agreed that Mr Thomas Doughtie & John Sympsone meet at Mr Aldermans house one Frydaye next to take & see the accounts of assessments & other accounts belonging to this borough.

Uppon complainte this courte made by divers taylers freemen of this borough againste one Jeffery Hinde a stranger for using the trade of a tayler being noe freeman of this borough ytt was ordered a distresse be sente out against him for xxs for using the trade of a tayler nott being made free and a warrante to be sente out against him to the constables of Grantham for attaching the said Hindes for disobeying the courte order.

Att this courte ytt was ordered & agreed that the constables of every ward shall forthwith give to all persons within this borough to meet uppon a day Mr Alderman shall appoynte to see what benevolences they will give towards setting the poore one worke.

Ytt was this courte alsoe agreed that John Dawson of Walkergate shall have the lease of the house where he dwelleth in Walkergate graunted unto him for one & twentie yeares to begine after the expiracon of his olde lease he payeing twentie marks fine for the same viz twentie nobles next courte daye.

Att this courte Tymothie Mattkine had day given him till nexte courte daye to give his answere for taking his lease of the houses he holdeth of this borough where he dwelleth in the High Streete.

Eighteenth Court of John Bee 18 September 1649

Att this courte ytt was agreed that Mr Hartley now payeing into this court five pounds parte tenn pounde & putting in securitie to free & discharge this borough of anie chardge or trouble concerning anie childe of Robert Cliftons & to release & dischardge this borough of anie sutes or other troubles which maye hereafter arise concerning Cliftons houses. This courte is contente to give him five pounds againe of the £x he was inioyned to paye to this borough toward repaire of Cliftons houses by a former order.

Timothy Matkine was this courte offered a lease of the houses he holdeth of this borough for tenn pounds & had daye given him to consider of ytt till the next court daye.

Richard Bristowe hath likewise tyme given him till the courte daye to consider what he will give for a fine of his house.

Att this courte ytt was moved by Mr Alderman concerning the lecturers dinners providing and that there shold be a cattalogue of theire names made & putt upp in the church that thereby they maye know theire severall dayes to lecture in whereuppon ytt was now agreed theire dinners shold be provided for att Mr John Watsons att the George & he is contente & hath promised to provide for Mr Alderman & the ministers as formerlie hath bine.

Mr Alderman further moved this courte concerning benevolences to be given & graunted for providing meanes to sett the poore on worke those present in courte giving in theire names what everie man will give, and Wednesday nexte appointed to meete to see what those that are absente & other inhabitants will give.

Agreed Mr Aldermans dinner to be made uppon his choyce daye to be made att Richard Pooles.

Ytt was this court ordered & agreed that the chamberline to paye such money as is due & owing to Mr Alderman by the towne or that hee hath taken uppe for the townes use.

f. 200 Seventeenth Court of John Bee 5 October 1649

Att this courte uppon a mocone made by Mr Alderman concerning benevolences to be given concerning the setting the poore on worke & for the paiment of the towne debts. Ytt was this court ordered & agreed that all those whoe had nott yett graunted to contribute should forthwith be demanded what they wolde give. And for the towne debts ytt was ordered & agreed that twoe thousand poundes sholde be taken uppe to be payed by £200 per annum.

Att this courte itt was ordered & agreed that Mr Conie, Mr William Clarke, William Poole & Morice Dalton sholde speake with Mr Recorder, Doctor Hurst, Mr Welby, Mr Clarke & Mr Trevillian about the said money borowing of them.

Att this court ytt was ordered that Mr Clarke shold veiwe the houses belonging to this towne now in the tenure of one Clarke of Spittlegate & the said Clarke on the courte daye to give his answere what he will give the towne for a fine for the said messuage & houses.

Ytt was this courte ordered that the Alderman now or hereafter to be chosen shall provide himself an newe gowne against his choyce or within three weekes after.

Att this courte ytt is concluded & agreed that an assessmente of thirtie poundes shall be made for the payemente of constables & other towne occassions assessors nominated & appointed viz Mr Cony, Mr Trevillian, Henry Cole, Thomas Graunt, William Parker & Daniell Coddington this assessmente forthwith to be made & to be collected & gathered & payed in att the court day. The constables to gather the assessment.

Att this court it is ordered & agreed upon that two men be nominated & chosen to looke to the towne mills every moneth & to give an accompt thereof monethly.

Eighteenth Court of John Bee 10 October 1649

Att this court it is ordered & agreed upon that the order made the last court for Mr Alderman now to be chosen concerning his makeing & providing himself of a new gowne, be confirmed, unlesse the twenty pounds formerly payed & allowed the Alderman for his choyce dinner be taken away & then he to doe as he pleases for the providing of his said gowne.

Att this court it is ordered & agreed upon that two men be monethly chosen for this next yeare to looke unto & oversee & receive the monethly profitte arising from the Towne Mills, which two men att the end of every moneth to make an instant accompt to Mr Alderman & the bretheren of the benifitt & profitt they shall amounte unto & pay in the same. And for the first moneth begining on Friday last being the first of this instant October Mr Richard Cony & Hugh Wilkinson are nominated & chosen to be the men & have now in open court taken upon them the said charge.

Att this court the townes debts were read & openly made knowne amounting to the summe of two thousand pounds & upwards whereupon Mr Alderman moved the court whether they were willing & content that two thousand pounds should be taken upp of Doctor Hurst, Mr William Welby, Mr William Clarke & Mr Robert Trevillian as att a former court was to this purpose agreed upon, for payment whereof this burrough to pay two hundred pounds yearly for twenty one yeares, to which mocon this court did very freely condiscend & agree & whereupon Doctor Hurst being present in court desired Mr Alderman & his bretheren to lette him knowe when they would have & receive their money that assurances might be be drawne for securing the payment of the said two hundred pounds per annum which (with great thanks to Doctor Hurst for his love & furtherance to the town in this busines) was agreed to about the _____ November next comeing. Hereupon Doctor Hurst againe moved the court that if the towne would be content to free them from all taxes & assessments to be charged upon them for the £200 they now to receive yearly for their £2000 for the said terme they would allow the towne yearly for the said tenn pounds, and instead of their two hundred pounds per annum receive & take from the towne of their £2000 only £190 per annum during the said terme of 21 yeares.

Likewise Doctor Hurst out of his love & respecte to the towne made offer to this court that if Mr Alderman & the court had occasion to use any money before Friday of the receipt of the whole some & protecting their assurances he would furnish them therein & whereupon it was agreed that the summes mencioned should be borrowed of him vizt £18 13s 4d owing to Mr Greenwood

> £12 00s 0d to Mr Tailer
> £11 00s 0d to Mr Ashton
> £08 16s 0d to John Withy
> £16 00s 0d to Mr Alderman
> £08 00s 0d to Susan Ferman
> £74 09s 4d.

f. 201 Att this court it is fully ordered concluded & agreed upon that the twenty pound heretofore given and allowed Mr Alderman towardes the making of his dinner on the choyce day shall now & hereafter be with holden for the use & benefitt of the towne and Mr Alderman the first & second twelve & comoners belonging to the court to pay for their owne dinners those as following vizt The first twelve iis vid p peece The second twelve xviiid p peece The Comoners xiid p peece.

Whereas there is a difference growne between the town & soke concerning assessmente imposed upon them whereby this corporacon hath for a long tyme beene oppressed & overcharged by reason of the said soak. And in regard the Committee for the County doe now sitt att Lincoln for the regulating & composing of differences of this nature, by & before whome there is hopes that relief & a friendly composure may be obtayned & had in the premisisses. It is this court ordered that Mr Alderman. Mr Richard Cony, Mr Robert Trevillian, Henry Ferman & William Poole be desired to goe to the Committee att Lincoln upon Friday next & use their best endeavours to gett some redress therein if they can.

Nineteenth & Ultimate Court of John Bee 18 October 1649.

Att this court it is agreed by a generall consent that during the tyme of Parliament assessment there is tenn pounds to be payed & allowed yearly toward the said assessment by Mr William Welby, Doctor Hurst, Mr William Clarke & Mr Robert Trevillian out of the two hundred pounds per annum assured unto them from this towne for one & twenty years. And if the said Parliament assessment shall cease during the continuance & before the expiracon of the said xxi years then it is left to their court side what they will give.

Att this court it is ordered & agreed by a generall consent that Mr William Parkins for his tenn pounds & charges in procureing the house late Mr Asteleys of Mr Acout for the poore shall have the tenn pounds out of the house by fiftie shillings per annum untill it be upp except there can be meanes to gett it of Mr Lloyd whoe of right ought to pay it.

Att this court it is ordered & agreed that Mr Robert Clerk the Town Clerke being not able to officiate the place by reason of his age & weaknesse that there be inquiries made against the court for a more able man & that Mr Clerk be allowed a sallary for his life as shalbe thought fit.

The Accompt of Mr George Briggs comburgesse coroner for the towne & soake of Grantham for parte of the yeare 1648 & 1649.

He saith that there were miscausualties following his yeare,of two that made away themselves vizt Widdow Allain of Manthorpe & one Bullimore a boy of Great Paunton but neither of them had lands or tenements goods or chattells whereby anything did growe due to the Comonwealth or for the benefitt of this corporacon. And so he hath nothing to accompt for.

The Accompt of Robert Trevillian comburgesse & escheater for the towne & soak of Grantham.

He sayth that nothing did escheate in his yeare whereby any profitte did grow due to the Comonwealth or this corporacon & so hath nothing to accompt for.

The Accompt of Mr William Clarke comburgesse of the town & soak of Grantham & John Fisher collectors for the Schoolehouse rents

The totall sume of the whole yeares rent is	£46	17s	08d
Payd forth	34	19	00
payed in open court in money	08	02	00
Totall payd	43	01	00
Remaining uncollected	3	16	08

Phillip Hollingworth & Henry Ferman Churchwardens
Phillip Hollingworth fined in open court for not bringing in his accompt according to court order xxs which was layed downe by the said Phillipp & taken by the court and further ordered that if he bring not in his accompt perfected by the next court day to be fined five pounds.

202 The Accompt of Henry Cole & Maurice Dalton chamberlaines.

Henry Cole his accompt	227	07	06
His Payments	225	00	03
Rest in his hands	002	07	03

Which was payed in open court
Maurice Dalton hath tyme till next court to perfect his Accompt.

Att this court it is ordered that Mr William Bury have his rent of two shillings per annum payed him next weeke for the lane in the Sand Pitte if it be found to be due.

Itt is agreed upon that the Draught for the townes securitie for the two thousand pound drawne by Mr Recorder, be delivered to Mr Thornton to be ingrossed.

That Mr Clarke doe enjoy his old lease for the pingle and to have itt for 28 yeares longer.

Att this court John Dawson payed to the chamberlaines the remainder of his fine for his house viz £vi xiis iiiid and the court iiiid to seale his lease by the first of November next.

Att this court Timothy Matkin hath payed to the chamberlaines the summe of tenn pounds for a fine of his house and he was to have his lease sealed by the first of November next.

Att this court it is ordered that Mr John Phiper be payed 53s 4d the next court day. (To Henry Ferman)

Paid to Phillipp Hollingworth & John Ferin the Markett
Place overseers for the repaire of the pompe   iis   vid
Paid Ashton Lord & Christopher Hanley   iis   vid
Paid Hugh Wilkinson for Westgate Well   iis   vid
Paid Daniell Coddington for Swinegate Well   iis   vid

Att this court the boxe was opened wherein was nineteen
shillings and three pence whereof
Paid to _____   00   07   06
Paid to Timothy Matkin   00   02   06
Paid to Thomas Dawkin for makeing Mr Hartleys bond   00   00   06
Paid to John Hanley that was given out of boxe besides what
was collected   00   06   08

At this court it is agreed by a generall consent that the succeeding Alderman
shall have for the next yeare the Sessions fines upon condicon he will be content
to pay a parte for the dinner which wilbe seaven pounds. And the Comoners are
content and have given it under their hands that they will pay five pounds
towards the payment of the same out of the comon stock to the succeeding
Alderman at Christ tide next.

Att this court it is agreed & ordered that the chamberlaines lend to Mr Gibson
and William Poole £xx untill Friday come a night & towards the payment of the
last 3 months assessment of £64 13s 4d.

INDEX OF PERSONS

INDEX OF PLACES
In Lincolnshire unless otherwise described

INDEX OF SUBJECTS

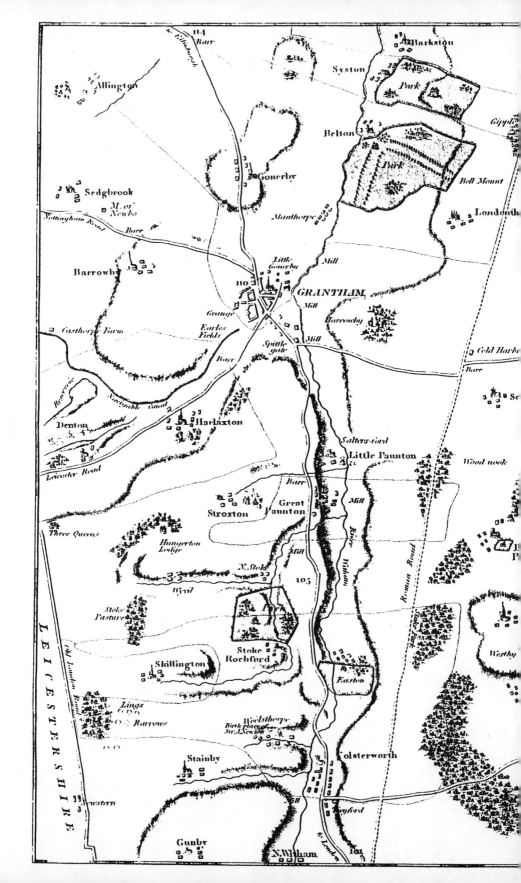